SOURCES FOR *FORGING AMERICA*

SOURCES FOR FORGING AMERICA

A CONTINENTAL HISTORY OF THE UNITED STATES

VOLUME TWO: SINCE 1863

EDITED BY

Felicia Angeja Viator
SAN FRANCISCO STATE UNIVERSITY

Stefan Lund
UNIVERSITY OF VIRGINIA

OXFORD
UNIVERSITY PRESS

Oxford University Press is a department of the University of Oxford.
It furthers the University's objective of excellence in research, scholarship,
and education by publishing worldwide. Oxford is a registered trade mark
of Oxford University Press in the UK and in certain other countries.

Published in the United States of America by Oxford University Press
198 Madison Avenue, New York, NY 10016, United States of America.

Library of Congress Cataloging-in-Publication Data

Names: Stern, Alexandra E., editor. | Lund, Stefan (Writer on the Civil
    War), editor. | Viator, Felicia Angeja, 1978—editor.
Title: Sources for "Forging America" : a continental history of the United
    States / edited by Alexandra E. Stern, The City College of New York;
    Stefan Lund, University of Virginia; Felicia Angeja Viator, San
    Francisco State University.
Other titles: Continental history of the United States
Identifiers: LCCN 2023017235 (print) | LCCN 2023017236 (ebook) | ISBN
    9780197657072 (v. 1 ; paperback) | ISBN 9780197657119 (v. 2 ; paperback)
    | ISBN 9780197657102 (v. 1 ; ebook) | ISBN 9780197657140 (v. 2 ; ebook)
Subjects: LCSH: United States—History—Sources.
Classification: LCC E173 .S689 2024 (print) | LCC E173 (ebook) | DDC
    973—dc23/eng/20230419
LC record available at https://lccn.loc.gov/2023017235
LC ebook record available at https://lccn.loc.gov/2023017236

Printed by Integrated Books International, United States of America

CONTENTS

HOW TO READ A PRIMARY SOURCE

This sourcebook is composed of eighty-four primary sources. A primary source is any text, image, or other source of information that gives us a first-hand account of the past by someone who witnessed or participated in the historical events in question. While such sources can provide significant and fascinating insight into the past, they must also be read carefully to limit modern assumptions about historical modes of thought. Here are a few elements to keep in mind when approaching a primary source.

AUTHORSHIP

Who produced this source of information? A male or a female? A member of the elite or of the lower class? An outsider looking in at an event or an insider looking out? What profession or lifestyle does the author pursue, which might influence how they are recording their information?

GENRE

What type of source are you examining? Different genres—categories of material—have different goals and stylistic elements. For example, a personal letter meant exclusively for the eyes of a distant cousin might include unveiled opinions and relatively trivial pieces of information, like the writer's vacation plans. On the other hand, a political speech intended to convince a nation of a leader's point of view might subdue personal opinions beneath artful rhetoric and focus on large issues like national welfare or war. Identifying genre can be useful for deducing how the source may have been received by an audience.

AUDIENCE

Who is reading, listening to, or observing the source? Is it a public or private audience? National or international? Religious or nonreligious? The source may be geared toward the expectations of a particular group; it may be recorded in a language that is specific to a particular group. Identifying audience can help us understand why the author chose a certain tone or why they included certain types of information.

HISTORICAL CONTEXT

When and why was this source produced? On what date? For what purposes? What historical moment does the source address? It is paramount that we approach primary sources in context to avoid anachronism (attributing an idea or habit to a past era where it does not belong) and faulty judgment. For example, when considering a medieval history, we must take account of the fact that in the Middle Ages, the widespread understanding was that God created the world and could still interfere in the activity of humankind—such as sending a terrible storm when a community had sinned. Knowing the context (Christian, medieval, views of the world) helps us to avoid importing modern assumptions—like the fact that storms are caused by atmospheric pressure—into historical texts. In this way we can read the source more faithfully, carefully, and generously.

BIAS AND FRAMING

Is there an overt argument being made by the source? Did the author have a particular agenda? Did any political or social motives underlie the reasons for writing the document? Does the document exhibit any qualities that offer clues about the author's intentions?

STYLISTIC ELEMENTS

Stylistic features such as tone, vocabulary, word choice, and the manner in which the material is organized and presented should also be considered when examining a source. They can provide insight into the writer's perspective and offer additional context for considering a source in its entirety.

SOURCES FOR *FORGING AMERICA*

CHAPTER 15

ENDING THE WAR AND (RE)CONSTRUCTING THE NATION, 1863–1865

15.1 ABRAHAM LINCOLN, PROCLAMATION OF AMNESTY AND RECONSTRUCTION (1863)*

Throughout 1863 the Confederate armies suffered a series of significant defeats across the country. Hoping to appeal to wavering Confederates, President Abraham Lincoln (1809–1865) announced his Proclamation of Amnesty and Reconstruction (sometimes called the Ten Percent Plan) in December of that year. Lincoln presented lenient terms, offering a pardon and the restoration of rights and property (except enslaved persons) to any individual who swore their future loyalty to the Union. Only Confederate leaders were ineligible for amnesty. Lincoln also announced that Confederate states could form new loyal state governments and rejoin the Union once 10 percent of the 1860 electorate took a loyalty oath. Lincoln hoped to use Union loyalists in occupied states such as Arkansas, Louisiana, and Tennessee to model that he would allow former Confederate states to peacefully return to the Union. The proclamation was printed in large legible type and circulated throughout the South.

Lincoln's proclamation was popular in the Union states, where many saw it as an important step to weaken the rebellion, restore the Union, and quicken the end of the war. Most rebels scorned the proclamation, however, unwilling to give up on the Confederate nation despite its misfortunes.

* Abraham Lincoln, *Proclamation of Amnesty and Reconstruction*, Tuesday, December 8, 1863. Abraham Lincoln papers: ser. 1, General Correspondence, 1833 to 1916. Manuscript/Mixed Material, Library of Congress, https://www.loc.gov/resource/mal.2849300/?sp=1&st=text&r=-0.359,-0.086,1.719,1.719,0.

Dec. 8, 1863
Proclamation.[1]

Whereas in and by the Constitution of the United States, it is provided that the President "shall have power to grant reprieves and pardons for offences against the United States, except in cases of impeachment," and

Whereas a rebellion now exists whereby the loyal State governments of several States have for a long time been subverted, and many persons have committed, and are now guilty of treason against the United States, and

Whereas, with reference to said rebellion and treason, laws have been enacted by Congress, declaring forfeitures, and confiscations of property, and liberation of slaves, all upon terms and conditions therein stated, and also declaring that the President was thereby authorized at any time thereafter, by proclamation, to extend to persons who may have participated in the existing rebellion, in any State or part thereof, pardon and amnesty, with such exceptions, and at such time, and on such conditions, as he may deem expedient for the public welfare, and

Whereas the Congressional declaration for limited and conditional pardon, accords with well established judicial exposition of the pardoning power, under the British, and American Constitutions, and

Whereas, with reference to said rebellion, the President of the United States has issued several proclamations, with provisions in regard to the liberation of slaves, and

Whereas it is now desired by some persons heretofore engaged in said rebellion, to resume their allegiance to the United States, and to re-inaugurate loyal State governments within and for their respective States, therefore

I, Abraham Lincoln, President of the United States, do proclaim, declare, and make known, to all persons who have, directly or by implication, participated in the existing rebellion, except[2] that a full pardon is

hereby granted to them and each of them, with restoration of all rights of property, except as to slaves, and upon the condition that every such person shall take and subscribe an oath, and thenceforward keep and maintain said oath inviolate; and which oath shall be registered for permanent preservation and shall be of the tenor and effect following, towit:

I do solemnly swear in presence of Almighty God, that I will henceforth faithfully support, protect, and defend the Constitution of the United States, and the Union of the States thereunder; and that I will, in like manner, abide by, and faithfully support all Acts of Congress passed during the existing rebellion, with reference to slaves, so long, and so far, as not repealed, modified, or held void by Congress, or by decision of the Supreme Court; and that I will, in like manner, abide by and faithfully support, all proclamations of the President made during the existing rebellion, having reference to slaves, so long, and so far as not modified, or declared void by decision of the Supreme Court, so help me God.*[3]

*[The following paragraph was written out as an addition on a separate slip] The persons excepted from the benefits of the foregoing provisions are all who are, or shall have been civil or diplomatic officers or agents of the so-called Confederate government; all who have left judicial stations under the United States to aid the rebellion; all who are, or shall have been military or naval officers of said so-called confederate government, above the rank of Colonel in the Army, or of lieutenant in the Navy; all who left seats in the United States Congress to aid the rebellion; all who resigned commissions in the army or navy of the United States, and afterwards aided the rebellion; and all who have engaged in any way, in treating colored persons, or white persons in charge of such, otherwise than lawfully as prisoners of war, and which persons may have been found in the United States service as soldiers, seamen, or in any other capacity.

---

1   Both the date and the heading "Proclamation" appear to be in another hand, not Lincoln's.
2   In the official copy, the words "as hereinafter excepted," follow at this point.

3   The asterisk indicates the insertion point for a paragraph written out as an addition on a separate slip. The list of exceptions is based on War Department, Memoranda for Proclamation of Amnesty and Reconstruction, December, 1863 (q. v.), a document which was provided Lincoln to aid in preparing this proclamation.

And I do further proclaim, declare, and make known that whenever, in any of the States of Arkansas, Texas, Louisiana, Mississippi, Tennessee, Alabama, Georgia, Florida, South-Carolina, and North Carolina, a number of persons, not less than one tenth in number of the votes cast at in such state, at the Presidential election of the year of our Lord, one thousand eight hundred and sixty, each having taken the oath aforesaid, and not having since violated it, and being a qualified voter by the election law of the state, existing immediately before the so-called act of secession, and excluding all others, shall re-establish a State government, which shall be republican, and in no wise contravening said oath, such shall be recognized as the true government of the State, and the State shall receive thereunder the benefits of the Constitutional provision which declares that "The United States shall guaranty to every State in the Union a republican form of government, and shall protect each of them against invasion, and on application of the legislature, or the executive (when the legislature can not be convened against domestic violence)."

And I do further proclaim, declare, and make known that any provision which may be adopted by such State government in relation to the freed people of such State, which shall recognize and declare their permanent freedom, provide for their education, and which may yet be consistent, as a temporary arrangement, with their present condition as a laboring, landless, and homeless class, shall not be objected to by the national executive.*4

---

4 The asterisk indicates the insertion point for the addition to the text that follows. For preliminary drafts of this passage, see the memorandum on the reverse side of Lincoln's draft of a letter to George Opdyke, December 2, 1863.

*[The following paragraph was written out as an addition on a separate slip] And it is suggested as not improper that in constructing a loyal State government in any State, the name of the State, the boundary, the subdivisions, the Constitution, and the general code of laws, as before the rebellion, be maintained, subject only to the modifications made necessary by the conditions hereinbefore stated, and such others, if any, not contravening said conditions, and which may be deemed expedient by those framing the new State government.

To avoid misunderstanding it may be proper to say that this paper proclamation, so far as it relates to State governments, has no reference to States wherein loyal State governments have all the while been maintained. And for the same reason it may be proper to further say that whether members sent to Congress from any State shall be admitted to seats constitutionally rests exclusively with the respective Houses, and not to any extent with the executive.

And still further that this proclamation is intended to present the people of the States wherein the national authority has been suspended, and loyal State governments have been subverted, a mode in and by which the national authority and loyal States governments may be re-established within said States, or in any of them; and, while the mode presented is the best the executive can present suggest, with his present impressions, it must not be understood that no other possible mode would be acceptable.

Given under my hand at the City of Washington, the 8th of December, A. D. one thousand eight hundred and sixty three, and of the independence of the United States of America the eightyeighth.

Abraham Lincoln

QUESTIONS TO CONSIDER

1. Lincoln made important exceptions in his offer of amnesty. What are these exceptions and why did Lincoln make them?

2. By requiring only 10 percent of 1860 voters to declare their loyalty before a new government could be formed, Lincoln set a low threshold for a rebellious state to rejoin the Union. What was his purpose in allowing former Confederates to rejoin the Union so easily?

15.2 NANCY JOHNSON, TESTIMONY BY A GEORGIA FREEDWOMAN ABOUT HOW UNION TROOPS STOLE HER PROPERTY (1873)*

As Union armies made their way through Georgia in 1864, soldiers removed or destroyed anything of military value, which often included food and livestock. In 1871 Congress established the Southern Claims Commission with the purpose of reimbursing loyal Americans whose property had been taken or destroyed by the Union Army during the war. Over a hundred special commissioners fanned out across the South to hold hearings, and they eventually forwarded twenty-two thousand cases with testimony from more than two hundred thousand witnesses to Washington for judgment.

Neither Congress nor the commissioners expected formerly enslaved people to bring many cases, as they understood them to have been deprived of any opportunity to own property during their enslavement. However, hundreds of formerly enslaved people did bring cases, describing how the livestock, foodstuffs, and other possessions they had accrued through their hard work had been seized by Union soldiers. Contrary to the expectations of white Northerners, many enslaved people had been industrious, shrewd, and proud of the personal possessions they had acquired.

Testimony by a Georgia Freedwoman before the Southern Claims Commission

[Savannah, Ga., March 22, 1873]

General Interrogatories by Special Com'r—My name is Nancy Johnson. I was born in Ga. I was a slave and became free when the army came here. My master was David Baggs. I live in Canoochie Creek. The claimant is my husband. He was a good Union man during the war. He liked to have lost his life by standing up for the Union party. He was threatened heavy. There was a Yankee prisoner that got away & came to our house at night; we kept him hid in my house a whole day. He sat in my room. White people didn't visit our house then. My husband slipped him over to a man named Joel Hodges & he conveyed him off so that he got home. I saw the man at the time of the raid & I knew him. He said that he tried to keep them from burning my house but he couldn't keep them from taking everything we had. I was sorry for them though a heap. The white people came hunting this man that we kept over night; my old master sent one of his own grandsons & he said if he found it that they must put my husband to death, & I had to tell a story to save life. My old master would have had him killed. He was bitter. This was my master David Baggs. I told him that I had seen nothing of him. I did this to save my husbands life. Some of the rebel soldiers deserted & came to our house & we fed them. They were opposed to the war & didn't own slaves & said they would die rather than fight. Those who were poor white people, who didn't own slaves were some of them Union people. I befriended them because they were on our side. I don't know that he ever did any thing more for the Union; we were way back in the country, but his heart was right & so was mine. I was served mighty mean before the Yankees came here. I was nearly frostbitten: my old

* Testimony of Nancy Johnson, March 22, 1873. GA case files, Approved Claims, series 732, Southern Claims Commission, 3rd Auditor, US General Accounting Office, Record Group 217, National Archives. (Published in Ira Berlin, ed., *Freedom: A Documentary History of Emancipation*, ser. I, vol. 1: *The Destruction of Slavery* (Cambridge, UK: Cambridge University Press, 2010), 150–54, http://www.freedmen.umd.edu/NJohnson.html.

Missus made me weave to make clothes for the soldiers till 12 o'clock at night & I was so tired & my own clothes I had to spin over night. She never gave me so much as a bonnet. I had to work hard for the rebels until the very last day when they took us. The old man came to me then & said if you won't go away & will work for us we will work for you; I told him if the other colored people were going to be free that I wanted to be. I went away & then came back & my old Missus asked me if I came back to behave myself & do her work & I told her no that I came to do my own work. I went to my own house & in the morning my old master came to me & asked me if I wouldn't go and milk the cows: I told him that my Missus had driven me off–well said he you go and do it—then my Mistress came out again & asked me if I came back to work for her like a "nigger"—I told her no that I was free & she said be off then & called me a stinking bitch. I afterwards wove 40 yds. Of dress goods for her that she promised to pay me for; but she never paid me a cent for it. I have asked her for it several times. I have been hard up to live but thank God, I am spared yet. I quit then only did a few jobs for her but she never did anything for me except give me a meal of victuals, you see I was hard up then, I was well to do before the war.

Second Set of Interrogatories by Spec'l Com'r.

1   I was present when this property was taken.
2   I saw it taken.
3   They said that they didn't believe what I had belonged to me & I told them that I would swear that it belonged to me. I had tried to hide things. They found our meat, it was hid under the house & they took a crop of rice. They took it out & I had some cloth under the house too & the dishes & two fine bed-quilts. They took them out. These were all my own labor & night labor. They took the bole of cloth under the house and the next morning they came back with it made into pantaloons. They were starved & naked almost. It was Jan & cold, They were on their way from Savannah. They took all my husbands clothes, except what he had on his back.
4   These things were taken from David Bagg's place in Liberty County. The Yankees took them. I should think there were thousands of them. I could not count them. They were about a day & a night.

5   There were present my family, myself & husband & this man Jack Walker. He is way out in Tatnal Co. & we can't get him here.
6   There were what we called officers there. I don't know whether they ordered the property taken. I put a pot on and made a pie & they took it to carry out to the head men. I went back where the officers camped & got my oven that I cooked it in back again. They must have ordered them or else they could not have gone so far & they right there. They said that they stood in need of them. They said that we ought not to care what they took for we would get it all back again; that they were obliged to have something to eat. They were mighty fine looking men.
7   They took the mare out of the stable; they took the bacon under the house, the corn was taken out of the crib, & the rice & the lard. Some of the chickens they shot & some they run down; they shot the hogs.
8   They took it by hand the camp was close by my house.
9   They carried it to their camps; they had lots of wagons there.
10 They took it to eat, bless you! I saw them eating it right there in my house. They were nearly starved.
11 I told one of the officers that we would starve & they said no that we would get it all back again, come & go along with us; but I wouldn't go because the old man had my youngest child hid away in Tatnal Co: he took her away because she knew where the gold was hid & he didn't want her to tell. My boy was sent out to the swamp to watch the wagons of provisions & the soldiers took the wagons & the boy, & I never saw him anymore. He was 14 yrs. old. I could have got the child back but I was afraid my master would kill him; he said that he would & I knew that he would or else make his children do it: he made his sons kill 2 men big tall men like you. The Lord forgive them for the way they have treated me. The child could not help them from taking the horses. He said that Henry (my boy) hallooed for the sake of having the Yankees find him; but the Yankees asked him where he was going & he didn't know they were soldiers & he told them that he was going to Master's mules.

12   I didn't ask for any receipt.

13   It was taken in the day time, not secretly.

14   When they took this property, the army was en-
     camped. Some got there before the camps were up.
     Some was hung up in the house. Some people told
     us that if we let some hang up they wouldn't touch
     the rest, but they did, they were close by. They
     commenced taking when they first came. They
     staid there two nights. I heard a heap of shooting,
     but I don't think that they killed anybody. I didn't
     know any of the officers or quartermasters.

15   This horse was as fine a creature as ever was & the
     pork &c were in good order.

16   Item No. 1. I don't know how old the mare was. I
     know she was young. She was medium sized. She
     was in nice order, we kept a good creature. My hus-
     band bought it when it was a colt, about 2 years
     old. I think he had been using it a year & a little
     better. Colored people when they would work
     always had something for themselves, after work-
     ing for their masters. I most forgot whether he paid
     cash or swapped cows. He worked & earned
     money, after he had done his masters work. They
     bridled & carried her off; I think they jumped right
     on her back

        Item No. 2. We had 7 hogs & we killed them
        right there. It was pickled away in the barrel:
        Some was done hung up to smoke, but we
        took it down & put it into the barrels to keep
        them from getting it. He raised the hogs. He
        bought a sow and raised his own pork & that is
        the way he got this. He did his tasks & after that
        he worked for himself & he got some money &
        bought the hogs and then they increased. He
        worked Sundays too; and that was for our-
        selves. He always was a hardworking man. I
        could not tell how much these would weigh;
        they were monstrous hogs, they were a big
        breed of hogs. We had them up feeding. The
        others were some two years old, & some more.

It took two men to help hang them up. This
was the meat from 7 hogs.

Item No. 3. I had half a barrel of lard. It was in
gourds, that would hold half a bushel a piece.
We had this hid in the crib. This was lard from
the hogs.

Item No. 4 I could not tell exactly how much
corn there was but there was a right smart. We
had 4 or 5 bushels ground up into meal & they
took all the corn besides. They carried it off in
bags and my children's undershirts, tied them
like bags & filled them up. My husband made
baskets and they toted some off in that way.
They toted some off in fanners & big blue tubs.

Item No. 5. I don't know exactly how much
rice there was; but we made a good deal. They
toted it off in bundles, threshed out—It was
taken in the sheaf. They fed their horses on it. I
saw the horses eating it as I passed there. They
took my tubs, kettles &c. I didn't get anything
back but an oven.

Item No. 7. We had 11 hogs. They were 2 or 3
years old. They were in pretty good order. We
were intending to fatten them right next year—
they killed them right there.

Item No. 8. I had 30 or 40 head of chickens.
They took the last one. They shot them. This
property all belonged to me and my husband.
None of it belonged to Mr. Baggs I swore to the
men so, but they wouldn't believe I could have
such things. My girl had a changable silk dress
& all had [talanas?] & they took them all—It
didn't look like a Yankee person would be so
mean. But they said if they didn't take them the
whites here would & they did take some of my
things from their camps after they left.

                                          her
                              Nancy X Johnson
                                         mark

QUESTIONS TO CONSIDER

1.   How did the war impact the lives of Nancy Johnson and her family members?

2.   How does Johnson's description of her interactions with her former masters compare to her ex-
     perience with the Union soldiers?

15.3 EXCERPT FROM THE VIRGINIA BLACK CODES (1866)*

After the end of the Civil War, new state governments in the former Confederate states passed a series of laws to define the rights of freedpeople, commonly called "Black Codes." While these laws often granted freedpeople new rights they had not had while enslaved—such as to marry and make contracts—the primary focus of these laws was to control the working conditions of Black Southerners. Although the laws varied from state to state, they generally required freedpeople to sign months-long contracts for plantation labor and forbade them from changing employers if someone offered them better wages or working conditions. These laws defined freedpeople who would not sign these contracts as "vagrants," and allowed anyone detained for vagrancy to be forcibly set to work. "Black Codes" ran contrary to many Black Southerners' hopes and expectations of freedom. Many freedpeople desired to cease working on plantations and move around as they wished throughout their county and state, choices that had been denied to them while enslaved. By forcing them into plantation labor and denying their choice in whether or where to work, lawmakers tried to re-create the antebellum conditions of slave labor as closely as they could.

AN ACT to regulate contracts for labor between white and colored persons, and to impose a fine on persons enticing laborers from the service of their employers under such contracts.

1. *Be it enacted by the general assembly*, That no contract between a white person and a colored person for the labor or service of the latter for a longer period than two months shall be binding on such colored person, unless the contract be in writing, signed by such white person, or his agent, and by such colored person duly acknowledged before a justice or notary public, or clerk of the country or corporation court, or overseer of the poor, or two or more credible witnesses in the county or corporation in which the white person may reside, or in which the service or labor is to be performed. And it shall be the duty of the justice, notary, clerk, or overseer of the poor, or the witnesses, to read and explain the contract to the colored person before taking his acknowledgment thereof, and to state that this has been done in the certificate of the acknowledgement of the contract.

2. If any person shall entice away from the service of another any laborer employed by him under a contract as provided by this act, knowing of the existence of such contract, or shall knowingly employ a laborer bound to service to another under such contract, he shall forfeit to the party aggrieved not less than ten nor more than twenty dollars for every such offence, to be recovered by warrant before any justice of the peace.

---

* Excerpts from Virginia Black Codes (1866), in "Laws in Relation to Freedmen," US Senate 39th Congress, 2nd Session, Senate Executive Doc. No. 6 (Washington, DC: War Department, Bureau of Refugees, Freedmen, and Abandoned Lands, 1866–67), 227–29, Library of Congress, https://memory.loc.gov/cgi-bin/ampage?collId=ody_llmisc&fileName=ody/ody0517/ody0517page.db&recNum=226&itemLink=r%3Fammem%2Faaodyssey%3A%40ofield%28NUMBER%2B%40oband%28llmisc%2Body0517%29%29&linkText=0.

3. This act shall be in force from and after the first day of April, eighteen hundred and sixty-six, and the first section shall not apply to any contract made prior to that date.

Passed February 20, 1866.

AN ACT to amend and re-enact the 14th section of chapter 108 of the code of Virginia for 1860, in regard to registers of marriage and to legalize the marriages of colored persons now cohabiting as husband and wife.

1. *Be it enacted by the general assembly*, That the fourteenth section of chapter one hundred and eight of the code of Virginia for eighteen hundred and sixty, be, and the same is hereby, amended and re-enacted so as to read as follows, to wit: "Henceforth, it shall be the duty of every minister, or other person, celebrating a marriage, and of the clerk or keeper of the records of any religious society which solemnizes marriages, by the consent of the parties, in open congregation, at once to make a record of every marriage between white persons, or between colored persons, solemnized by or before him, stating in such record whether the persons be white or colored, and, within two months after such marriage, to return a copy thereof, signed by him, to the clerk of the county or corporation in which the same is solemnized. The clerk issuing any marriage license shall at the time ascertain from the party obtaining such license a certificate setting forth, as near as may be, the date and place of the proposed marriage, the full names of both the parties, their ages and condition before marriage, whether single or widowed, the places of their birth and residence, the names of their parents, and the occupation of the husband."

2. That where colored persons, before the passage of this act, shall have undertaken and agreed to occupy the relation to each other of husband and wife, and shall be cohabiting together as such at the time of its passage, whether the rites of marriage shall have been celebrated between them or not, they shall be deemed husband and wife, and be entitled to the rights and privileges, and subject to the duties and obligations of that relation, in like manner as if they had been duly married by law; and all their children shall be deemed legitimate, whether born before or after the passage of this act. And when the parties have ceased to cohabit before the passage of this act, in consequence of the death of the woman, or from any other cause, all the children of the woman, recognized by the man to be his, shall be deemed legitimate.

3. This act shall be in force from its passage.

Passed February 27, 1866.

AN ACT to amend and re-enact the 9th section of chapter 103 of the code of Virginia for 1860, defining a Mulatto, providing for the punishment of offences by colored persons, and for the admission of their evidence in legal investigations, and to repeal all laws in relation to slaves and slavery, and for other purposes.

1. *Be it enacted by the general assembly*, That every person having one-fourth or more of negro blood, shall be deemed a colored person: and every person, not a colored person, having one-fourth or more of Indian blood, shall be deemed an Indian.

2. All laws in respect to crimes and punishments, and in respect to criminal proceedings, applicable to white persons, shall apply in like manner to colored persons and to Indians, unless when it is otherwise specially provided.

3. The following acts and parts of acts are hereby repealed, namely: All acts and parts of act relating to slaves and slavery; chapter one hundred and seven of the code of eighteen hundred and sixty, relating to free negroes; chapter two hundred of said code, relating to offences by negroes; chapter two hundred and twelve of said code, relating to proceedings against negroes; chapter ninety-eight of said code, relating to patrols; sections twenty-five to forty-seven, both inclusive, of chapter one hundred and ninety-two of said code; sections twenty-six to thirty, both inclusive, and sections thirty-three to thirty-seven, both inclusive, of chapter one hundred and ninety-eight of said code; the fifth paragraph, as enumerated in section two of chapter two hundred and three of said code; all acts and parts of acts imposing on negroes the penalty of stripes, where the same penalty is not imposed on white persons; and all other acts and parts of acts inconsistent with this act.

4. This act shall be in force from its passage.
   Passed February 27, 1866.

AN ACT in relation to the testimony of colored persons.

1. *Be it enacted by the general assembly*, That colored persons and Indians shall, otherwise competent and subject to the rules applicable to other persons, shall be admitted as witnesses in the following cases:

1. In all civil cases and proceedings at law and in equity in which a colored person or an Indian is a party, or may be directly benefited or injured by the result.

2. In all criminal proceedings, in which a colored person or an Indian is a party or which arise out of an injury done, attempted or threatened to person, property, or rights of a colored person or Indian, or in which it is alleged in the presentment, information or indictment, or in which the court is of opinion, from the other evidence, that there is probable cause to believe that the offence was committed by a white person in conjunction or co-operation with a colored person or Indian.

3. The testimony of colored persons shall in all cases and proceedings, both at law and in equity, be given *ore tenus* and not by deposition; and in suits in equity and in all other cases in which the deposition of the witness would be regularly part of the record, the court shall, if desired by any party or if deemed proper by itself, certify the facts proved by such witness or the evidence given by him as far as credited by the court, and one or the other may be proper, under the rules of law applicable to the case; and such certificate shall be made part of the record.

4. This act shall be in force from its passage.
   Passed February 28, 1866.

AN ACT providing for the punishment of vagrants.

1. *Be it enacted by the general assembly*, That the overseers of the poor, or other officers having charge of the poor, or the special county police, or the police of any corporation, or any one or more of such persons, shall be and are hereby empowered and required, upon discovering any vagrant or vagrants within their respective counties or corporations, to make information thereof to any justice of the peace of their county or corporation, and to require a warrant for apprehending such vagrant or vagrants, to be brought be before him or some other justice; and if upon due examination it shall appear that the person or persons are within the true description of a vagrant, as hereinafter mentioned, such justice shall, by warrant, order such vagrant or vagrants to be employed in labor for any term not exceeding three months, and, but any constable of such county or corporation to be hired out for the best wages that can be procured; to be applied, except as hereafter provided, for the use of the vagrant or his family, as ordered by the justice. And if any such vagrant or vagrants shall, during such time of service, without sufficient case, run away from the person so employing him or them, he or they shall be apprehended on the warrant of a justice, and returned to the custody of such hirer, who shall have, free of any further hire, the services of said vagrant for one month in addition to the original term of hiring; and said employer shall then have the power, if authorized by the justice, to work said vagrant confined with ball and chain; or should said hirer decline to receive again said vagrant, then said vagrant shall be taken by the officer, upon the order of a justice, to the poor or work house, if there be any such in said county or corporation; or, if authorized by the justice, to work him, confined with ball and chain, for the period for which he would have had to serve his late employer, had he consented to receive him again; or should there be, when said runaway vagrant is apprehended, any public work going on in said county or corporation, then said vagrant, upon the order of a justice, shall be delivered over by said officer to the superintendent of such public work, who shall, for the like last mentioned period, work said vagrant on said public works, confined with ball and chain, if so authorized by the justice. But if there be no poor or work house in said county or cooperation, and no public work then in progress therein, then, in that event, said justice, may cause said vagrant to be delivered to any person who will take charge of him, said person to have his services free of charge. . . .

QUESTIONS TO CONSIDER

1. What rights do the Virginia Black Codes grant to freedpeople and what restrictions do they impose on those rights?
2. The Black Codes were a series of laws governing several different aspects of Black Southerners' social, legal, and familial lives. How do these several laws work together to limit and control the living conditions of Black Southerners?

15.4 VISUAL SOURCE: BATTLEGROUND RUINS IN CHARLESTON, SOUTH CAROLINA (c. 1860–1865)*

Charleston, South Carolina, held particular significance for Americans on both sides of the Civil War. As one of the largest cities in the Confederacy, the home of some outspoken proslavery ideologues, and the location of Fort Sumter where the war had begun, Charleston represented the heart of slavery and the secession. South Carolina, spurred on by a hotbed of secessionists in Charleston, had been the first state to secede in 1860. The Union government hoped to capture the city, both to close the port and to seize this important Confederate symbol. The Union Navy blockaded Charleston for over eighteen months between July 1863 and February 1865, when Confederate forces eventually evacuated, retreating ahead of a Union Army advancing north from Georgia.

Over a year of naval bombardment reduced much of the city to ruins. The building pictured in the foreground of this photograph was a church; one of its remaining columns stands prominently in the center of the image, while to the right a hole in the wall exposes the brickwork of the crumbling building. Though no people appear in the picture, signs of human habitation are evident in the path through the debris.

---

* Courtesy National Archives, photo no. III-B-4667

QUESTIONS TO CONSIDER

1. The column at the center of the image is relatively undamaged compared to the ruins all around it. What thoughts or feelings was the photographer trying to evoke by focusing his image on this architecture?
2. Many towns were captured during the Civil War without experiencing significant physical damage. What would the capture and destruction of Charleston have meant to those on different sides of the war?

15.5 VISUAL SOURCE: THOMAS NAST, *PARDON AND FRANCHISE* (1865)*

In the wake of the Civil War, the United States had to determine how to integrate former Confederates and Black Americans into the body politic. In this image published in *Harper's Weekly*, famous cartoonist Thomas Nast (1840–1902) juxtaposes former rebels seeking pardons from a disdainful feminine Columbia (representing an idealized United States) with Columbia's praise for a Black veteran wounded in battle.

---

* Courtesy of the Library of Congress

In May 1865, President Andrew Johnson (1808–1875) issued an amnesty proclamation for all former Confederates who would swear loyalty to the Union. However, Confederate leaders and major landholders were excepted and had to apply to Johnson personally for a pardon. Thanks to Johnson's pardon, many former rebels could participate in postwar elections and help guide the course of early reconstruction efforts. In contrast, no state had expanded voting opportunities for Black Americans by the end of the war, although Lincoln had endorsed the expansion of voting rights to some Black Americans, including soldiers. With former rebels allowed to vote in Southern states, where the overwhelming majority of Black people lived, the likelihood of a meaningful expansion of Black voting rights looked slim. Unable to vote themselves, Black veterans faced the prospect of having their rights curtailed by governments elected by the former rebels they had fought against.

QUESTIONS TO CONSIDER

1. The concept of loyalty is central to the contrast Nast draws in this image. What hypocrisy is he trying to highlight with this illustration?
2. Political cartoons in the nineteenth century frequently used Columbia to represent a civilized, idealized, and virtuous United States. How does Nast use this character to make his opinions clear to the reader?

CHAPTER 16

THE PROMISE AND LIMITS OF RECONSTRUCTION, 1865–1877

16.1 THADDEUS STEVENS, SPEECH TO CONGRESS (1867)*

Following the Confederate surrender at Appomattox, Virginia, in April 1865, President Andrew Johnson (1808–1875) and Republican lawmakers such as Thaddeus Stevens (1792–1868) disagreed over how to integrate former rebels into the Union. Johnson claimed that the authority to reconstruct the seceded states fell under his power as chief executive. He issued blanket pardons to many former rebels and installed governors of his own choosing in former Confederate states. Johnson made no attempt to enfranchise the millions of freedpeople who lived in the former Confederacy. In opposition to this approach, Stevens argued that Congress, as the legislative body elected by the American people, was the correct authority to determine the course of reconstruction. He feared that Johnson's pardons and refusal to grant Black Southerners the vote would lead the new Southern state governments to be dominated by former Confederates, endangering Black and white Southerners who had remained loyal to the Union throughout the war.

In the wake of the Civil War, Johnson, himself a white Southerner, thought it best to re-establish the Union as quickly as possible, with as little change as possible. Stevens argued that unless significant changes were instituted to prevent those who launched the rebellion from taking power again, then the war would have been fought for nothing.

---

* Thaddeus Stevens, "Speech on Reconstruction," January 3, 1867, Teaching American History, https://teachingamericanhistory .org/document/speech-on-reconstruction-2/.

This is a bill designed to enable loyal men, so far as I could discriminate them in these States, to form governments which shall be in loyal hands, that they may protect themselves from . . . outrages. . . . In states that have never been restored since the rebellion from a state of conquest, and which are this day held in captivity under the laws of war, the military authorities, under this decision and its extension into disloyal states, dare not order the commanders of departments to enforce the laws of the country. . . .

Since the surrender of the armies of the confederate States of America a little has been done toward establishing this Government upon the true principles of liberty and justice. . . . But in what have we enlarged their liberty of thought? In what have we taught them the science and granted them the privilege of self-government? . . . Call you this a free Republic when four millions are subjects but not citizens? . . . I pronounce it no nearer to a true Republic now when twenty-five million of a privileged class exclude five million from all participation in the rights of government. . . .

What are the great questions which now divide the nation? In the midst of the political Babel which has been produced by the intermingling of secessionists, rebels, pardoned traitors, hissing Copperheads, and apostate Republicans, such a confusion of tongues is heard that it is difficult to understand either the questions that are asked or the answers that are given. Ask, what is the "President's policy?" and it is difficult to define it. Ask, what is the "policy of Congress?" and the answer is not always at hand.

A few moments may be profitably spent in seeking the meaning of each of these terms. Nearly six years ago a bloody war arose between different sections of the United States. Eleven States, possessing a very large extent of territory, and ten or twelve million people, aimed to sever their connection with the Union, and to form an independent empire, founded on the avowed principle of human slavery and excluding every free State from this confederacy. . . . The two powers mutually prepared to settle the question by arms. . . .

President Lincoln, Vice President Johnson, and both branches of Congress repeatedly declared that the belligerent States could never again intermeddle with the affairs of the Union, or claim any right as members of the United States Government until the legislative power of the Government should declare them entitled thereto. . . . For whether their states were out of the Union as they declared, or were disorganized and "out of their proper relations" to the Government, as some subtle metaphysicians contend, their rights under the Constitution had all been renounced and abjured under oath, and could not be resumed on their own mere motion. . . .

The Federal arms triumphed. The confederate armies and government surrendered unconditionally. The law of nations then fixed their condition. They were subject to the controlling power of the conquerors. No former laws, no former compacts or treaties existed to bind the belligerents. They had all been melted and consumed in the fierce fires of the terrible war. The United States . . . appointed military provisional governors to regulate their municipal institutions until the law-making power of the conqueror should fix their condition and the law by which they should be permanently governed. . . . No one then supposed that those States had any governments, except such as they had formed under their rebel organization. . . . Whoever had then asserted that those States [were] entitled to all the rights and privileges which they enjoyed before the rebellion and were on a level with their loyal conquerors would have been deemed a fool. . . .

In this country the whole sovereignty rests with the people, and is exercised through their Representatives in Congress assembled. . . . No Government official, from the president and the Chief Justice down, can do any one single act which is not prescribed and directed by the legislative power. . . .

. . . This I take to be the great question between the President and Congress. He claims the right to reconstruct by his own power. Congress denies him all power in the matter, except those of advice, and has determined to maintain such denial. . . .

. . . [President Johnson] desires that the States created by him shall be acknowledged as valid States, while at the same time he inconsistently declares that the old rebel States are in full existence, and always have been, and have equal rights with the loyal States. . . .

Congress refuses to treat the States created by him as of any validity, and denies that the old rebel States have any existence which gives them any rights under the Constitution. . . . Congress denies that any State lately in rebellion has any government or constitution known to the Constitution of the United States. . . .

It is to be regretted that inconsiderate and incautious Republicans should ever have supposed that the slight amendments already proposed to the Constitution, even when incorporated into that instrument, would satisfy the reforms necessary for the security of the Government. Unless the rebel States, before admission, should be made republican in spirit, and placed under the guardianship of loyal men, all our blood and treasure will have been spent in vain. I waive now the question of punishment which, if we are wise, will still be inflicted by moderate confiscations, both as a reproof and example. Having these States, as we all agree, entirely within the power of Congress, it is our duty to take care that no injustice shall remain in their organic laws. Holding them "like clay in the hands of the potter," we must see that no vessel is made for destruction. Having now no governments, they must have enabling acts. . . . Impartial suffrage, both in electing the delegates and ratifying their proceedings, is now the fixed rule. There is more reason why colored voters should be admitted in the rebel States than in the Territories. In the States they form the great mass of the loyal men. Possibly with their aid loyal governments may be established in most of those States. Without it all are sure to be ruled by traitors; and loyal men, black and white, will be oppressed, exiled, or murdered. There are several good reasons for the passage of this bill. In the first place, it is just. I am now confining my arguments to Negro suffrage in the rebel States. Have not loyal blacks quite as good a right to choose rulers and make laws as rebel whites? In the second place, it is a necessity in order to protect the loyal white men in the seceded States. The white Union men are in a great minority in each of those States. With them the blacks would act in a body; and it is believed that in each of said States, except one, the two united would form a majority, control the States, and protect themselves.

Now they are the victims of daily murder. They must suffer constant persecution or be exiled. . . .

Another good reason is, it would insure the ascendancy of the Union party. Do you avow the party purpose? exclaims some horror-stricken demagogue. I do. For I believe, on my conscience, that on the continued ascendancy of that party depends the safety of this great nation. If impartial suffrage is excluded in the rebel States then everyone of them is sure to send a solid rebel representative delegation to Congress, and cast a solid rebel electoral vote. They, with their kindred Copperheads of the North, would always elect the President and control Congress. While slavery sat upon her defiant throne, and insulted and intimidated the trembling North, the South frequently divided on questions of policy between Whigs and Democrats, and gave victory alternately to the sections. Now, you must divide them between loyalists, without regard to color, and disloyalists, or you will be the perpetual vassals of the free-trade, irritated, revengeful South. For these, among other reasons, I am for Negro suffrage in every rebel State. If it be just, it should not be denied; if it be necessary, it should be adopted; if it be a punishment to traitors, they deserve it.

But it will be said, as it has been said, "This is Negro equality!" What is Negro equality. . .? It means . . . just this much, and no more: every man, no matter what his race or color; every earthly being who has an immortal soul, has an equal right to justice, honesty, and fair play with every other man; and the law should secure him these rights. The same law which condemns or acquits an African should condemn or acquit a white man. The same law which gives a verdict in a White man's favor should give a verdict in a black man's favor on the same state of facts. Such is the law of God and such ought to be the law of man. This doctrine does not mean that a Negro shall sit on the same seat or eat at the same table with a white man. That is a matter of taste which every man must decide for himself. . . . If there be any who are afraid of the rivalry of the black man in office or in business, I have only to advise them to try and beat their competitor in knowledge and business capacity, and there is no danger that his white neighbors will prefer his African rival to himself. . . .

QUESTIONS TO CONSIDER

1. According to Stevens, what are some of the "great questions" Americans must decide in the wake of the Civil War?
2. Stevens is very conscious of white Americans' prejudice against freedpeople and other Black Americans. How does he address this issue in his speech?

16.2 TESTIMONY OF MERVIN GIVENS TO CONGRESS ABOUT KU KLUX KLAN ACTIVITY IN SOUTH CAROLINA (1871)*

Beginning in 1866, Republicans in the United States Congress passed a series of laws and constitutional amendments meant to reconstruct former Confederate states. These policies established temporary military governorships in those states, enfranchised all men including freedmen, and barred some rebel leaders from holding political office. In response, many white Southerners engaged in violent campaigns of terror, primarily targeting Black Southerners as well as white Unionists. These attacks were often carried out by white supremacist groups such as the Ku Klux Klan, the White League, and the Red Shirts. Often attacking at night and in disguise, the terrorists would intimidate, harass, assault, mutilate, and kill men and women who they believed supported Republican, Unionist, or racially egalitarian policies. Although these groups were relatively unorganized at first, in the early 1870s they grew in size, incorporating Confederate veterans and adopting a more paramilitary character. In response to the testimony of people like Mervin Givens, Congress passed Enforcement Acts in 1870 and 1871, which President Ulysses S. Grant (1822–1885) used to effectively, if temporarily, curtail white supremacist terrorism in the South.

SPARTANBURG, SOUTH CAROLINA, July 12, 1871 MERVIN GIVENS (colored) sworn and examined. By Mr. Stevenson:

QUESTION: Your name in old times was Mery Moss?
ANSWER: Yes, sir; but since freedom I don't go by my master's name. My name now is Givens.
QUESTION: What is your age?
ANSWER: About forty I expect.
QUESTION: Where do you live?
ANSWER: With Silas Miles.

QUESTION: Where is that?
ANSWER: Five miles from here on the straight Columbia road.
QUESTION: Is it at General Bates's place?
ANSWER: No sir; it is on the road by Cedar Springs.
QUESTION: Did you not live on General Bates's place?
ANSWER: No, sir.
QUESTION: Have you ever been visited by the Ku-Klux?
ANSWER: Yes, sir.
QUESTION: When?

* *Report of the Joint Select Committee to Inquire into the Condition of Affairs in the Late Insurrectionary States, made to the two Houses of Congress, February 19, 1872*, Internet Archive, 698–700, https://archive.org/details/reportofjointselo4unit/page/698/mode/2up?q=givens.

ANSWER: About the last of April.

QUESTION: Tell what they said and did.

ANSWER: I was asleep when they came to my house, and did not know anything about them until they broke in on me.

QUESTION: What time of night was it?

ANSWER: About twelve o'clock at night. They broke in on me and frightened me right smart, being asleep. They ordered me to get up and make a light. As quick as I could gather my senses I bounced up and made a light, but not quick enough. They jumped at me and struck me with a pistol, and made a knot that you can see there now. By the time I made the light I catched the voice of them, and as soon as I could see by the light, I looked around and saw by the size of the men and voice so that I could judge right off who it was. By that time they jerked the case off the pillow and jerked it over my head and ordered me out of doors. That was all I saw in the house. After they carried me out of doors I saw nothing more. They pulled the pillow-slip over my head and told me if I took off they would shoot me. They carried me out and whipped me powerful.

QUESTION: With what?

ANSWER: With sticks and hickories. They whipped me powerful.

QUESTION: How many lashes?

ANSWER: I can't tell. I have no knowledge at all about it. May be a hundred or two. Two men whipped me and both at once.

QUESTION: Did they say anything to you?

ANSWER: They cursed me and told me I had voted the radical ticket, and they intended to beat me so I would not vote it again.

QUESTION: Did you know any of them?

ANSWER: Yes, sir; I think I know them.

QUESTION: What were their names?

ANSWER: One was named John Thomson and the other was John Zimmerman. Those are the two men I think it was.

QUESTION: How many were there in all?

ANSWER: I didn't see but two. After they took me out, I was blindfolded; but I could judge from the horse tracks that there were more than two horses there. Some were horses and some were mules. It was a wet, rainy night; they whipped me stark naked. I had a brown undershirt on and they tore it clean off.

QUESTION: Could you not judge whether there were more than two?

ANSWER: No, sir; they would not give me time. They whirled me right around and told me to go when they got through whipping, and I just split right off without trying to see anything more.

QUESTION: How far did you live from General Bates's place then?

ANSWER: I expect it was five miles.

QUESTION: Did you know what the Ku-Klux had done there?

ANSWER: No, sir. I didn't live in the settlement at all. I heard a heap, but I didn't know it.

QUESTION: Did you know whether the people were driven off of his place?

ANSWER: I think a good many were.

QUESTION: Did you know any of them who lived there?

ANSWER: I used to know them in old times, but I have almost forgotten, people have changed about so.

By Mr. Van Trump:

QUESTION: There were, then, two men who came to your house?

ANSWER: Yes, sir; that was all I could see.

QUESTION: Were they disguised?

ANSWER: Yes, sir.

QUESTION: How?

ANSWER: They had on some sort of gray-looking clothes, and much the same sort of thing over their face. One of them had a sort of high hat with tassel and sort of horns.

QUESTION: How far did John Thomson live from there?

ANSWER: I think it is two or three miles.

QUESTION: Were you acquainted with him?

ANSWER: Yes, sir.

QUESTION: Where?

ANSWER: At my house. My wife did a good deal of washing for them both. I was very well-acquainted with their size and their voices. They were boys I was raised with. John Zimmerman is a play-boy I have been with all my life.

QUESTION: How old is John?

ANSWER: About twenty-five years.

QUESTION: A married man?

ANSWER: No, sir, single.

QUESTION: How old is John Thomson?

ANSWER: I don't know his age. They lived farther below. The way I got acquainted with him, they kept a grocery shop.

QUESTION: Does living below make any difference about your knowing his age?

ANSWER: I never got acquainted with him until last winter.

QUESTION: Can you not form an idea of his age?

ANSWER: He may be the same age; he is a young gentleman.

QUESTION: Not married?

ANSWER: No, sir.

QUESTION: Were their faces completely covered?

ANSWER: Yes, sir; I could not see them.

QUESTION: Then it is only by judging their voices and size that you believe it was them?

ANSWER: Yes, sir.

QUESTION: Did you tell anybody else it was John Thomson?

ANSWER: I have never named it.

QUESTION: Why?

ANSWER: I was afraid to.

QUESTION: Are you afraid now?

ANSWER: I am not afraid to own the truth as nigh as I can.

QUESTION: Is there any difference in owning to the truth on the 12th of July and on the 1st of April?

ANSWER: The black people have injured themselves very much by talking, and I was afraid.

QUESTION: Are you not afraid now?

ANSWER: No, sir; because I hope there will be a stop put to it.

QUESTION: Why do you hope so?

ANSWER: Because I believe that gentlemen have got it in hand that is coming to do something for us.

QUESTION: Do you think we three gentlemen can stop it?

ANSWER: No, sir; but I think you can get some help.

QUESTION: Has anybody been telling you that?

ANSWER: No, sir; nobody told me that.

QUESTION: You did not see any horses when Thomson and Zimmerman came up to the house in the night?

ANSWER: No, sir; but over where they whipped, I went down next morning after my shirt, and the horses were hitched within about ten steps of the fence.

QUESTION: You thought there were more than Thomson and Zimmerman, judging by the horse tracks?

ANSWER: Yes, sir.

QUESTION: You said some were horse and some were mule tracks; can you tell the difference?

ANSWER: Yes, sir; I can tell the difference in the size of a horse's track and a mule's.

QUESTION: Is there much difference?

ANSWER: Yes, sir.

QUESTION: If both are shod?

ANSWER: Yes, sir; there is a great difference in the shape, and I have shod horses and mules, and I am very well acquainted with both kinds of feet.

QUESTION: Why did you not commence a prosecution against Thomson and Zimmerman?

ANSWER: I am like the rest, I reckon; I am too cowardly.

QUESTION: Why do you not do it now; you are not cowardly now?

ANSWER: I shouldn't have done it now.

QUESTION: I am talking about bringing suit for that abuse on that night. Why do you not have them arrested?

ANSWER: It ought to be done.

QUESTION: Why do you not do it?

ANSWER: For fear they would shoot me. If I were to bring them up here and could not prove the thing exactly on them, and they were to get out of it, I would not expect to live much longer.

QUESTIONS TO CONSIDER

1. Givens believed he knew the men who attacked him, despite their efforts to blindfold him. What does Givens's previous relationship with his attackers indicate about the postwar South and white supremacist violence there?

2. Givens and his questioners allude to other similar incidents of violence in nearby areas. How has Givens's life been impacted by this violence in his community?

16.3 VISUAL SOURCE: DISTINGUISHED MEMBERS, RECONSTRUCTED CONSTITUTION OF LOUISIANA (1868)*

Between 1867 and 1869, former Confederate states held conventions to establish new state constitutions that would codify political and civil rights for Black Americans. Over 250 Black delegates were elected to these conventions, and they constituted a majority in states such as Louisiana and South Carolina. This was a remarkable change from the antebellum period in which free and enslaved Black people made up a substantial minority, or even the majority, of state populations but were not considered part of the body politic. These representatives came from a variety of backgrounds. Most were ministers, craftsmen, teachers, or farmers; only a few had been manual laborers. Unusually, almost all Black convention delegates in Louisiana had been born free.

The constitutions these delegates helped write codified substantial changes to the prewar state governments. Many existing property qualifications (such as for jury service) were abandoned, punishments reminiscent of slavery such as whipping were outlawed, and government-funded public schools were established where there had been none. Although Black delegates were divided over some issues, such as whether to disenfranchise former rebels, they formed a solid bloc throughout the South in favor of expanded civil rights and public education.

* Courtesy of the Library of Congress

QUESTIONS TO CONSIDER

1. The delegates pictured here are surrounded by martial imagery such as battle flags, cannons, and bayonets. What is the illustrator trying to convey about the delegates with these symbols?
2. This image was included with a printing of the constitution the delegates eventually produced. What might have been the purpose of including this picture in the publication?

16.4 VISUAL SOURCE: PHILADELPHIA MAYORAL ELECTION POSTER ON RACIAL SEGREGATION ON PUBLIC TRANSIT (1868)*

While the national political focus remained on the former Confederacy and the fate of the freed-people there, Black communities in Northern states campaigned for equal treatment by their local governments. Although the Northern states had abolished slavery decades previously, many still had a variety of restrictive statutes that controlled when, where, and how Black Americans could work, travel, and live. The purpose of many of these laws was to keep Black Americans on the margins of society, to segregate Black communities from their white neighbors.

For decades Philadelphia housed one of the largest and most politically active Black communities in the Northern states. Following the Civil War, Black Philadelphians began to challenge racial segregation on the city's trolley car line. Segregation on the trolley cars not only curtailed Black Philadelphians' ability to travel but was a public rebuke of Black claims to social equality. For three years, Black Philadelphians protested these restrictions until an 1867 law finally forbade racial segregation on public transport in Pennsylvania. Segregation in public spaces remained a salient political issue, as this poster from the 1868 Philadelphia mayoral election demonstrates.

* Courtesy of the Library of Congress

QUESTIONS TO CONSIDER

1. How does the author use fonts and phrasing to frame the issue of segregation on municipal public transport?
2. The poster says Fox not only opposes integration on public transport but also "all social and political equality" with Black Americans. Why is racial equality a concern for Fox and his supporters at this particular moment—in 1868?

16.5 VISUAL SOURCE: THOMAS NAST, *UNCLE SAM'S THANKSGIVING DINNER* (1869)*

The German-born American cartoonist Thomas Nast (1840–1902) designed this idealistic portrayal of prosperity and racial equality for the Thanksgiving holiday in 1869. Following the ratification of the Fourteenth Amendment in 1868, which established equal citizenship for those born or naturalized in the United States, Nast's illustration portrays many different American ethnic groups participating in a shared feast. White, Black, Chinese, and Native American people of all ages feast together, seated at a table below portraits of presidents Washington, Lincoln, and Grant. The centerpiece of the table displays the slogans "Self Government" and "Universal Suffrage," while captions in the corner offer an invitation reading "Come One, Come All, Free and Equal."

Here Nast offers a deliberately aspirational portrayal of a truly egalitarian American society. The US government had attacked, enslaved, and proscribed all of the non-white groups represented, but here at "Uncle Sam's Thanksgiving Dinner" past wrongs are forgotten or forgiven. Nast illustrates the radical implications of the equality promised by the Fourteenth Amendment and highlights the hypocrisy of those who clung to racial prejudice while claiming to support the Constitution.

QUESTIONS TO CONSIDER

1. Examine the diners closely. Note which groups Nast depicts and how they interact with one another. How does Nast use the diners to represent his message?
2. What does Nast believe to be core American values? How can you tell this from his illustration?

---

* Courtesy of the Library of Congress

CHAPTER 17

CAPITALISM AND THE GILDED AGE, 1873–1890

17.1 WALT WHITMAN, "TO A LOCOMOTIVE IN WINTER" (1876)*

The expansion of railway networks throughout the United States—especially west of the Mississippi—in the 1870s and 1880s had profound implications for the country. Miles of new track were laid by a plethora of railroad corporations, connecting far-flung hamlets to major urban centers and spawning new settlements all along their line. These new companies required scores of wage laborers to keep them running, building tracks, feeding coal into engines, and loading freight. Railroads encouraged financial speculation and corruption, and their speed, size, and lack of safety precautions contributed to a dramatic increase in accidental deaths among American men.

This poem by Walt Whitman (1819–1892), one of the most influential poets in American history, rhapsodizes on the beauty and power of an inhuman form. However, Whitman's muse is not a natural phenomenon like a waterfall or sunset, but a man-made railroad engine. He draws the reader's mind to the details of the engine's structure and celebrates the imperious "fierce-throated beauty" that follows its own course. Whitman's poem expresses awe at a novel technology that had quickly begun to collapse barriers of space and time and reorder American society.

Thee for my recitative,
Thee in the driving storm even as now, the snow,
    the winter-day declining,
Thee in thy panoply, thy measur'd dual throbbing
    and thy beat convulsive,
Thy black cylindric body, golden brass and silvery
    steel,
Thy ponderous side-bars, parallel and
    connecting rods, gyrating, shuttling
    at thy sides,

Thy metrical, now swelling pant and roar, now
    tapering in the distance,

Thy great protruding head-light fix'd in front,
Thy long, pale, floating vapor-pennants, tinged
    with delicate purple,
The dense and murky clouds out-belching from
    thy smoke-stack,
Thy knitted frame, thy springs and valves, the
    tremulous twinkle of thy wheels,

---

* Walt Whitman, "To a Locomotive in Winter," *New-York Tribune*, February 19, 1876, p. 4. Library of Congress.

Thy train of cars behind, obedient, merrily
   following,
Through gale or calm, now swift, now slack, yet
   steadily careering;
Type of the modern—emblem of motion and
   power—pulse of the continent,
For once come serve the Muse and merge in verse,
   even as here I see thee,
With storm and buffeting gusts of wind and falling
   snow,
By day thy warning ringing bell to sound its notes,
By night thy silent signal lamps to swing.

Fierce-throated beauty!
Roll through my chant with all thy lawless music,
   thy swinging lamps at night,
Thy madly-whistled laughter, echoing, rumbling
   like an earthquake, rousing all,
Law of thyself complete, thine own track firmly
   holding,
(No sweetness debonair of tearful harp or glib
   piano thine,)
Thy trills of shrieks by rocks and hills return'd,
Launch'd o'er the prairies wide, across the lakes,
To the free skies unpent and glad and strong.

QUESTIONS TO CONSIDER

1. In this short poem Whitman pays meticulous attention to many details of the locomotive. What is he trying to convey to the reader by describing the train so specifically?
2. Trains and the railroad companies that ran them represented many things to nineteenth-century Americans: speed and technological progress, but also death and the temptation of corruption. What word choices or turns of phrase indicate how Whitman feels about the locomotive?

17.2 MRS. SPOTTED HORN BULL, TESTIMONY ON THE BATTLE OF THE GREASY GRASS (LITTLE BIGHORN) (N.D.)*

The Battle of the Greasy Grass, often known in the United States as the Battle of the Little Bighorn or simply as Custer's Last Stand, was a major battle of the Great Sioux War that took place between June 25–26, 1876, in southern Montana. The war began months earlier, following several years of incursions by US miners and cavalry into the Sioux reservation in the Black Hills of South Dakota. In June 1876, US Lt. Col. George Armstrong Custer led the US 7th Cavalry to scout the Little Bighorn river valley, where they encountered and attacked a large village of Sioux and Cheyenne. The poorly planned attack failed, and the well-armed Sioux and Cheyenne overwhelmed Custer's command, killing over 270 men.

   This passage comes from a description of the battle as experienced by the unnamed wife of Spotted Horn Bull, a chief of the Hunkpapas, an oyáte, or tribe, of the Lakota Sioux. She recalls the conflict from the perspective of Native noncombatants who were a primary target of Custer's attack.

---

* James McLaughlin, *My Friend the Indian* (Boston: Houghton Mifflin, 1910), 167–72.

US Army forces targeted noncombatant Native people either to kill them, to destroy a village, or to hold them hostage as leverage in negotiations.

---

ike that the soldiers were upon us. Through the tepee poles their bullets rattled. The sun was several hours high and the tepees were empty. Bullets coming from a strip of timber on the west bank of the Greasy Grass passed through the tepees of the Blackfeet and Hunkpapa. The broken character of the country across the river, together with the fringe of trees on the west side, where our camp was situated, had hidden the advance of a great number of soldiers, which we had not seen until they were close upon us and shooting into our end of the village, where, from seeing the direction taken by the soldiers we were watching, we felt comparatively secure.

The women and children cried, fearing they would be killed, but the men, the Hunkpapa and Blackfeet, the Oglala and Minniconjou, mounted their horses and raced to the Blackfeet tepees. We could still see the soldiers of Long Hair marching along in the distance, and our men, taken by surprise, and from a point whence they had not expected to be attacked, went singing the song of battle into the fight behind the Blackfeet village. And we women wailed over the children, for we believed that the Great Father had sent all his men for the destruction of the Sioux. Some of the women put loads on the travois and would have left, but that their husbands and sons were in the fight. Others tore their hair and wept for the fate that they thought was to be the portion of the Sioux, through the anger of the Great Father, but the men were not afraid, and they had many guns and cartridges. Like the fire that, driven by a great wind, sweeps through the heavy grass-land where the buffalo range, the men of the Hunkpapa, the Blackfeet, the Oglala, and the Minniconjou rushed through the village and into the trees, where the soldiers of the white chief had stopped to fire. The soldiers [Reno's] had been sent by Long Hair to surprise the village of my people. Silently had they moved off around the hills, and keeping out of sight of the young men of our people, had crept in, south of what men now call Reno Hill; they had crossed the Greasy Grass and climbed the bench from the bank.

The way from the river to the plateau upon which our tepees stood was level, but the soldiers were on foot when they came in sight of the Blackfeet. Then it was that they fired and warned us of their approach. . . .

The shadow of the sun had not moved the width of a tepee pole's length from the beginning to the ending of the first fight. . . . Even the women, who knew nothing of warfare, saw that Reno had struck too early, and the warriors who were generals in planning, even as Long Hair was, knew that the white chief would attempt to carry out his plan of the attack, believing that Reno had beaten our young men. There was wild disorder in our camp, the old women and children shrieked and got in the way of the warriors, and the women were ordered back out of the village, so that they might not be in the way of our soldiers. And our men went singing down the river, confident that the enemy would be defeated, even as we believed that all of Reno's men had been killed. And I wept with the women for the brave dead and exulted that our braves should gain a great victory over the whites led by Long Hair, who was the greatest of their chiefs, and whose soldiers could then be plainly seen across the river. From a hill behind the camp, at first, and then from the bank of the river, I watched the men of our people plan to overthrow the soldiers of the Great Father; and before a shot was fired, I knew that no man who rode with Long Hair would go back to tell the tale of the fight that would begin when the soldiers approached the river at the lower end of the village. . . .

From across the river I could hear the music of the bugle and could see the column of soldiers turn to the left, to march down to the river to where the attack was to be made. All I could see was the warriors of my people. They rushed like the wind through the village, going down the ravine as the women went out to the grazing-ground to round up the ponies. It was done very quickly. There had been no council the night before—there was no need for one; nor had there been a scalp-dance: nothing but the merry-making of the young men and the maidens. When we did not know there was to be a fight, we could not be prepared for it. And our camp was not pitched anticipating a battle. The warriors would not have picked out such a place for a fight with white men, open to attack from both ends and from the west side. No; what was done that day was done while the sun stood still and the white men were delivered into the hands of the Sioux. . . .

I cannot remember the time. When men fight and the air is filled with bullets, when the screaming of horses that are shot drowns the war-whoop of the warriors, a woman whose husband and brothers are in the battle does not think of the time. But the sun was no longer overhead when the war-whoop of the Sioux sounded from the river-bottom and the ravine surrounding the hill at the end of the ridge where Long Hair had taken his last stand. The river was in sight from the butte, and while the whoop still rung in our ears and the women were shrieking, two Cheyennes tried to cross the river and one of them was shot and killed by Longo Hair's men. Then the men of the Sioux nation, led by Crow King, Hump, Crazy Horse, and many great chiefs, rose up on all sides of the hill, and the last we could see from our side of the river was a great number of gray horses. The smoke of the shooting and the dust of the horses shut out the hill, and the soldiers fired many shots, but the Sioux shot straight and the soldiers fell dead. The women crossed the river after the men of our village, and when we came to the hill there were no soldiers living and Long Hair lay dead among the rest. There were more than two hundred dead soldiers on the hill, and the boys of the village shot many who were already dead, for the blood of the people was hot and their hearts bad, and they took no prisoners that day.

QUESTIONS TO CONSIDER

1. Mrs. Spotted Horn Bull describes the behavior of US Armed Forces led by Reno and Custer (Long Hair). How does she understand the motives and behavior of the US Army and its intentions toward the Sioux?
2. What emotions do Mrs. Spotted Horn Bull and her fellow villagers experience? How do they respond to the sudden threat posed by the US Army?

17.3 FRANK LLOYD WRIGHT, ON SEEING HIS FIRST AMERICAN CITY (1887)*

Frank Lloyd Wright (1867–1959) was one of the most significant American architects of the twentieth century. His designs often emphasized the environment surrounding a building and sought to harmonize human habitation with the natural world. A pioneer in modernist architecture, Wright worked in Chicago and the surrounding area for decades.

In his 1932 autobiography, Wright describes first arriving in Chicago in 1887 at the age of twenty. Chicago had experienced exponential growth and had nearly doubled its population to

* Frank Lloyd Wright, "Frank Lloyd Wright Sees His First American City," in *An Autobiography Frank Lloyd Wright* (New York: Duell, Sloan and Pearce, 1932), 63–64.

over a million in the 1880s alone. Shortly after Wright's arrival, Chicago outstripped Philadelphia to become America's second-largest city. When Wright first viewed Chicago, many of the buildings were of recent construction, both because of the dramatic population increase and because of a devastating fire that had burned through the city in 1871. Wright describes himself as unimpressed with much of the cityscape, commenting that the buildings are all designed with "the same thought or lack of it," in a "savage, outrageous attempt at variety." He is similarly disoriented by the city's scale, depicting one of his first experiences as being swept up in a "brutal, hurrying crowd."

Wells Street Station: Six o'clock in late Spring, 1887. Drizzling. Sputtering white arc-light in the station and in the streets, dazzling and ugly. I had never seen electric lights before.

Crowds. Impersonal, intent on seeing nothing.

Somehow I didn't like to ask anyone anything. Followed the crowd. . . .

I wondered where Chicago was—if it was near. Suddenly the clanging of a bell. The crowd began to run. I wondered why: found myself alone and realized why in time to get off but stayed on as the bridge swung out with me into the channel and a tug, puffing clouds of steam, came pushing along below, pulling at an enormous iron grain boat, towing it slowly along through the gap.

Stood there studying the river-sights in the drizzling rain until the bridge followed after and closed to open the street again. Later, I never crossed the river without being charmed by somber beauty.

Wondered where to go for the night. But again if I thought to ask anyone, there was only the brutal, hurrying crowd, trying hard not to see.

Drifted south.

This must be Chicago now. So cold, black, blue-white and wet.

The horrid blue-white glare of arc-lights was over everything.

Shivering. Hungry. Went into an eating place near Randolph Street and parted with seventy cents, ten per cent of my entire capital.

Got into the street again to find it colder raining harder. . . .

. . . Wabash Avenue. Cottage-Grove Avenue cable cars were running there. My first sight of the cable car. So, curious, I got on the grip-car beside the gripman and tried to figure it all out, going south in the process

until the car stopped and "all out!" That car was going to the barn.

Got on the one coming out headed north now. Not sleepy nor tired. Half resentful because compelled to read the signs pressing on the eyes everywhere. They claimed your eyes for this, that, and everything beside. They lined the car above the windows. They lined the way, pushing, crowding and playing all manner of tricks on the desired eye.

Tried to stop looking at them. Compelled to look again. Kept on reading until reading got to be torture.

There were glaring signs on the glass shop-fronts against the lights inside, sharp signs in the glare of the sputtering arc-lamps outside.

HURRAH signs. STOP signs. COME ON IN signs. HELLO signs set out before the blazing windows on the sidewalks. Flat fences lettered both sides, man-high, were hanging out across above the sidewalks and lit by electric lamps. . . .

Supersensitive eyes were fixed by harsh dissonance and recovered themselves: reasoned and fought for freedom. Compelled again—until the procession of saloons, food shops, barber shops, eating houses, saloons, restaurants, groceries, laundries—and saloons, saloons, tailors, dry goods, candy shops, bakeries and saloons, became chaos in a wilderness of Italian, German, Irish, Polak, Greek, English, Swedish, French, Chinese and Spanish names in letters that began to come off, and get about, interlace and stick and climb and swing again.

Demoralization of the eye began: names obliterating everything. Names and what they would do for you or with you or to you for your money. Shutting your eyes didn't end it, for then you heard them louder than you saw them. They would begin to mix with absurd effect and you need take nothing to get the effect of another extravaganza. Letters this time. Another ballet, of A. B. C. D. E. F. G., L. M. N. O. P., X. Y. and Z the premier danseuse, intervening in fantastic dances. . . .

Chicago architecture! Where was it? Not the Exposition Building, a rank, much-domed yellow shed on the lake front. No, nor the rank and file along the streets. The rank and file all pretty much alike, industriously varied but with no variety. All the same thought or lack of it. Were all American cities like this one, so casual, so monotonous in their savage, outrageous attempts at variety? All competing for the same thing in the same way? Another senseless competition never to be won?

QUESTIONS TO CONSIDER

1. Wright's family moved around frequently during his childhood but rarely settled in a town of more than ten thousand people. What features of the comparatively huge city of Chicago most surprise Wright in his first impression?

2. In what way does Wright's description of nineteenth-century Chicago resemble modern American metropolises? What stands out as different?

17.4 VISUAL SOURCE: WILLIAM HOLBROOK BEARD, *THE BULLS AND BEARS IN THE MARKET, WALL STREET* (1879)*

American painter William Holbrook Beard (1824–1900) frequently used animals to satirize human behavior in his work. In this composition painted in oil on linen, he portrays a cavalcade of bulls and bears meant to represent investors in the New York Stock Exchange. His choice of animals corresponds to recently developed slang terms: a "bull" investor aggressively bought stocks believing their value would increase, while a cautious "bear" investor believed the market was headed for a downturn. Beard painted this piece during the economic depression resulting from the Panic of 1873, a financial crisis caused in part by zealous overvaluing of railroad bonds.

Beard places his stampede in the center of the New York financial district. To the left the New York Stock Exchange is clearly visible, while the columns of the United States Sub-Treasury are visible to the right.

* Photography © New-York Historical Society

QUESTIONS TO CONSIDER

1. Beard's choice of setting and animals made it clear that he intended to satirize the expanding American financial system. What is Beard saying with this piece about the behavior of Wall Street bankers and investors?

2. Note the bears throughout the painting. How do their behaviors compare to those of the bulls in their midst and why is this significant?

17.5 VISUAL SOURCE: SOLOMON D. BUTCHER, *THE SHORES FAMILY NEAR WESTERVILLE, CUSTER COUNTY, NE (1887)*

American photographer Solomon Butcher (1856–1927) produced thousands of images in his lifetime, primarily of homesteaders in central Nebraska where he lived. Beginning in 1862, the US Congress passed a series of Homestead Acts that offered to sell federal land in the western states

---

* Nebraska State Historical Society, [Digital ID nbhips 10527]

and territories to aspiring farmers. Homesteaders paid a small price for their acreage as long as they agreed to remain and farm the land. With the end of the Civil War and the expansion of western railroads, homesteaders flooded into the Great Plains. Nebraska's population ballooned from less than thirty thousand in 1860 to over a million in 1890.

This portrait shows the family of Jerry Shores, a formerly enslaved man who emigrated to central Nebraska and took up a homestead with his brothers Moses Speese and Henry Webb. Although many freed people sought a new life on homesteads around Omaha and western Nebraska, they made up only a relatively small portion of the state's population. Shores's farm building is constructed of prairie sod, a standard building material among Great Plains homesteaders who had little access to wood or other building materials.

QUESTIONS TO CONSIDER

1. What does this image tell you about living conditions on nineteenth-century Great Plains homesteads?
2. What made a homestead farm in the western states appealing to Black families like the Shores?

17.6 VISUAL SOURCE: THE DESTRUCTION OF THE BUFFALO (c. 1892)*

American bison, sometimes colloquially known as buffalo, are large grazing animals that once dominated much of the central North American continent. Living in huge herds and numbering in the tens of millions, the bison were essential to the livelihoods of many Native peoples of the Great Plains such as the Comanche, Lakota, and Blackfoot. Hunting bison provided important supplies to these groups such as large amounts of meat and skins that could be used to make clothing. The bison also held immense spiritual significance for many of these groups.

During the latter half of the 1800s, as the US Army continually went to war with Great Plains Indians, army officials began ordering the slaughter of bison to deprive the Native peoples of this valuable resource. By killing this integral animal, the army hoped to render their nomadic life impossible, making it easier to force them onto reservations. Numerous hunters also engaged in massive bison hunts, and, along with the army, they killed millions of bison, almost driving them extinct. In this photograph, two men pose with an enormous pile of bison skulls.

* public domain / Wikipedia

QUESTIONS TO CONSIDER

1. How are the men in this photograph posed? How do they feel about the destruction of the buffalo?
2. How does this photograph use scale to capture the magnitude of the killing?

CAULDRONS OF PROTEST, 1873–1896

18.1 BOB HART, "THE EIGHT-HOUR SYSTEM" (N.D.)*

The labor organization the Knights of Labor popularized the concept of the eight-hour day as it grew to prominence during the 1870s. At the time, many Americans, especially manual laborers, were expected to work ten hours a day or more—a schedule that was not only exhausting but also left little time for other pursuits or relationships. Unlike other labor organizations, the Knights were open to almost every sort of laborer, even those who did work that was not considered skilled, and shortening the workday was an issue that workers of all sorts could rally behind. The slogan "Eight hours for work, eight hours for rest, eight hours for what we will!" captured the idea that a worker's life should not be entirely controlled or "monopolized" by his employer. Working men, the Knights and their allies claimed, had a right to the time they needed to live full and fruitful lives. A shorter workday meant more time to spend with family, to pursue education and improvement, to participate in politics and culture, and to rest. Although broadly understood as normal today, in the late nineteenth century the eight-hour day represented a radical change in Americans' working conditions.

Respectfully Dedicated to Mr. James Davis and Employees.
Composed and sung by Bob Hart, Academy of Music.

Air—*Whack row-de-row.*
Come, workmen, all, both great and small,
    Pay attention to my ditty,
'Tis something interests you all
    That labour in this city.
Be wide awake,
An interest take—
    Don't wait for legislation;

The greatest aim of all mankind,
It is self-preservation.

CHORUS.
Whack row-de-row,
How are you, eight-hour system;
Whack row-de-row,
We are bound to put it through.

Our claims are just—we know they're right,
    As honest men will all agree;
We wage no war on capital,

---

* The Eight-Hour System. Monographic. Online Text. https://www.loc.gov/item/amss.as103300/.

That every one can see.
If you want to know,
We can soon show,
 Without any exaggeration,
We'll do as much in eight now
 With a little more exertion.

CHORUS. Whack row-de-row, &c.

We will take the hours of the day,
 And divide them up by three;
First, take eight for labour, say,
 Which we'll do honestly;
Eight for rest,
Which, at the best,
 Gives our strength time to recover;
And eight more to attend the wants
 Of our distressed worthy brothers.

CHORUS. Whack, row-de-row, &c.

You may talk about your heroes,

But where is one so grand,
Who kindness to his fellows shows,
 And rightly understands.
One of this kind
You're sure to find,
 If the trouble you will take, sirs.
At twenty-seven Julia street,
 Is the prince of boiler-makers.

CHORUS. Whack row-de-row, &c.

Here the honest sons of Vulcan
 In their glory you may find;
Their hammers click, the time flies quick,
 They never are behind.
The secret's one
That all may own,
 It will cost you but the trial,
The eight-hour system is the thing—
 It's a fact, and there's no denial.

CHORUS. Whack row-de-row, &c.

QUESTIONS TO CONSIDER

1. What arguments does the songwriter advance for the justice of an eight-hour workday?
2. The lyrics declare that "The aim of all mankind/It is self-preservation." How does this sentiment resonate with the demand for an eight-hour workday?

18.2 COLORED FARMERS' ALLIANCE ON VIOLENCE AGAINST BLACK FARMERS (1889)*

The Farmers' Alliance was one of a variety of labor organizations that encouraged mutualism and cooperation among farmers and laborers while opposing monopolies. White members of the Alliance barred Black farmers from joining its Southern branches, so Black farmers established their own Colored Farmers' Alliance. An important way in which the Alliance tried to aid farmers was by establishing cooperative stores that would offer agricultural supplies at a more affordable rate.

 White Southerners had a long history of using mob violence to enforce white supremacy and prevent what they saw as interference with the racial status quo. They understood attempts by Black

---

* "Dispatch from a Mississippi Colored Farmers' Alliance," *The Forum* 9, no. 6 (New York: Forum Publishing Company, 1890), 716–17, https://www.americanyawp.com/reader/16-capital-and-labor/dispatch-from-a-mississippi-colored-farmers-alliance-1889/.

Americans to organize and improve their livelihoods as a threat to white supremacy. They accused organizations like the Alliance of taking advantage of Black Southerners' supposed "ignorance" and asserted that their "supervision" was therefore necessary. Meetings and lists of resolutions as seen in this article were used by perpetrators of mob violence and white supremacist attacks to portray their actions as the reasonable response of a "united and outraged community."

Some Knights of Labor in Louisiana ventured to ask their employers for a larger share of the plantation crops; they were called rioters, and shot down in cold blood. Such occurrences have taken place in various sections. Take, for instance, the case of the suppression of the Farmers' Alliances at Minter City, Mississippi. Minter City is in the rich, cotton-growing region of Tallahatchie County. White lecturers of the Farmers' Alliances went there and organized Alliance stores. Colored people joined the organizations. The Alliance at Durant, on the Illinois Central Railroad, advanced supplies. The farmers began to patronize these stores, instead of the local traders, who had charged them enormous profits, swallowing up their little earnings. These local traders determined that the Alliances should be broken up. The annexed extracts from the St. Louis "Globe-Democrat," in a dispatch dated December 2, 1889, tell how it was done.

"Of all the 'Nigger killings' charged up to Mississippi, the recent campaign in the Tallahatchie country was the worst. The smallest estimate of the number shot is 20. The largest return of casualties is 200 dead. Probably 40 Negroes were murdered before the work ceased. The sole offense which called for such a terrible lesson was the organization of a Colored Farmers' Alliance, and the attempt to put in practice the plan of patronizing an Alliance store. Against the right of the Negro to enjoy the benefits of the Farmers' Alliance organization, the white store-keepers and planters of the Tallahatchie country banded themselves together. They began by exiling Cromwell, the agent of the commercial company. The usual reports now went out that the Negroes were organizing and arming for a race conflict. Then the killing began. . . . There was no battle. There was no resistance by the Negroes. The white store-keepers and planters, armed with Winchesters, rode through the country picking out their victims. . . . The condemned man was made to stand facing a tree, and a volley was fired at his back. Then

the white store-keepers and planters rode on to the next place. It is known that at least 20 Negroes were killed in this way. . . . The outline of facts comes from white men and Democrats. . . . When the white store-keepers and planters had concluded their work they met and adopted the following resolutions:

"Whereas, it is the sense of this meeting that the organization known here as the Colored Farmers' Alliance is being diverted from its original or supposed purpose,

"Resolved, that we, the planters and citizens of Tallahatchie River, hereby request the Durant Commercial Company to desist from selling goods or loaning money to said organization . . . and we hereby serve notice that goods or other things shipped to the secretaries or managers of said Alliance shall not be delivered. . . . We do not intend to, and we will not submit to, a combination subversive of our fortunes, our lives, and our property.

"Resolved, that the secretary of this meeting be required to notify the editor of the Colored Farmers' 'Alliance Advocate,' published at Valden, Miss., that the issuance of copies of his paper to subscribers at the Shell Mound, McNutt, Sunnyside, Minter City, Graball, and Sharkey post offices shall be stopped, and to notify him further that a disregard of this notice will be treated as it should deserve by a united and outraged community.

"Resolved, that the members of this meeting pledge themselves individually and collectively to carry out these resolutions in letter and spirit.

"Resolved, that the Secretary forward a copy of the proceedings of this meeting to said Durant Commercial Company and the editor of the Colored Farmers' 'Alliance Advocate,' by mail."

The local Tallahatchie county paper says:

"These resolutions look harsh and arbitrary, but when the fearful ignorance and prejudice of the Negroes are taken into account, it is indisputable that a combination of any kind among them is dangerous and needs more or less surveillance. They frequently prostitute their churches and benevolent orders to wrongful purposes."

In view of the incidents and purposes of the foregoing brutal and bloody Minter City tragedy, well does the "Globe-Democrat" ask: "What will the National Farmers' Alliance do about this?" On the other hand, what, may we ask, will not the southern Democrats do when the southern Farmers' Alliances not only organize co-operative stores, but also undertake to elect members of the Farmers' Alliances as State officers and congressmen?

We give the answer: they will not be allowed a free canvass or an honest count. They will be trampled under foot by reckless southern Democrats. Free politics does not exist at the South. Freedom is there a mockery to the black man; suffrage is a sham to all Republicans. All that a national law can accomplish toward fair elections at the South, both for the Republican and Farmers' Alliance candidates, should be done. But more than that is needed. When southern Democrats like Senator Pugh openly proclaim that national laws, constitutionally enacted, are to be resisted at the South unto bloodshed, there should be aroused everywhere at the North a sentiment of indignation; and this, growing stronger each day, should at last resemble that northern uprising of former days, which, overcoming commercial cowardice and dough-faced subserviency, first thrust slavery back to its gloomy lair, and next, on due provocation, invaded its precincts and destroyed the monster forever.

QUESTIONS TO CONSIDER

1. How does the Colored Farmers' Alliance connect the attacks in Mississippi to other problems in the South? What solutions does the Alliance propose?
2. How do the attackers use their resolutions to justify their murders? What do they want readers to believe about the violence they committed?

18.3 LUCY PARSONS, SPEECH TO THE INDUSTRIAL WORKERS OF THE WORLD (1905)*

Lucy Parsons (1851–1942) was an anarchist and labor organizer in Chicago between the 1870s and 1930s. Parsons was born into slavery, although she rarely spoke about the circumstances of her birth and upbringing. Her husband, Albert Parsons, was one of four anarchist organizers controversially convicted and executed for the Haymarket bombing. She was a founding member of numerous labor organizations, including the Industrial Workers of the World (IWW), an international union founded in 1905 that sought to unionize workers across a range of professions and industries. Parsons contributed to a variety of anarchist and labor-related publications but was best known as a powerful orator.

In this speech to the founding convention of the IWW, Parsons addresses several topics including the experience of women under capitalism, the need for a general strike, and the legacy of the

* "Lucy Parsons Speech to the IWW," in *Proceedings of the First Convention of the Industrial Workers of the World* (New York Labor News Co., 1905), 167–72.

Haymarket bombing. Speaking to a union that was meant to organize a wide variety of workers, she stresses the need for unified action, encouraging her listeners to "sink such differences as nationality, religion, and politics."

I can assure you that after the intellectual feast that I have enjoyed immensely this afternoon, I feel fortunate to appear before you now in response to your call. I do not wish you to think that I am here to play upon words when I tell you that I stand before you and feel much like a pigmy before intellectual giants, but that is only the fact. I wish to state to you that I have taken the floor because no other woman has responded, and I feel that it would not be out of place for me to say in my poor way a few words about this movement.

We, the women of this country, have no ballot even if we wished to use it, and the only way that we can be represented is to take a man to represent us. You men have made such a mess of it in representing us that we have not much confidence in asking you; and I for one feel very backward in asking the men to represent me. We have no ballot, but we have our labor. I think it is August Bebel, in his *Woman in the Past, Present and Future*—a book that should be read by every woman that works for wages—I think it is Bebel that says that men have been slaves throughout all the ages, but that woman's condition has been worse, for she has been the slave of a slave. I think there was never a greater truth uttered. We are the slaves of the slaves. We are exploited more ruthlessly than men. Wherever wages are to be reduced the capitalist class use women to reduce them, and if there is anything that you men should do in the future it is to organize the women.

And I tell you that if the women had inaugurated a boycott of the State street stores since the teamsters' strike they would have surrendered long ago. (Applause). I do not stand before you to brag. I had no man connected with that strike to make it of interest to me to boycott the stores, but I have not bought one penny's worth there since that strike was inaugurated. I intended to boycott all of them as one individual at least, so it is important to educate the women. Now I wish to show my sisters here that we fasten the chains of slavery upon our sisters, sometimes unwittingly, when we go down to the department store and look around for cheap bargains and go home and exhibit what we have got so cheap. When we come to reflect it simply means the robbery of our sisters, for we know that the things cannot be made for such prices and give the women who made them fair wages.

I wish to say that I have attended many conventions in the twenty-seven years since I came here to Chicago, a young girl, so full of life and animation and hope. It is to youth that hope comes; it is to age that reflection comes. I have attended conventions from that day to this of one kind and another and taken part in them. I have taken part in some in which our Comrade Debs had a part. I was at the organization that he organized in this city some eight or ten years ago. Now, the point I want to make is that these conventions are full of enthusiasm. And that is right; we should sometimes mix sentiment with soberness; it is a part of life. But, as I know from experience, there are sober moments ahead of us, and when you go out of this hall, when you have laid aside your enthusiasm, then comes solid work. Are you going out with the reflection that you appreciate and grasp the situation that you are to tackle? Are you going out of here with your minds made up that the class in which we call ourselves, revolutionary Socialists so-called—that that class is organized to meet organized capital with the millions at its command? It has many weapons to fight us. First it has money. Then it has legislative tools. Then it has its judiciary; it has its army and its navy; it has its guns; it has armories; and last, it has the gallows. We call ourselves revolutionists. Do you know what the capitalists mean to do to you revolutionists? I simply throw these hints out that you young people may become reflective and know what you have to face at the first, and then it will give you strength. I am not here to cause any discouragement, but simply to encourage you to go on in your grand work.

Now, that is the solid foundation that I hope this organization will be built on; that it may be built not like a house upon the sand, that when the waves of adversity come it may go over into the ocean of oblivion; but that it shall be built upon a strong, granite, hard foundation; a foundation made up of the hearts and aspirations of the men and women of this twentieth century who have set their minds, their bands, their hearts and their heads against the past with all its miserable poverty, with its wage slavery, with its children ground into dividends, with its miners away down under the earth and with never the light of sunshine, and with its women selling the holy name of womanhood for a day's board. I hope we understand that this organization has set its face against that iniquity, and that it has set its eyes to the rising star of liberty, that means fraternity, solidarity, the universal brotherhood of man. I hope that while politics have been mentioned here—I am not one of those who, because a man or woman disagrees with me, cannot act with them—I am glad and proud to say I am too broad-minded to say they are a fakir or fool or a fraud because they disagree with me. My view may be narrow and theirs may be broad; but I do say to those who have intimated politics here as being necessary or a part of this organization, that I do not impute to them dishonesty or impure motives. But as I understand the call for this convention, politics had no place here; it was simply to be an economic organization, and I hope for the good of this organization that when we go away from this hall, and our comrades go some to the west, some to the east, some to the north and some to the south, while some remain in Chicago, and all spread this light over this broad land and carry the message of what this convention has done, that there will be no room for politics at all. There may be room for politics; I have nothing to say about that; but it is a bread and butter question, an economic issue, upon which the fight must be made.

Now, what do we mean when we say revolutionary Socialist? We mean that the land shall belong to the landless, the tools to the toiler, and the products to the producers. (Applause.) Now, let us analyze that for just a moment, before you applaud me. First, the land belongs to the landless. Is there a single land owner in this country who owns his land by the constitutional rights given by the constitution of the United States who will allow you to vote it away from him? I am not such a fool as to believe it. We say, "The tools belong to the toiler." They are owned by the capitalist class. Do you believe they will allow you to go into the halls of the legislature and simply say, "Be it enacted that on and after a certain day the capitalist shall no longer own the tools and the factories and the places of industry, the ships that plow the ocean and our lakes?" Do you believe that they will submit? I do not. We say, "The products belong to the producers." It belongs to the capitalist class as their legal property. Do you think that they will allow you to vote them away from them by passing a law and saying, "Be it enacted that on and after a certain day Mr. Capitalist shall be dispossessed?" You may, but I do not believe it. Hence, when you roll under your tongue the expression that you are revolutionists, remember what that word means. It means a revolution that shall turn all these things over where they belong to the wealth producers. Now, how shall the wealth producers come into possession of them? I believe that if every man and every woman who works, or who toils in the mines, the mills, the workshops, the fields, the factories and the farms in our broad America should decide in their minds that they shall have that which of right belongs to them, and that no idler shall live upon their toil, and when your new organization, your economic organization, shall declare as man to man and women to woman, as brothers and sisters, that you are determined that you will possess these things, then there is no army that is large enough to overcome you, for you yourselves constitute the army. (Applause). Now, when you have decided that you will take possession of these things, there will not need to be one gun fired or one scaffold erected. You will simply come into your own, by your own independence and your own manhood, and by asserting your own individuality, and not sending any man to any legislature in any State of the American Union to enact a law that you shall have what is your own; yours by nature and by your manhood and by your very presence upon this earth.

Nature has been lavish to her children. She has placed in this earth all the material of wealth that is necessary to make men and women happy. She has given us brains to go into her store house and bring from its recesses all that is necessary. She has given us these two hands and these brains to manufacture them suited to the wants of men and women. Our civilization stands on a parallel with all other civilizations. There is just one thing we lack, and we have only ourselves to blame if we do not become free. We simply lack the intelligence to take possession of that which we have produced. (Applause). And I believe and

I hope and I feel that the men and women who constitute a convention like this can come together and organize that intelligence. I must say that I do not know whether I am saying anything that interests you or not, but I feel so delighted that I am talking to your heads and not to your hands and feet this afternoon. I feel that you will at least listen to me, and maybe you will disagree with me, but I care not; I simply want to shed the light as I see it. I wish to say that my conception of the future method of taking possession of this is that of the general strike: that is my conception of it. The trouble with all the strikes in the past has been this: the workingmen like the teamsters in our cities, these hard-working teamsters, strike and go out and starve. Their children starve. Their wives get discouraged. Some feel that they have to go out and beg for relief, and to get a little coal to keep the children warm, or a little bread to keep the wife from starving, or a little something to keep the spark of life in them so that they can remain wage slaves. That is the way with the strikes in the past. My conception of the strike of the future is not to strike and go out and starve, but to strike and remain in and take possession of the necessary property of production. If any one is to starve—I do not say it is necessary—let it be the capitalist class. They have starved us long enough, while they have had wealth and luxury and all that is necessary. You men and women should be imbued with the spirit that is now displayed in far-off Russia and far-off Siberia where we thought the spark of manhood and womanhood had been crushed out of them. Let us take example from them. We see the capitalist class fortifying themselves to-day behind their Citizens' Associations and Employers' Associations in order that they may crush the American labor movement. Let us cast our eyes over to far-off Russia and take heart and courage from those who are fighting the battle there, and from the further fact shown in the dispatches that appear this morning in the news that carries the greatest terror to the capitalist class throughout all the world—the emblem that has been the terror of all tyrants through all the ages, and there you will see that the red flag has been raised. (Applause). According to the Tribune, the greatest terror is evinced in Odessa and all through Russia because the red flag has been raised. They know that where the red flag has been raised whoever enroll themselves beneath that flag recognize the universal brotherhood of man; they recognize that the red current that flows through the veins of all humanity is identical, that the ideas of all humanity are identical; that those who raise the red flag, it matters not where, whether on the sunny plains of China, or on the sun-beaten hills of Africa, or on the far-off snow-capped shores of the north, or in Russia or in America—that they all belong to the human family and have an identity of interest. (Applause). That is what they know.

So when we come to decide, let us sink such differences as nationality, religion, politics, and set our eyes eternally and forever towards the rising star of the industrial republic of labor; remembering that we have left the old behind and have set our faces toward the future. There is no power on earth that can stop men and women who are determined to be free at all hazards. There is no power on earth so great as the power of intellect. It moves the world and it moves the earth.

Now, in conclusion, I wish to say to you—and you will excuse me because of what I am going to say and only attribute it to my interest in humanity. I wish to say that nineteen years ago on the fourth of May of this year, I was one of those at a meeting at the Haymarket in this city to protest against eleven workingmen being shot to pieces at a factory in the southeastern part of this city because they had dared to strike for the eight-hour movement that was to be inaugurated in America in 1886. The Haymarket meeting was called primarily and entirely to protest against the murder of comrades at the McCormick factory. When that meeting was nearing its close some one threw a bomb. No one knows to this day who threw it except the man who threw it. Possibly he has rendered his account with nature and has passed away. But no human being alive knows who threw it. And yet in the soil of Illinois, the soil that gave a Lincoln to America, the soil in which the great, magnificent Lincoln was buried in the State that was supposed to be the most liberal in the union, five men sleep the last sleep in Waldheim under a monument that, has been raised there because they dared to raise their voices for humanity. I say to any of you who are here and who can do so, it is well worth your time to go out there and draw some inspiration around the graves of the first martyrs who fell in the great industrial struggle for liberty on American soil. (Applause). I say to you that even within the sound of my voice, only two short blocks from where we meet to-day, the scaffold was erected on which those five men paid the penalty for daring to raise their voices against the iniquities of the age in which we live. We are assembled here for the same purpose. And do any of you older men remember the telegrams that were sent out from Chicago while our comrades were not yet even cut down from the cruel gallows? "Anarchy is dead, and these miscreants have been put out of the way." Oh, friends, I am sorry that I even had to use that word, "anarchy" just now in your presence, which was not in my mind at the outset. So if any of you wish to go out there and look at this monument that has been raised by those who believed in their comrades' innocence and sincerity, I will ask you, when you have gone out and looked at the monument, that you will go to the reverse side of the monument and there read on the reverse side the words of a man, himself the purest and the noblest man who ever sat in the gubernatorial chair of the State of Illinois, John P. Altgeld. (Applause). On that monument you will read the clause of his message in which he pardoned the men who were lingering then in Joliet. I have nothing more to say. I ask you to read the words of Altgeld, who was at that time the governor, and had been a lawyer and a judge, and knew whereof he spoke, and then take out your copy books and copy the words of Altgeld when he released those who had not been slaughtered at the capitalists' behest, and then take them home and change your minds about what those men were put to death for.

Now, I have taken up your time in this because I simply feel that I have a right as a mother and as a wife of one of those sacrificed men to say whatever I can to bring the light to bear upon this conspiracy and to show you the way it was. Now, I thank you for the time that I have taken up of yours. I hope that we will meet again some time, you and I, in some hall where we can meet and organize the wage workers of America, the men and women, so that the children may not go into the factories, nor the women into the factories, unless they go under proper conditions. I hope even now to live to see the day when the first dawn of the new era of labor will have arisen, when capitalism will be a thing of the past, and the new industrial republic, the commonwealth of labor, shall be in operation. I thank you. (Applause.)

QUESTIONS TO CONSIDER

1. Parsons opens her speech with a discussion of the role of women in society and the economy. According to Parsons, what makes the experience of women unique and how do their experiences relate to the larger labor struggle?
2. Why does Parsons advocate for a general strike?

18.4 VISUAL SOURCE: THOMAS NAST, *DIFFICULT PROBLEMS SOLVING THEMSELVES* (1879)*

Prolific cartoonist Thomas Nast (1840–1902) often reflected social controversy in his illustrations, as in this example where he tackles prejudice against Black Americans and Chinese Americans. Many white Americans subscribed to a host of negative stereotypes about both groups, seeing their presence in and around white communities as a problem. White Americans were suspicious of the non-Christian, overwhelmingly male Chinese immigrant populations and believed them to be prone

---

* Courtesy of the Library of Congress

to vice and unwilling or unable to form families or assimilate. Black Americans were stereotyped as lazy, uncouth, and unintelligent—suited only for roles as manual laborers. These prejudices led many white Americans to believe that Black Americans and Chinese Americans could not be competent, industrious citizens of the republic, and that their presence was thus a threat to good order.

In this cartoon published in *Harper's Weekly*, Nast rejects these biases, arguing that these "problems" would "solve themselves" if Black Americans and Chinese Americans were welcomed and encouraged to participate in the growing United States. The signs beckon the Chinese immigrant away from enclaves on the Pacific Coast toward new opportunity in the prosperous eastern United States. The Black freedman, on the other hand, is encouraged to go west, to carve out a new life in the western states.

DIFFICULT PROBLEMS SOLVING THEMSELVES.

QUESTIONS TO CONSIDER

1. What choices did Nast make in his illustrations of the Black and Chinese everyman to make them seem respectable, in contrast to prevailing stereotypes?
2. Why did Nast choose to picture both a Black American and a Chinese American in this cartoon? What parallels is he drawing between the treatment of these groups in the United States?

18.5 VISUAL SOURCE: *THE ANARCHIST-LABOR TROUBLES IN CHICAGO (1886)**

Nineteenth-century Chicago was a rapidly industrializing urban metropolis and a center of labor activism. On May 4th, 1886, Chicago police officers attempted to disperse a peaceful rally in support of the eight-hour workday. An unknown assailant threw a homemade bomb which detonated in front of the officers, killing one officer immediately and severely wounding several others. The police then opened fire on the rally, killing four protesters and wounding dozens of others. Chicago police assumed that foreign-born anarchists were responsible and arrested eight anarchist activists with no proven connection to the attack. Following a trial marked by political and ethnic prejudice, seven of the defendants were sentenced to death. Two sentences were commuted to life imprisonment, one convict committed suicide, and the other four were executed. Those executed were celebrated by labor activists as martyrs to lethal state violence, but the aftermath of the Haymarket bombing proved to be a setback for the labor movement as the trial had produced significant negative press. The accompanying illustration published in *Frank Leslie's Illustrated Newspaper* is one such example, prominently featuring armed "murderous rioters" firing into a mass of officers and labelling the protest "the anarchist troubles."

* Courtesy of the Library of Congress

QUESTIONS TO CONSIDER

1. Consider the depiction of the crowd and the accompanying text.[1] What does the illustrator want the reader to understand about the labor movement and the protest at Haymarket Square?

2. Who does the illustrator consider to be the victims of Haymarket? How do you know?

_____

1 The caption underneath the illustration reads "Illinois.—The anarchist labor troubles in Chicago—the police charging the murderous rioters in Old Haymarket Square on the night of May 4th."

CHAPTER 19

CONSTRUCTING PROGRESSIVISM, 1886–1914

19.1 UPTON SINCLAIR, EXCERPTS FROM *THE JUNGLE* (1906)*

Upton Sinclair (1878–1968) was a socialist writer commonly associated with the muckrakers, journalists who wrote investigative exposés of corruption. In his 1906 novel *The Jungle*, Sinclair told the story of a Lithuanian immigrant named Jurgis who comes to Chicago and begins working at a slaughterhouse called Durham. Jurgis witnesses the appalling treatment suffered by both workers and animals as men suffer injury and maiming while processing diseased animals for human consumption. Although the story is fictional, it was based on Sinclair's own research in Chicago. Durham was clearly meant to represent Armour, Chicago's largest meatpacker, and much of the malpractice Sinclair described was confirmed in subsequent investigations.

Sinclair had intended his descriptions of the suffering of workers to inspire sympathy for the socialist cause. Instead, readers were disgusted by the practices of industrial meatpacking. The book quickly became a bestseller and spurred readers to demand new regulations to ensure food safety. Within a year of its publication, Congress passed two new laws providing for meat inspections and banning dangerous food additives.

The people of Chicago saw the government inspectors in Packingtown, and they all took that to mean that they were protected from diseased meat; they did not understand that these hundred and sixty-three inspectors had been appointed at the request of the packers, and that they were paid by the United States government to certify that all the diseased meat was kept in the state. They had no authority beyond that; for the inspection of meat to be sold in the city and state the whole force in Packingtown consisted of three henchmen of the local political machine!

And shortly afterward one of these, a physician, made the discovery that the carcasses of steers which had been condemned as tubercular by the government

---

* Upton Sinclair, *The Jungle* (1906; Project Gutenberg eBook, 2006), https://www.gutenberg.org/cache/epub/140/pg140-images.html.

inspectors, and which therefore contained ptomaines, which are deadly poisons, were left upon an open platform and carted away to be sold in the city; and so he insisted that these carcasses be treated with an injection of kerosene—and was ordered to resign the same week! So indignant were the packers that they went farther, and compelled the mayor to abolish the whole bureau of inspection; so that since then there has not been even a pretense of any interference with the graft. There was said to be two thousand dollars a week hush money from the tubercular steers alone; and as much again from the hogs which had died of cholera on the trains, and which you might see any day being loaded into boxcars and hauled away to a place called Globe, in Indiana, where they made a fancy grade of lard.

Jurgis heard of these things little by little, in the gossip of those who were obliged to perpetrate them. It seemed as if every time you met a person from a new department, you heard of new swindles and new crimes. There was, for instance, a Lithuanian who was a cattle butcher for the plant where Marija had worked, which killed meat for canning only; and to hear this man describe the animals which came to his place would have been worthwhile for a Dante or a Zola. It seemed that they must have agencies all over the country, to hunt out old and crippled and diseased cattle to be canned. There were cattle which had been fed on "whisky-malt," the refuse of the breweries, and had become what the men called "steerly"—which means covered with boils. It was a nasty job killing these, for when you plunged your knife into them they would burst and splash foul-smelling stuff into your face; and when a man's sleeves were smeared with blood, and his hands steeped in it, how was he ever to wipe his face, or to clear his eyes so that he could see? It was stuff such as this that made the "embalmed beef" that had killed several times as many United States soldiers as all the bullets of the Spaniards; only the army beef, besides, was not fresh canned, it was old stuff that had been lying for years in the cellars.

Then one Sunday evening, Jurgis sat puffing his pipe by the kitchen stove, and talking with an old fellow whom Jonas had introduced, and who worked in the canning rooms at Durham's; and so Jurgis learned a few things about the great and only Durham canned goods, which had become a national institution. They were regular alchemists at Durham's; they advertised a mushroom-catsup, and the men who made it did not know what a mushroom looked like. They advertised "potted chicken,"—and it was like the boardinghouse soup of the comic papers, through which a chicken had walked with rubbers on. Perhaps they had a secret process for making chickens chemically—who knows? said Jurgis' friend; the things that went into the mixture were tripe, and the fat of pork, and beef suet, and hearts of beef, and finally the waste ends of veal, when they had any. They put these up in several grades, and sold them at several prices; but the contents of the cans all came out of the same hopper. And then there was "potted game" and "potted grouse," "potted ham," and "deviled ham"—de-vyled, as the men called it. "De-vyled" ham was made out of the waste ends of smoked beef that were too small to be sliced by the machines; and also tripe, dyed with chemicals so that it would not show white; and trimmings of hams and corned beef; and potatoes, skins and all; and finally the hard cartilaginous gullets of beef, after the tongues had been cut out. All this ingenious mixture was ground up and flavored with spices to make it taste like something. Anybody who could invent a new imitation had been sure of a fortune from old Durham, said Jurgis' informant; but it was hard to think of anything new in a place where so many sharp wits had been at work for so long; where men welcomed tuberculosis in the cattle they were feeding, because it made them fatten more quickly; and where they bought up all the old rancid butter left over in the grocery stores of a continent, and "oxidized" it by a forced-air process, to take away the odor, rechurned it with skim milk, and sold it in bricks in the cities! Up to a year or two ago it had been the custom to kill horses in the yards—ostensibly for fertilizer; but after long agitation the newspapers had been able to make the public realize that the horses were being canned. Now it was against the law to kill horses in Packingtown, and the law was really complied with—for the present, at any rate. Any day, however, one might see sharp-horned and shaggy-haired creatures running with the sheep and yet what a job you would have to get the public to believe that a good part of what it buys for lamb and mutton is really goat's flesh!

There was another interesting set of statistics that a person might have gathered in Packingtown—those of the various afflictions of the workers. When Jurgis had first inspected the packing plants with Szedvilas, he had marveled while he listened to the tale of all the things that were made out of the carcasses of animals, and of all the lesser industries that were maintained there; now he found that each one of these lesser industries was a separate little inferno, in its way as horrible as the killing beds, the source and fountain of them all. The workers in each of them had their own peculiar diseases. And the wandering visitor might be skeptical about all the swindles, but he could not be skeptical about these, for the worker bore the evidence of them about on his own person—generally he had only to hold out his hand.

There were the men in the pickle rooms, for instance, where old Antanas had gotten his death; scarce a one of these that had not some spot of horror on his person. Let a man so much as scrape his finger pushing a truck in the pickle rooms, and he might have a sore that would put him out of the world; all the joints in his fingers might be eaten by the acid, one by one. Of the butchers and floorsmen, the beef-boners and trimmers, and all those who used knives, you could scarcely find a person who had the use of his thumb; time and time again the base of it had been slashed, till it was a mere lump of flesh against which the man pressed the knife to hold it. The hands of these men would be criss-crossed with cuts, until you could no longer pretend to count them or to trace them. They would have no nails,—they had worn them off pulling hides; their knuckles were swollen so that their fingers spread out like a fan. There were men who worked in the cooking rooms, in the midst of steam and sickening odors, by artificial light; in these rooms the germs of tuberculosis might live for two years, but the supply was renewed every hour. There were the beef-luggers, who carried two-hundred-pound quarters into the refrigerator-cars; a fearful kind of work, that began at four o'clock in the morning, and that

wore out the most powerful men in a few years. There were those who worked in the chilling rooms, and whose special disease was rheumatism; the time limit that a man could work in the chilling rooms was said to be five years. There were the wool-pluckers, whose hands went to pieces even sooner than the hands of the pickle men; for the pelts of the sheep had to be painted with acid to loosen the wool, and then the pluckers had to pull out this wool with their bare hands, till the acid had eaten their fingers off. There were those who made the tins for the canned meat; and their hands, too, were a maze of cuts, and each cut represented a chance for blood poisoning. Some worked at the stamping machines, and it was very seldom that one could work long there at the pace that was set, and not give out and forget himself and have a part of his hand chopped off. There were the "hoisters," as they were called, whose task it was to press the lever which lifted the dead cattle off the floor. They ran along upon a rafter, peering down through the damp and the steam; and as old Durham's architects had not built the killing room for the convenience of the hoisters, at every few feet they would have to stoop under a beam, say four feet above the one they ran on; which got them into the habit of stooping, so that in a few years they would be walking like chimpanzees. Worst of any, however, were the fertilizer men, and those who served in the cooking rooms. These people could not be shown to the visitor,—for the odor of a fertilizer man would scare any ordinary visitor at a hundred yards, and as for the other men, who worked in tank rooms full of steam, and in some of which there were open vats near the level of the floor, their peculiar trouble was that they fell into the vats; and when they were fished out, there was never enough of them left to be worth exhibiting,—sometimes they would be overlooked for days, till all but the bones of them had gone out to the world as Durham's Pure Leaf Lard!

QUESTIONS TO CONSIDER

1. How does Sinclair use the experiences of Jurgis to criticize industrial capitalism?
2. Many people found the descriptions of unsafe meatpacking practices more disturbing than the terrible working conditions of the workers. Why might readers have had this reaction?

19.2 MARGARET SANGER, EXCERPTS FROM *WHAT EVERY GIRL SHOULD KNOW* (1916)*

Margaret Sanger (1879–1966) was an influential activist for sex education and birth control in the early twentieth century. She believed that women and girls ought to be able to make their own choices about how and when to have children and supported contraception and education about puberty and sexual reproduction. She faced prosecution and arrest for her writing on this subject due to federal laws that considered publishing that discussed contraception and abortion to be "obscene" and therefore criminal.

In her pamphlet *What Every Girl Should Know*, Sanger laid out her case for sex education, arguing that informed women should be able to make their own healthy decisions about their bodies. She also addressed criticism that her education on topics such as sexually transmitted disease ("venereal disease") would frighten young women and cause them to forego motherhood. Sanger argued instead that sexuality should be liberating and that education would allow women to choose to become mothers knowing both the potential joys and risks of that decision.

Students of vice, whether teachers, clergymen, social workers or physicians, have been laboring for years to find the cause and cure for vice, and especially for prostitution. They have failed so far to agree on either the cause or the cure, but it is interesting to know that upon one point they have been compelled to agree, and that is, that *ignorance of the sex functions* is one of the strongest forces that sends young girls into *unclean* living.

This, together with the knowledge of the rapidly increasing spread of venereal diseases and the realization of their subtle nature, has awakened us to the need of a saner and healthier attitude on the sex subject, and to the importance of *sex education* for boys and girls.

. . .

The whole object of teaching the child about reproduction through evolution is to clear its mind of any shame or mystery concerning its birth and to impress it with the beauty and naturalness of procreation, in order to prepare it for the knowledge of puberty and marriage.

There must of necessity be special information for the pubescent boy and girl, for having arrived at the stage in their mental development they no longer take for granted what has been told them by the parents, but are keen to form their own ideas and gather information independently. It is right, therefore, to give them the facts as science has found them.

There are workers and philanthropists who say there is too much stress put upon the subject of venereal diseases; that the young girl after learning or hearing of the dangers she is likely to encounter in the sexual relation, is afraid to marry and consequently lives a life unloved and alone.

"Your treatment of this subject is dangerous," said a very earnest social worker a few weeks ago. "Such knowledge will prevent our young girls from marrying."

To which I replied that my object in telling young girls the truth is for the definite purpose of preventing them from entering into sexual relations whether in marriage or out of it, without thinking and knowing. Better a thousand times to live alone and unloved than to be tied to a man who has robbed her of health or of the joy of motherhood, or welcoming the pains of

---

* Margaret H. Sanger, *What Every Girl Should Know* (1916; Project Gutenberg eBook, 2016), 7–8, https://www.gutenberg.org/ebooks/52888.

motherhood, live in anxiety lest her sickly offspring be taken out of her life, or grow up a chronic invalid.

I have more faith in the force of love. I believe that two people convinced that they love each other and desire to live together will talk as frankly of their own health and natures as they do today of the house furnishings and salaries. Their love for each other will protect them from ill health and disease, and prompt them to procure of their own accord, a certificate of health if each has the right information and knowledge.

There are, however, different phases of nature, the knowledge of which binds and cements the love of two people, other than venereal diseases, for these diseases are only symptoms of a great social disorder.

Every girl should first understand herself; she should know her anatomy, including sex anatomy; she should know the epochs of a normal woman's life, and the unfoldment which each epoch brings; she should know the effect the emotions have on her acts, and finally she should know the fullness and richness of life when crowned by the flower of motherhood.

QUESTIONS TO CONSIDER

1. What does Sanger want to change about Americans' approach to motherhood?
2. What role does education play in Sanger's beliefs? Why is education so important to her?

19.3 JOSEPHINE ST. PIERRE RUFFIN, ADDRESS AT THE FIRST NATIONAL CONFERENCE OF BLACK WOMEN'S CLUBS (1895)*

Josephine St. Pierre Ruffin (1842–1924) was a Black activist, organizer, and publisher who advocated for civil rights and suffrage for Black women. Ruffin and her husband George were active in a variety of anti-slavery and other reform causes, but after George died in 1886 Josephine continued to advocate on behalf of Black women in particular. In 1890 Ruffin founded the *Woman's Era*, a newspaper that addressed the interests and issues of Black women. Throughout the 1890s she founded or helped found several women's clubs for Black women, part of a larger national movement in which women organized local clubs to advocate for social reform.

In this speech to the National Conference of Black Women's Clubs, Ruffin lays out what she sees as important priorities and challenges for Black women to address. She stresses the important role that Black women should play in improving their communities and emphasizes that their activism will benefit everyone in their communities.

---

* Josephine St. Ruffin Pierre, "Address at the First National Conference of Black Women's Clubs," *The Woman's Era* 2, no. 5 (August 1895), 13–15.

The reasons why we should confer are so apparent that it would seem hardly necessary to enumerate them, and yet there is none of them but demand our serious consideration. In first place we need to feel the cheer and inspiration of meeting each other; we need to gain the courage and fresh life that comes from the mingling of congenial souls, of those working for the same ends. Next we need to talk over not only those things which are of vital importance to us as women, but also the things that are of special interest to us as colored women, the training of our children, openings for boys and girls, how they can be prepared for occupations and occupations may be found or opened for them, what we especially can do in the moral education of the race with which we are identified, our mental elevation and physical development, the home training it is necessary to give our children in order to prepare them to meet the peculiar conditions in which they shall find themselves, how to make the most of our own, to some extent, limited opportunities, these are some of our own peculiar questions to be discussed. Besides these are the general questions of the day, which we cannot afford to be indifferent to: temperance, morality, the higher education, hygiene and domestic questions. If these things need the serious consideration of women more advantageously placed by reason of all the aid to right thinking and living with which they are surrounded, surely we, with everything to pull us back, to hinder us in developing, need to take every opportunity and means for the thoughtful consideration which shall lead to wise action.

. . .

Too long have we been silent under unjust and unholy charges; we cannot expect to have them removed until we disprove them through ourselves. It is not enough to try and disprove unjust charges through individual effort that never goes any further. Year after year southern women have protested against the admission of colored women into any national organization on the ground of [the] immorality of these women, and because all refutation has only been tried by individual work the charge has never been crushed, as it could and should have been at the first. Now with an army of organized women standing for purity and mental worth, we in ourselves deny the charge and open the eyes of the world to a state of affairs to which they have been blind, often willfully so, and the very fact that the charges, audaciously and flippantly made, as they often are, are of so humiliating and delicate a nature, serves to protect the accuser by driving the helpless accused into mortified silence. It is to break this silence, not by noisy protestations of what we are not, but by a dignified showing of what we are and hope to become that we are impelled to take this step, to make of this gathering an object lesson to the world.

For many and apparent reasons it is especially fitting that the women of the race take the lead in this movement, but for all this we recognize the necessity of the sympathy of our husbands, brothers and fathers. Our women's movement is woman's movement in that it is led and directed by women for the good of women and men, for the benefit of all humanity, which is more than any one branch or section of it. We want, we ask the active interest of our men, and, too, we are not drawing the color line; we are women, American women, as intensely interested in all that pertains to us as such as all other American women: we are not alienating or withdrawing, we are only coming to the front, willing to join any others in the same work and cordially inviting and welcoming any others to join us. If there is any one thing I would especially enjoin upon this conference it is union and earnestness. The questions that are to come before us are of too much import to be weakened by any trivialities or personalities. If any differences arise, let them be quickly settled, with the feeling that we are all workers to the same end, to elevate and dignify colored American womanhood.

QUESTIONS TO CONSIDER

1. What challenges does Ruffin believe Black women in particular face?
2. What role does Ruffin imagine for women's clubs in American society and culture? What issues does she think Black women can and should help to improve?

19.4 VISUAL SOURCE: GRANT E. HAMILTON, *OUT IN THE COLD* (1884)*

Although women had begun organizing to secure voting rights as early as the 1840s, by the 1880s the movement had fractured into rival groups and had made relatively little headway. Activists had suffered a setback in the 1860s when women were not included in the voting protections of the Fifteenth Amendment. While women were allowed to vote in several territories in 1884, there were no states that enfranchised them. Chinese Americans meanwhile had recently been denied citizenship by the 1882 Chinese Exclusion Act, which removed them from the protections of the Fifteenth Amendment that banned voting restrictions based on race. Due both to this act and local white hostility, few Chinese Americans had the opportunity to vote.

This comic illustration from the satirical magazine *Judge* makes light of women and Chinese Americans by showing them literally left out in the cold—i.e., excluded from voting—while inside, caricatured Irish American and Black American men smirk and mock the unenfranchised.

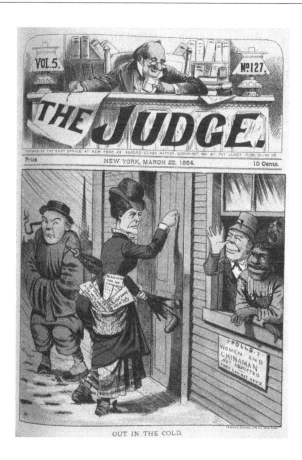

OUT IN THE COLD.

---

* Courtesy of the Library of Congress

QUESTIONS TO CONSIDER

1. What is the purpose of the Irish American and Black American men in the window?
2. What point is the illustrator making about the expansion of voting rights?

19.5 VISUAL SOURCE: AD FOR HORSFORD'S ACID PHOSPHATE BRAIN TONIC FOR "NERVOUSNESS" (1888)*

Branded or "patent" medicines such as Horsford's Acid Phosphate were a key industry progressives sought to reform. Patent medicines were medical products that typically promised relief from a wide variety of minor and often unrelated symptoms. Typically, they were concocted relatively cheaply, often using addictive substances such as opiates and alcohol, and there was little to no proof of their short- or long-term efficacy. Because these tonics were relatively easy to manufacture, the market was flooded with a variety of medicines of dubious efficacy all promising to relieve numerous ailments based on the expertise of an alleged doctor who created the mixture. As a result, the manufacturers of patent medicines engaged in early attempts at branding and advertising to differentiate their product from the dozens similar to it.

The 1906 Food and Drug Act was a key progressive legislative achievement, establishing the federal government's authority to ensure that food and medicine sold in the United States was safe for consumption. The key elements of this legislation were the requirements that patent medicines like Horsford's list an active ingredient and avoid certain addictive chemicals.

---

* Courtesy of the Library of Congress

QUESTIONS TO CONSIDER

1. What techniques does this advertisement use to appeal to as many potential customers as possible?
2. What is the purpose of the urban and frontier imagery in the advertisement? What does Horsford's want readers to associate with its product?

19.6 VISUAL SOURCE: RAND McNALLY AND COMPANY, *BIRD'S EYE VIEW OF THE WORLD'S COLUMBIAN EXPOSITION, CHICAGO (1893)**

Throughout the latter half of the nineteenth century, the United States and several European states hosted World's Expos or World's Fairs—massive exhibitions of industrial and cultural progress from around the world. Chicago's Columbian Exposition in 1893 was the largest World's Fair yet and it attracted nearly thirty million attendees during its six-month run. The technological marvels on display ranged from useful everyday innovations like the zipper to massive attractions such as a Ferris wheel.

---

* Courtesy of the Library of Congress

During the late nineteenth century, Chicago had grown dramatically to become one of the pre-eminent American cities. Despite a devastating fire in 1871, Chicago stood as the second largest US city in 1890, up from ninth largest in 1860. Two hundred temporary neoclassical buildings were constructed for the fairgrounds in Jackson Park along the shore of Lake Michigan. The white stucco plaster that was used gave the fairgrounds their nickname, the White City. The grandeur of the White City helped inspire the City Beautiful movement, an element of progressive reform that emphasized the beautification of American cities through the improvement of public spaces.

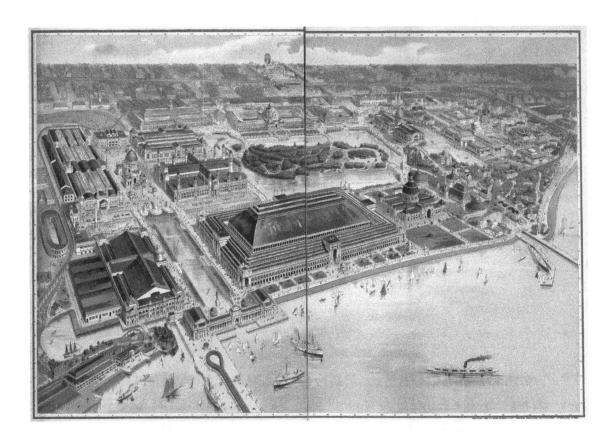

QUESTIONS TO CONSIDER

1. How is this illustration framed to emphasize the grandeur of the Columbian Exposition?
2. What elements of the Columbian Exposition as pictured here inspired the City Beautiful movement?

CHAPTER 20

EMPIRE AND RACE, 1890–1914

20.1 CITIZENS' COMMITTEE ON THE ANNEXATION OF HAWAII, "MEMORIAL TO THE PRESIDENT, THE CONGRESS, AND THE PEOPLE OF THE UNITED STATES OF AMERICA" (1897)*

This appeal was sent to the United States Congress when it debated the annexation of Hawai'i in late 1897. The Kingdom of Hawai'i opted to welcome and conciliate European and American missionaries and sailors who arrived in the islands more frequently in the early nineteenth century. In an effort to convince Europe and the United States that they were a civilized nation that must be treated as an equal, Hawai'i established legislatures and newspapers, and conformed to European-American property law. Although this gained Hawai'i formal international recognition, these westernization efforts also opened the door for American capitalists to establish large sugar plantations on the islands, importing a variety of foreign laborers, and changing both the population and economy of the archipelago. Two coups in 1887 and 1893 overthrew the indigenous Hawaiian monarchy and replaced it with a nominal republic under the control of American plantation interests. This American-controlled government soon succeeded in effecting the annexation of Hawai'i by the United States.

M EMORIAL
To the President, the Congress and the People of the United States of America.
This Memorial respectfully represents as follows:

I. That your memorialists are residents of the Hawaiian Islands; that the majority of them are aboriginal Hawaiians; and that all of them possess the qualifications provided for electors of representatives in the Hawaiian Legislature by the Constitution and laws prevailing in the Hawaiian Islands at the date of the overthrow of the Hawaiian Constitutional Government January 17, 1893.

* Available at Legal Foundation for Hawaiian Independence, https://www.hawaii-nation.org/memorial.html.

2. That the supporters of the Hawaiian Constitution of 1887 have been, thence to the present time, in the year 1897, held in subjection by the armed forces of the Provisional Government of the Hawaiian Islands, and of its successor, the Republic of Hawaii; and have never yielded, and do not acknowledge a spontaneous or willing allegiance or support to said Provisional Government, or to said Republic of Hawaii.

3. That the Government of the Republic of Hawaii has no warrant for its existence in the support of the people of these Islands; that it was proclaimed and instituted and has hitherto existed and now exists, without considering the rights and wishes of a great majority of the residents, native and foreign born, of the Hawaiian Islands; and especially that said Government exists and maintains itself solely by force of arms, against the rights and wishes of almost the entire aboriginal population of these Islands.

4. That said Republic is not and never has been founded or conducted upon a basis of popular government or republican principles; that its Constitution was adopted by a convention, a majority of whose members were self-appointed, and the balance of whose members were elected by a numerically insignificant minority of the white and aboriginal male citizens and residents of these Islands; that a majority of the persons so voting for delegates to such Constitutional Convention was composed of aliens, and that a majority of said aliens so voting were of then very recent residents, without financial interests or social ties in the Islands.

5. That the Constitution so adopted by said Convention has never been submitted to a vote of the people of these Islands; but was promulgated and established over the said Islands, and has ever since been maintained, only by force of arms, and with indifference to the will of practically the entire aboriginal population, and a vast majority of the whole population of these Islands.

6. That the said Government, so existing under the title of the Republic of Hawaii, assumes and asserts, the right to extinguish the Hawaiian Nationality, heretofore existing, and to cede and convey all rights of sovereignty in and over the Hawaiian Islands and their dependencies to a foreign power, namely, to the United States of America.

7. That your memorialists have learned with grief and dismay that the President of the United States has entered into, and submitted for ratification by the United States Senate, a Treaty with the Government of the Republic of Hawaii, whereby it is proposed to extinguish our existence as a Nation, and to annex our territory to the United States.

8. That the Hawaiian people, during more than half a century prior to the events hereinabove recited, had been accustomed to participate in the Constitutional forms of Government, in the election of Legislatures, in the administration of justice through regularly constituted magistrates, courts and juries, and in the representative administration of public affairs, in which the principle of government by majorities has been acknowledged and firmly established.

9. That your memorialists humbly but fervently protest against the consummation of this invasion of their political rights; and they earnestly appeal to the President, the Congress and the People of the United States, to refrain from further participating in the wrong so proposed; and they invoke in support of this memorial the spirit of that immortal Instrument, the Declaration of American Independence; and especially the truth therein expressed, that Governments derive their just powers from the consent of the governed, ---and here repeat, that the consent of the people of the Hawaiian Islands to the forms of Government imposed by the so-called Republic of Hawaii, and to said proposed Treaty of Annexation, has never been asked by and is not accorded, either to said Government or to said project of Annexation.

10. That the consummation of the project of Annexation dealt with in said Treaty would be subversive of the personal and political rights of these memorialists, and of the Hawaiian people and Nation, and would be a negation of the rights and principles proclaimed in the Declaration of American Independence, in the Constitution of the United States, and in the schemes of government of all other civilized and representative Governments.

11. Wherefore your memorialists respectfully submit that they, no less than the citizens of any American Commonwealth, are entitled to select, ordain and establish for themselves, such forms of Government as to them shall seem most likely to effect their safety and happiness; and that questions of such moment to the Hawaiian people as are proposed to be settled by said Treaty, are questions upon which said people have the right, in the forum of Conscience, to be heard; and that said Hawaiian people have thus far been denied the privilege of being heard upon said questions.

12. And your memorialists humbly pray the President, Congress and the people of the United States, that no further steps be taken toward the ratification of said Treaty, or toward the extinguishment of the Hawaiian Nationality, or toward the absorption of the Hawaiian people and territory into the body politic and territory of the United States of America, at least until the Hawaiian people, as represented by those citizens and residents of the Hawaiian Islands who, under the provisions of the Hawaiian Constitution, promulgated July 7, 1887, would be qualified to vote for representatives in the Legislature, shall have had the opportunity to express at the ballot box, their wishes as to whether such project of Annexation shall be accepted or rejected.

13. And your memorialists, for themselves, and in behalf of the Hawaiian people, and of the residents of the Hawaiian Islands, pledge their faith that if they shall be accorded the privilege of voting upon said questions, at a free and fair election to be held for that purpose; and if a fair count of the votes that shall be cast at such election shall show a majority in favor of such Annexation, these memorialists, and the Hawaiian people will yield a ready and cheerful acquiescence in said project.

Honolulu, Hawaii October 8, 1897

J. Kalua Hookano

Samuel K. Pua

F. J. Testa

C. B. Maile

Samuel K. Kamakaia, Citizens' Committee

James Keauiluna Kaulia, President of the Hawaiian Patriotic League

David Kalauokalani, President of the Hawaiian Political Association

QUESTIONS TO CONSIDER

1. How do the authors of this appeal identify themselves and why do you think the authors chose to describe themselves this way?

2. What evidence do the authors present to argue that the Republic of Hawai'i is an illegitimate government? What do the authors consider to be a legitimate basis for political power?

20.2 FREDERICK DOUGLASS, LETTER TO IDA B. WELLS (1892)*

Ida B. Wells (1862–1931) was a pioneering civil rights journalist, best known for her exposés on vigilante killings of Black Americans in the South. White Southerners routinely targeted Black men who had been formally or informally accused of a crime and executed them often by hanging or shooting in a crime commonly referred to as "lynching." Beginning in the 1890s, Wells began conducting investigations into lynchings in the South and published her conclusions both in the press and in pamphlets such as *Southern Horrors* (1892). Wells documented that lynching was a disturbingly common phenomenon and argued that the victims were often Black Southerners whose economic success made local white people feel threatened. She also observed that the alleged crime of the Black victims was often rape of a white woman, an accusation that often seemed spurious because white Southerners assumed any sexual relationship between a white woman and a Black man to be rape.

In this letter Frederick Douglass (c. 1818–1895), a famous Black journalist and activist of the previous generation, applauds Wells for her work exposing Southern lynching. Douglass, who escaped from slavery as a young man and became a leading advocate for the abolition of slavery, commends Wells for documenting how white Southerners continued to enforce white supremacy after slavery had been abolished.

Dear Miss Wells:

Let me give you thanks for your faithful paper on the lynch abomination now generally practiced against colored people in the South. There has been no word equal to it in convincing power. I have spoken, but my word is feeble in comparison. You give us what you know and testify from actual knowledge. You have dealt with the facts with cool, painstaking fidelity and left those naked and uncontradicted facts to speak for themselves.

Brave woman! you have done your people and mine a service which can neither be weighed nor measured. If American conscience were only half alive, if the American church and clergy were only half christianized, if American moral sensibility were not hardened by persistent infliction of outrage and crime against colored people, a scream of horror, shame and indignation would rise to Heaven wherever your pamphlet shall be read.

But alas! even crime has power to reproduce itself and create conditions favorable to its own existence. It sometimes seems we are deserted by earth and Heaven yet we must still think, speak and work, and trust in the power of a merciful God for final deliverance.

Very truly and gratefully yours,
FREDERICK DOUGLASS
Cedar Hill, Anacostia, D.C. Oct. 25, 1892

---

* Frederick Douglass to Ida B. Wells, letter, October 25, 1892, in Ida B. Wells, *Southern Horrors: Lynch Law in All Its Phases* (The New York Age Print, 1892).

QUESTIONS TO CONSIDER

1. Douglass compliments Wells's argumentative style, noting that she lets "naked and uncontradicted facts to speak for themselves." Why might Wells have thought this would be a useful approach to convincing Americans of the prevalence and violence of lynching?
2. Is Douglass optimistic that Wells's pamphlet will change Americans' minds?

20.3 SIMON POKAGON, "THE RED MAN'S GREETING" (1893)*

The Chicago World's Fair, sometimes known as the Columbian Exposition, was an exposition of achievements in arts, industry, and culture from around the world. Held in 1893, it also commemorated four centuries since Christopher Columbus had landed in what are now the Americas. The Fair was a massive undertaking: it involved building over two hundred temporary neoclassical buildings, featured exhibits and contributions from forty-six countries, and attracted over twenty-seven million visitors over the course of its six-month run.

Simon Pokagon was a Potawatomi activist from the Lake Michigan area known for his denunciations of colonialism and his embrace of temperance. He had his essay "Red Man's Greeting" stamped onto birchbark pages, bound, and sold or given away at the Fair. The essay was deliberately targeted to the predominantly white fairgoers to encourage them to reflect on injustices perpetrated against America's Indigenous peoples that had accompanied the various achievements displayed at the Fair. Calling European colonists "carrion crows," "locusts," and "barbarians," Pokagon argues that many problems faced by Indigenous Americans are the direct result of centuries of violence and deception by colonists and their descendants.

In behalf of my people, the American Indians, I hereby declare to you, the pale-faced race that has usurped our lands and homes, that we have no spirit to celebrate with you the Great Columbian Fair now being held in this Chicago city, the wonder of the world.

No; sooner would we hold high joy-day over the graves of our departed fathers, than to celebrate our own funeral, the discovery of America. And while you who are strangers, and you who live here, bring the offerings of the handiwork of your own lands, and your hearts in admiration rejoice over the beauty and grandeur of this young republic, and you say, "Behold the wonders wrought by our children in this foreign land," do not forget that this success has been at the sacrifice of *our* homes and a once happy race.

Where these great Columbian show-buildings stretch skyward, and where stands this "Queen City of the West," *once* stood the red man's wigwam; here met their old men, young men, and maidens; here blazed their council-fires. But now the eagle's eye can find no trace of them. Here was the center of their widespread hunting-grounds; stretching far eastward, and

---

* Simon Pokagon, *Red Man's Greeting* (Hartford, MI: C.H. Engle, 1893).

to the great salt Gulf southward, and to the lofty Rocky Mountain chain westward; and all about and beyond the Great Lakes northward roamed vast herds of buffalo that no man could number, while moose, deer, and elk were found from ocean to ocean. Pigeons, ducks, and geese in near bow-shot moved in great clouds through the air, while fish swarmed our streams, lakes, and seas close to shore. All were provided by the Great Spirit for our use; we destroyed none except for food and use; had plenty and were contented and happy.

But alas! the pale-faces came by chance to our shores, many times very needy and hungry. We nursed and fed them,—fed the ravens that were soon to pluck out our eyes, and the eyes of our children; for no sooner had the news reached the Old World that a new continent had been found, peopled with another race of men, than, locust-like, they swarmed on all our coasts; and, like the carrion crows in spring, that in circles wheel and clamor long and loud, and will not cease until they find and feast upon the dead, so these strangers from the East long circuits made, and turkey-like they gobbled in our ears, "Give us gold, give us gold;" "Where find you gold? Where find you gold?"

We gave for promises and "geegaws" all the gold we had, and showed them where to dig for more; to repay us, they robbed our homes of fathers, mothers, sons, and daughters; some were forced across the sea for slaves in Spain, while multitudes were dragged into the mines to dig for gold, and held in slavery there until all who escaped not, died under the lash of the cruel task-master. It finally passed into their history that, "the red man of the west, unlike the black man of the east, will die before he'll be a slave." Our hearts were crushed by such base ingratitude; and, as the United States has decreed, "No Chinaman shall land on our shores," so we then felt that no such barbarians as they, should land on *ours*.

In those days that tried our fathers' souls, tradition says: "A crippled, grey-haired sire told his tribe that in the visions of the night he was lifted high above the earth, and in great wonder beheld a vast spider-web spread out over the land from the Atlantic Ocean to the setting sun. Its net-work was made of rods of iron; along its lines in all directions rushed monstrous spiders, greater in strength, and larger far than any beast of earth, clad in brass and iron, dragging after them long rows of wigwams with families therein, outstripping

in their course the flight of birds that fled before them. Hissing from their nostrils came forth fire and smoke, striking terror to both foul and beast. The red men hid themselves in fear, or fled away, while the white man trained these monsters for the war path, as warriors for battle.

The old man who saw the visions claimed it meant that the Indian race would surely pass away before the pale-faced strangers. He died a martyr to his belief. Centuries have passed since that time, and we now behold in the vision, as in a mirror, the present net-work of railroads, and the monstrous engines with their fire, smoke, and hissing steam, with cars attached as they go sweeping through the land.

The cyclone of civilization rolled westward; the forests of untold centuries were swept away; streams dried up; lakes fell back from their ancient bounds; and all our fathers once loved to gaze upon was destroyed, defaced, or marred, except the sun, moon, and starry skies above, which the Great Spirit in his wisdom hung beyond their reach.

Still on the storm-cloud rolled, while before its lightning and thunder the beasts of the earth and the fowl of the air withered like grass before the flame--were shot for love of power to kill along, and left to spoil upon the plains. Their bleaching bones now scattered far and near, in shame declare the wanton cruelty of pale-faced men. The storm unsatisfied on land swept our lakes and streams, while before its clouds of hooks, nets, and glistening spears the fish vanished from our waters like the morning dew before the rising son. Thus our inheritance was cut off, and we were driven and scattered as sheep before the wolves.

Nor was this all. They brought among us fatal diseases our fathers knew not of; our medicine-men tried in vain to check the deadly plague; but they themselves died, and our people fell as fall the leaves before the autumn's blast.

To be just, we must acknowledge, there were some good men with these strangers, who gave their lives for ours, and in great kindness taught us the revealed will of the Great Spirit through his Son Jesus, the mediator between God and man. But while we were being taught to love the Lord our God with all our heart, mind, and strength, and our neighbors as ourselves, and our children were taught to lisp "Our Father who art in heaven, hallowed be thy name," bad men of the same race, whom we thought of the same belief, shocked our faith in the revealed will of the Father, as they came among us with bitter oaths upon their lips, something we had never heard before, and cups of fire-water in their hands, something we had never seen before. They pressed the sparkling glasses to our lips and said, "Drink, and you will be happy." We drank thereof, we and our children, but alas! like the serpent that charms to kill, the drink-habit coiled about the heart-strings of its victims, shocking onto death, friendship, love, honor, manhood—all that makes men good and noble; crushing out all ambition, and leaving naught but a culprit vagabond in the place of a man.

Now as we have been taught to believe that our first parents ate of the forbidden fruit, and fell, so we as fully believe this fire-water is the hard-cider of the white man's devil, made from the fruit of that tree that brought death in to the world, and all our woes. The arrow, the scalping-knife, and the tomahawk used on the war-path were *merciful* compared with it; *they* were used in our defense, but the accursed drink came like the serpent in the form of a dove. Many of our people partook of it without mistrust, as children pluck the flowers and clutch a scorpion in their grasp; only when they feel the sting, they let the flowers fall. But Nature's children had no such power; for when the viper's fangs they felt, they only hugged the reptile the more closely to their breasts, while friends before them stood pleading with prayers and tears that they would let the deadly serpent drop. But all in vain. Although they promised so to do, yet with laughing grin and steps uncertain like the fool, they still more frequently guzzled down this hellish drug. Finally conscience ceased to give alarm, and, led by deep despair to life's last brink, and goaded by demons on every side, they cursed themselves, they cursed their friends, they cursed their beggar babes and wives, they cursed their God, and died.

You say of us that we are treacherous, vindictive, and cruel; in answer to the charge, we declare to all the world with our hands uplifted before high Heaven, that before the white man came upon us, we were kind, outspoken, and forgiving. Our real character has been misunderstood because we have resented the breaking of treaties made with the United States, as we honestly understood them. The few of our children who are permitted to attend your schools, in great pride

tell us that they read in your own histories, how William Penn, a Quaker, and a good man, made treaties with nineteen tribes of Indians, and that neither he nor they ever broke them; and further, that during seventy years, while Pennsylvania was controlled by the Quakers, not a drop of blood was shed nor a war-whoop sounded by our people. Your own historians, and our traditions, show that for nearly two hundred years, different Eastern powers were striving for the mastery in the new world, and that our people were persuaded by the different factions to take the war-path, being generally led by white men who had been discharged from prisons for crimes committed in the Old World.

Read the following, left on record by Peter Martyr who visited our forefathers in the day of Columbia.

> "It is certain that the land among these people is as common as the sun and water, and that 'thine and mine,' the seed of all misery, have no place with them. They are content with so little, that in so large a country they have rather a superfluity than a scarceness: so that they seem to live in the golden world without toil, living in open gardens not intrenched with dykes, not divided with hedges, nor divided with walls. They deal truly one with another, without laws, without books, without judges. They take him for an evil and mischievous man, who taketh pleasure in doing hurt to another, and albeit they delight not in superfluities, yet they make provision for the increase of such roots whereof they make bread, content with such simple diet whereof health is preserved and disease is avoided."

Your own histories show that Columbus on his first visit to our shores, in a message to the king and queen of Spain, paid our forefathers this beautiful tribute:—

> "They are loving, uncovetous people: so docile in all things that I swear to your majesties there is not in the world a better race or more delightful country. They love their neighbors as themselves, and their talk is ever sweet and gentle, accompanied with smile: and though they be naked, yet their manners are decorous and praiseworthy."

But a few years passed away, and your historians left to be perused with shame, the following facts:—

> "On the islands of the Atlantic Coast and in the populous empires of Mexico and Peru, the Spaniards,

through pretense of friendship and religion, gained audience with chiefs and kings, their families and attendants. They were received with great kindness and courtesy, but in return they most treacherously seized and bound in chains the unsuspecting natives; and as a ransom for their release, demanded large sums of gold which were soon given by their subjects. But instead of granting them freedom as promised, they were put to death in a most shocking manner. Their subjects were then hunted down like wild beasts, with bloodhounds, robbed and enslaved; while under pretext to convert them to Christianity, the rack, the scourge, and the fagot were used. Some were burned alive in their thickets and fastnesses for refusing to work the mines as slaves."

Tradition says these acts of base ingratitude were communicated from tribe to tribe throughout the continent, and that a universal wail as one voice went up from all the tribes of the unbroken wilderness: "We must beat back these strangers from our shores before they seize our lands and homes, or slavery or death are ours."

Reader, pause here, close your eyes, shut out from your heart all prejudice against our race, and honestly consider the above records penned by the pale-faced historians centuries ago; and tell us in the name of eternal truth, and by all that is sacred and dear to mankind, was there ever a [people] without the slightest reason of offense, more treacherously imprisoned and scourged than we have been? And tell us, have crime, despotism, violence, and slavery ever been dealt out in a more wicked manner to crush out life and liberty? And was ever a people more mortally offended than our forefathers were?

Almighty Spirit of humanity, let thy arms of compassion embrace and shield us from the charge of treachery, vindictiveness, and cruelty, and save us from further oppression! And may the great chief of the United States appoint no more broken-down or disappointed politicians as agents to deal with us, but may he select good men that are tried and true, men who fear not to do the right. This is our prayer. What would remain for us if we were not allowed to pray? All else we acknowledge to be in the hands of this great republic.

It is clear that for years after the discovery of this country, we stood before the coming strangers, as a block of marble before the sculptor, ready to be shaped into a statue of grace and beauty; but in their greed for gold, the block was hacked to pieces and destroyed. Child-like we trusted in them with all our hearts; and as the young nestling while yet blind, swallows each morsel given by the parent bird, so we drank in all they said. They showed us the compass that guided them across the trackless deep, and as its needle swung to and fro, only resting to the north, we looked upon it as a thing of life from the eternal world. We could not understand the lightning and thunder of their guns, believing they were weapons of the gods; nor could we fathom their wisdom in knowing and telling us the exact time in which the sun or moon should be darkened; hence, we looked upon them as divine; we revered them—yes, we trusted in them, as infants trust in the arms of their mothers.

But again and again was our confidence betrayed, until we were compelled to know that greed for gold was all the balance-wheel they had. The remnants of the beasts are now wild and keep beyond the arrow's reach, the fowls fly high in air, the fish hide themselves in deep waves. We have been driven from the homes of our childhood and from the burial places of our kindred and friends, and scattered far westward into desert places, where multitudes have died from homesickness, cold, and hunger, and are suffering and dying still for want of food and blankets.

As the hunted dear close chased all day long, when night comes on, weary and tired, lies down to rest, mourning for companions of the morning herd, all scattered, dead, and gone, so we through weary years have tried to find some place to safely rest. But all in vain! Our throbbing hearts unceasing say, "The hounds are howling on our tracks." Our [sad] history has been told by weeping parents to their children from generation to generation; and as the fear of the fox in the duckling is hatched, so the wrongs we have suffered are transmitted to our children, and they look upon the white man with distrust as soon as they are born. Hence our worst acts of cruelty should be viewed by all the world with Christian charity, as being but the echo of bad treatment dealt out to us.

Therefore we pray our critics everywhere to be not like the thoughtless boy who condemns the toiling bees wherever found, as vindictive and cruel, because in robbing their homes he once received the poisoned darts that nature gave for their defense. Our strongest defense against the onward marching hordes, we fully realize is as useless as the struggles of a lamb born high in air, pierced to its heart, in the talons of the eagle.

We shall never be happy here any more; we gaze into the faces of our little ones, for smiles of infancy to please, and into the faces of our young men and maidens, for joys of youth to cheer advancing age, but alas! instead of smiles of joy we find but looks of sadness there. Then we fully realize in the anguish of our souls that their young and tender hearts, in keenest sympathy with ours, have drank in the sorrows we have felt, and their sad faces reflect it back to us again. No rainbow of promise spans the dark cloud of our afflictions; no cheering hopes are painted on our midnight sky. We only stand with folded arms and watch and wait to see the future deal with us no better than the past. No cheer of sympathy is given us; but in answer to our complaints we are told the Triumphal March of the Eastern race westward is by the unalterable decree of nature, termed by them "survival of the fittest." And so we stand upon the sea-shore, chained hand and foot, while the incoming tide of the great ocean of civilization rises slowly but surely to overwhelm us.

But a few more generations and the last child of the forest will have passed into the world beyond—into that kingdom where Tche-ban-you-booz, the Great Spirit, dwelleth, who loveth justice and mercy, and hateth evil; who has declared the "fittest" in his kingdom shall be those alone that hear and aid his children when they cry, and that love him and keep his commandments. In that kingdom many of our people in faith believe he will summon the pale-faced spirits to take position on his left, and the red spirits upon his right, and that he will say, "Sons and daughters of the forest, your prayers for deliverance from the iron heels of oppression through centuries past are recorded in this book now open before me, made from the bark of the white birch, a tree under which for generations past you have mourned and wept. On its pages silently has been recorded your sad history. It has touched my heart with pity and I will have compassion."

Then turning to his left he will say, "Sons and daughters of the East, all hear and give heed to my words. While on Earth I did great and marvelous things for you—I gave my only Son, who declared unto you

my will, and as you had freely received, to so freely give. A few of you have kept the faith; and through opposition and great tribulation have labored hard and honestly for the redemption of mankind regardless of race or color. To all such I now give divine power to fly on lightning throughout my universe. Now, therefore, listen; and when the great drum beats let all try their powers to fly. Only those can rise who acted well their part on earth to redeem and save the fallen."

The drum will be sounded, and the innumerable multitude will appear like some vast sea of wounded birds struggling to rise. We shall behold it, and shall hear their fluttering as the rumbling of an earthquake, and to our surprise shall see but a scattering few in triumph rise, and shall hear their songs re-echo through the vault of heaven as they sing, "Glory to the highest who hath redeemed and saved us."

Then the Great Spirit will speak with a voice of thunder to the remaining shame-faced multitude: "Hear ye: it is through great mercy that you have been permitted to enter these happy hunting-grounds. Therefore I charge you in presence of these red men that you are guilty of having tyrannized over them in many and strange ways. I find you guilty of having made wanton wholesale butchery of their game and fish, I find you guilty of having used tobacco, a poisonous weed made only to kill parasites in plants and lice on men and beast. You found it with the red men, who used it only in smoking the pipe of peace, to confirm their contracts, in place of a seal. But you multiplied its use, not only in smoking, but in chewing, and snuffing, thus forming unhealthy, filthy habits, and by cigarettes, the abomination of abominations, learned little children to hunger and thirst after the father and mother of palsy and cancers.

"I find you guilty of tagging after the pay agents sent out by the great chief of the United States, among the Indians, to pay off their birth-right claims to homes, and liberty, and native lands, and then sneaking about their agencies by deceit and trickery, cheating and robbing them of their money and goods, thus leaving them poor and naked. I also find you guilty of following the trail of Christian missionaries into the wilderness among the natives, and when they had set up my altars, and the great work of redemption had just begun, and some in faith believed, you then and there most wickedly set up the idol of Man-tchi-man in-to (the devil) and there stuck out your sign, SAMPLE ROOMS. You then dealt out to the sons of the forest a most damnable drug, fitly termed on earth by Christian women, "a beverage of hell," which destroyed both body and soul, taking therefore, all their money and blankets, and scrupling not to take in pawn the Bibles given them by my servants.

"Therefore know ye, this much abused race shall enjoy the liberties of these happy-hunting-grounds, while I teach them my will, which you were in duty-bound to do while on earth. But instead, you blocked up the highway that led to Heaven, that the car of salvation might not pass over. Had you done your duty, they as well as you would now be rejoicing in glory with my saints with whom you, fluttering, tried this day in vain to rise. But now I say unto you, Stand back! you shall not tread upon the heels of my people, nor

tyrannize over them any more. Neither shall you with gatling-gun or otherwise disturb or break-up their prayer meetings in camp any more. Neither shall you practice with weapons of lightning and thunder any more. Neither shall you use tobacco in any shape, way, or manner. Neither shall you touch, taste, handle, make, buy, or sell anything that can intoxicate any more. And know ye, ye cannot buy out the law or skulk by justice here; and if any attempt is made on your part to break these commandments, I shall forthwith grant these red men of America great power, and delegate them to cast you out of Paradise, and hurl you headlong through its outer gates into the endless abyss beneath—far beyond, where darkness meets with light, there to dwell, and thus shut you out from my presence and the presence of angels and the light of heaven forever and ever."

QUESTIONS TO CONSIDER

1. What sources does Pokagon cite when he compares the lives of Indigenous Americans before and after colonization? Why do you think he chose those sources in particular?
2. Pokagon saves some of his strongest condemnation for "fire-water" or alcoholic beverages. How does his denunciation of alcohol support his larger critique of colonialism?

20.4 ENRIQUE DUPUY DE LÔME, LETTER TO JOSÉ CANALEJAS (1898)*

What was supposed to be a private letter from Spanish ambassador Enrique Dupuy de Lôme (1851–1904) to Spanish prime minister José Canalejas (1854–1912) was leaked to the *New York Journal* in 1898. The candid remarks from de Lôme, who described US president William McKinley as a "weak" and vacillating amateur politician, eager for popular attention, drew an angry response from the American public. Along with the explosion on the USS *Maine* a week later, the de Lôme letter helped solidify American public opinion against Spain.

The *New York Journal*, which published the leaked letter, was the flagship publication of newspaper magnate William Randolph Hearst. Hearst's *Journal* and its rival, Joseph Pulitzer's *New York*

---

* "Letter from Señor Don Enrique Dupuy de Lôme to Señor Don José Canelejas," 1898. Notes from Foreign Missions, 1789–1906, General Records of the Department of State, Record Group 59; National Archives at College Park, College Park, MD.

World, were notorious practitioners of "Yellow Journalism"—reporting that emphasized sensationalism and scandal. The *Journal's* focus on inflammatory news from Spain such as the de Lôme letter and its subsequent calls for de Lôme's resignation made it the most significant public opposition to Spain in the lead up to the Spanish–American War.

His Excellency
Don José Canalejas.
My distinguished and dear friend:
You have no reason to ask my excuses for not having written to me, I ought also to have written to you but I have put off doing so because overwhelmed with work and nous sommes quittes.

The situation here remains the same. Everything depends on the political and military outcome in Cuba. The prologue of all this, in this second stage (phase) of the war, will end the day when the colonial cabinet shall be appointed and we shall be relieved in the eyes of this country of a part of the responsibility for what is happening in Cuba while the Cubans, whom these people think so immaculate, will have to assume it.

Until then, nothing can be clearly seen, and I regard it as a waste of time and progress, by a wrong road, to be sending emissaries to the rebel camp, or to negotiate with the autonomists who have as yet no legal standing, or to try to ascertain the intentions and plans of this government. The (Cuban) refugees will keep on returning one by one and as they do so will make their way into the sheep-fold, while the leaders in the field will gradually come back. Neither the one nor the other class had the courage to leave in a body and they will not be brave enough to return in a body.

The Message has been a disillusionment to the insurgents who expected something different; but I regard it as bad (for us).

Besides the ingrained and inevitable bluntness (grosería) with which is repeated all that the press and public opinion in Spain have said about Weyler, it once more shows what McKinley is, weak and a bidder for the admiration of the crowd besides being a would-be politician (politicastro) who tries to leave a door open behind himself while keeping on good terms with the jingoes of his party.

Nevertheless, whether the practical results of it (the Message) are to be injurious and adverse depends only upon ourselves.

I am entirely of your opinions; without a military end of the matter nothing will be accomplished in Cuba, and without a military and political settlement there will always be the danger of encouragement being give to the insurgents, buy a part of the public opinion if not by the government.

I do not think sufficient attention has been paid to the part England is playing.

Nearly all the newspaper rabble that swarms in your hotels are Englishmen, and while writing for the Journal they are also correspondents of the most influential journals and reviews of London. It has been so ever since this thing began.

As I look at it, England's only object is that the Americans should amuse themselves with us and leave her alone, and if there should be a war, that would the better stave off the conflict which she dreads but which will never come about.

It would be very advantageous to take up, even if only for effect, the question of commercial relations and to have a man of some prominence sent hither, in order that I may make use of him here to carry on a propaganda among the senators and others in opposition to the Junta and to try to win over the refugees.

So, Amblard is coming. I think he devotes himself too much to petty politics, and we have got to do something very big or we shall fail.

Adela returns your greeting, and we all trust that next year you may be a messenger of peace and take it as a Christmas gift to poor Spain.

Ever your attached friend and servant,
ENRIQUE DUPUY de LÔME.

QUESTIONS TO CONSIDER

1. How does de Lôme assess the American government? How does he explain the behavior of US politicians and what does he think can be done to influence them?

2. What parts of the de Lôme letter do you think Americans found infuriating and why?

20.5 PLATT AMENDMENT (1903)*

Named for Connecticut senator Orville H. Platt (1827–1905), the Platt Amendment was an addition to the Army Appropriations Bill passed by the US Congress that defined under what terms the United States would cease its occupation of Cuba. Following the conclusion of the Spanish–American War, Cubans had hoped the United States might help them establish their independence as Congress had already promised that it did not intend to annex the island.

President William McKinley (1843–1901) and members of his administration, however, did not believe that Cubans were capable of governing themselves and establishing an orderly and peaceful state. As a result, the United States imposed several conditions on Cuba before it would agree to leave, forcing the Cubans to incorporate the Platt Amendment into their own constitution. Cuba authorized future US military intervention on the island, formally approved everything the US Army had done during its current occupation and required it to see and lease land on the island for US naval bases. Cuba did not get the independence it hoped for, and instead was forced to agree to American dominance.

Whereas the Congress of the United States of America, by an Act approved March 2, 1901, provided as follows:

Provided further, That in fulfillment of the declaration contained in the joint resolution approved April twentieth, eighteen hundred and ninety-eight, entitled "For the recognition of the independence of the people of Cuba, demanding that the Government of Spain relinquish its authority and government in the island of Cuba, and withdraw its land and naval forces from Cuba and Cuban waters, and directing the President of the United States to use the land and naval forces of the United States to carry these resolutions into effect,"

the President is hereby authorized to "leave the government and control of the island of Cuba to its people" so soon as a government shall have been established in said island under a constitution which, either as a part thereof or in an ordinance appended thereto, shall define the future relations of the United States with Cuba, substantially as follows:

"I. That the government of Cuba shall never enter into any treaty or other compact with any foreign power or powers which will impair or tend to impair the independence of Cuba, nor in any manner authorize or permit any foreign power

---

* "Treaty Between the United States and the Republic of Cuba Embodying the Provisions Defining Their Future Relations as Contained in the Act of Congress Approved March 2, 1901," 1903. Perfected Treaties, 1778–1945, General Records of the United States Government, Record Group 11; National Archives Building, Washington, DC.

or powers to obtain by colonization or for military or naval purposes or otherwise, lodgement in or control over any portion of said island."

"II. That said government shall not assume or contract any public debt, to pay the interest upon which, and to make reasonable sinking fund provision for the ultimate discharge of which, the ordinary revenues of the island, after defraying the current expenses of government shall be inadequate."

"III. That the government of Cuba consents that the United States may exercise the right to intervene for the preservation of Cuban independence, the maintenance of a government adequate for the protection of life, property, and individual liberty, and for discharging the obligations with respect to Cuba imposed by the treaty of Paris on the United States, now to be assumed and undertaken by the government of Cuba."

"IV. That all Acts of the United States in Cuba during its military occupancy thereof are ratified and validated, and all lawful rights acquired thereunder shall be maintained and protected."

"V. That the government of Cuba will execute, and as far as necessary extend, the plans already devised or other plans to be mutually agreed upon, for the sanitation of the cities of the island, to the end that a recurrence of epidemic and infectious diseases may be prevented, thereby assuring protection to the people and commerce of Cuba, as well as to the commerce of the southern ports of the United States and the people residing therein."

"VI. That the Isle of Pines shall be omitted from the proposed constitutional boundaries of Cuba, the title thereto being left to future adjustment by treaty."

"VII. That to enable the United States to maintain the independence of Cuba, and to protect the people thereof, as well as for its own defense, the government of Cuba will sell or lease to the United States lands necessary for coaling or naval stations at certain specified points to be agreed upon with the President of the United States."

"VIII. That by way of further assurance the government of Cuba will embody the foregoing provisions in a permanent treaty with the United States."

QUESTIONS TO CONSIDER

1. Which requirements of the Platt Amendment made it impossible for Cuba to behave as a fully independent country?
2. Based on this amendment, what sort of future relationship do you think the US Congress imagined for the United States and Cuba?

20.6 VISUAL SOURCE: GRANT E. HAMILTON, *I RATHER LIKE THAT IMPORTED AFFAIR* (1904)*

This caricature of President Theodore Roosevelt (1858–1919) by political cartoonist Grant E. Hamilton (1862–1926) portrays him rejecting the legacy established by other wartime and former-soldier presidents as represented by the hats of Grant, Lincoln, and Washington. Roosevelt, dressed in his cavalry uniform, instead covets a distinctly European and un-American

* Courtesy of the Library of Congress

"imported" crown representing imperialist values. Both as a cabinet secretary and later as president, Roosevelt had favored involvement in military conflict and the annexation of far-flung territories such as the Philippines and the Panama Canal Zone. As president, he announced what came to be known as the Roosevelt Corollary, a policy that justified US military intervention in other countries in the Americas at the discretion of the president. These policies were opposed by anti-imperialists who felt that if the United States conquered overseas territories, it would be no different from European colonizers and that the inclusion of more non-white people in the US polity threatened white supremacy.

QUESTIONS TO CONSIDER

1. What visual cues does the illustrator use to make Roosevelt an object of ridicule? What is the political significance of these elements of the illustration?
2. What is the significance of the contrast between the "European" hat Roosevelt favors, as opposed to the other options in the background?

20.7 VISUAL SOURCE: LEADERS OF THE PHILIPPINE REVOLUTION (c. 1898)*

This photograph shows leaders of the Katipunan, a Philippine revolutionary movement that sought to free the Philippines islands from Spanish colonial rule. Throughout the late nineteenth and early twentieth centuries, the Katipunan waged a revolt first against the Empire of Spain and then, after Spain ceded the Philippines to the United States following the Spanish–American War, against the United States. Although the Katipunan struggle was popular among Filipinos, the movement was also split by factional infighting. Andrés Bonifacio, an influential early leader in the movement, had already been executed by rival Emilio Aguinaldo by the time this photo was taken.

Aguinaldo and other leaders initially hoped that the United States would ally with them in their war against Spain, recognize their independence, and sympathize with their goals of ending colonialism and establishing a modern, Western-style republic. The McKinley administration disappointed these hopes, however, viewing Filipinos as incapable of self-government and treating the Philippine islands as a mere territory to be used as a stepping stone to American ambitions in China.

* Archivo General de Indias, Sevilla

QUESTIONS TO CONSIDER

1. What social or economic class do you think the leaders pictured here belong to? What indications can you find of their relative wealth or social standing?
2. What similarities and differences exist between the Philippine and American wars for independence?

CHAPTER 21

WAR, REVOLUTION, AND REACTION, 1910–1925

21.1 WOODROW WILSON, "FOURTEEN POINTS" (1918)*

President Woodrow Wilson (1856–1924) outlined his hopes for the peace that would follow World War I in a message to Congress nine months after the United States had entered the war. At the time, the US was not generally considered a true global power and Wilson's stated goal of reorienting the world away from war and encouraging peaceful self-determination of peoples was an ambitious goal for an American president. Coming after years of war that had left tens of millions dead and wounded, Wilson's Fourteen Points were an optimistic hope for a postwar world.

Wilson sought "peace without victory"—that is, the establishment of a permanent peace without the usual annexations and indemnity payments demanded by the victors. In some ways his hopes were reflected in the Treaty of Versailles, which ended the war: new countries such as Finland, Poland, and Yugoslavia were carved out of old empires, and a global association called the League of Nations was formed to help prevent future conflicts. Ultimately, however, the treaty looked little like what Wilson had laid out, its demands including massive punitive payments from Germany and the expansion of British and French colonial holdings. Wilson could not convince Americans to ratify the treaty, and the United States never joined the League of Nations.

It will be our wish and purpose that the processes of peace, when they are begun, shall be absolutely open and that they shall involve and permit henceforth no secret understandings of any kind. The day of conquest and aggrandizement is gone by; so is also the day of secret covenants entered into in the interest of particular governments and likely at some unlooked-for moment to upset the peace of the world. It is this happy fact, now clear to the view of every public man whose thoughts do not still linger in an age that is dead and gone, which makes it possible for every nation whose purposes are consistent with justice and

* President Wilson's Message to Congress, January 8, 1918, Records of the United States Senate, Record Group 46, Records of the United States Senate, National Archives.

the peace of the world to avow now or at any other time the objects it has in view.

We entered this war because violations of right had occurred which touched us to the quick and made the life of our own people impossible unless they were corrected and the world secure once for all against their recurrence. What we demand in this war, therefore, is nothing peculiar to ourselves. It is that the world be made fit and safe to live in; and particularly that it be made safe for every peace-loving nation which, like our own, wishes to live its own life, determine its own institutions, be assured of justice and fair dealing by the other peoples of the world as against force and selfish aggression. All the peoples of the world are in effect partners in this interest, and for our own part we see very clearly that unless justice be done to others it will not be done to us. The programme of the world's peace, therefore, is our programme; and that programme, the only possible programme, as we see it, is this:

I.   Open covenants of peace, openly arrived at, after which there shall be no private international understandings of any kind but diplomacy shall proceed always frankly and in the public view.

II.   Absolute freedom of navigation upon the seas, outside territorial waters, alike in peace and in war, except as the seas may be closed in whole or in part by international action for the enforcement of international covenants.

III. The removal, so far as possible, of all economic barriers and the establishment of an equality of trade conditions among all the nations consenting to the peace and associating themselves for its maintenance.

IV.   Adequate guarantees given and taken that national armaments will be reduced to the lowest point consistent with domestic safety.

V.   A free, open-minded, and absolutely impartial adjustment of all colonial claims, based upon a strict observance of the principle that in determining all such questions of sovereignty the interests of the populations concerned must have equal weight with the equitable claims of the government whose title is to be determined.

VI.   The evacuation of all Russian territory and such a settlement of all questions affecting Russia as

will secure the best and freest cooperation of the other nations of the world in obtaining for her an unhampered and unembarrassed opportunity for the independent determination of her own political development and national policy and assure her of a sincere welcome into the society of free nations under institutions of her own choosing; and, more than a welcome, assistance also of every kind that she may need and may herself desire. The treatment accorded Russia by her sister nations in the months to come will be the acid test of their good will, of their comprehension of her needs as distinguished from their own interests, and of their intelligent and unselfish sympathy.

VII. Belgium, the whole world will agree, must be evacuated and restored, without any attempt to limit the sovereignty which she enjoys in common with all other free nations. No other single act will serve as this will serve to restore confidence among the nations in the laws which they have themselves set and determined for the government of their relations with one another. Without this healing act the whole structure and validity of international law is forever impaired.

VIII. All French territory should be freed and the invaded portions restored, and the wrong done to France by Prussia in 1871 in the matter of Alsace-Lorraine, which has unsettled the peace of the world for nearly fifty years, should be righted, in order that peace may once more be made secure in the interest of all.

IX.   A readjustment of the frontiers of Italy should be effected along clearly recognizable lines of nationality.

X.   The peoples of Austria-Hungary, whose place among the nations we wish to see safeguarded and assured, should be accorded the freest opportunity to autonomous development.

XI.   Rumania, Serbia, and Montenegro should be evacuated; occupied territories restored; Serbia accorded free and secure access to the sea; and the relations of the several Balkan states to one another determined by friendly counsel along historically established lines of allegiance and nationality; and international guarantees of the political and economic independence and territorial integrity of the several Balkan states should be entered into.

XII. The Turkish portion of the present Ottoman Empire should be assured a secure sovereignty, but the other nationalities which are now under Turkish rule should be assured an undoubted security of life and an absolutely unmolested opportunity of autonomous development, and the Dardanelles should be permanently opened as a free passage to the ships and commerce of all nations under international guarantees.

XIII. An independent Polish state should be erected which should include the territories inhabited by indisputably Polish populations, which should be assured a free and secure access to the sea, and whose political and economic independence and territorial integrity should be guaranteed by international covenant.

XIV. A general association of nations must be formed under specific covenants for the purpose of affording mutual guarantees of political independence and territorial integrity to great and small states alike.

In regard to these essential rectifications of wrong and assertions of right we feel ourselves to be intimate partners of all the governments and peoples associated together against the Imperialists. We cannot be separated in interest or divided in purpose. We stand together until the end.

For such arrangements and covenants we are willing to fight and to continue to fight until they are achieved; but only because we wish the right to prevail and desire a just and stable peace such as can be secured only by removing the chief provocations to war, which this programme does remove. We have no jealousy of German greatness, and there is nothing in this programme that impairs it. We grudge her no achievement or distinction of learning or of pacific enterprise such as have made her record very bright and very enviable. We do not wish to injure her or to block in any way her legitimate influence or power. We do not wish to fight her either with arms or with hostile arrangements of trade if she is willing to associate herself with us and the other peace-loving nations of the world in covenants of justice and law and fair dealing. We wish her only to accept a place of equality among the peoples of the world,—the new world in which we now live,—instead of a place of mastery.

QUESTIONS TO CONSIDER

1. What were Wilson's goals as he explained them in the Fourteen Points? How did he hope the measures he proposed would accomplish them?

2. Which of Wilson's goals do you think might have been achievable? What might have needed to happen to make the vision outlined in the Fourteen Points possible?

21.2 ALAN SEEGAR, "I HAVE A RENDEZVOUS WITH DEATH" (1919)*

Alan Seeger (1888–1916) was an American serving with the French Foreign Legion during World War I when he wrote this poem, possibly during the winter of 1915–1916. Originally from New York, Seeger had moved to Paris and enlisted in the French army soon after the outbreak of war. He was killed in battle during the first days of the Somme River Offensive in the summer of 1916, a battle in which over a million men were killed and wounded. This poem was published posthumously.

In this poem Seeger reflects on soldierly duty, mortality, and the fear of death. He repeats his conviction that he will meet his death in spring, the time of year when battle often resumed following a pause in fighting imposed by winter. Seeger expresses an acceptance of the inevitability of death; though he acknowledges the joyful and satisfying experiences he will miss, he articulates minimal regret. Seeger sees his meeting with death as a duty, an obligation which he is resolved not to fail.

I have a rendezvous with Death,
    At some disputed barricade,
When Spring comes back with rustling shade
    And apple blossoms fill the air—
I have a rendezvous with Death,
    When Spring brings back blue days and fair.

It may be he shall take my hand
    And lead me into his dark land
And close my eyes and quench my breath
    It may be I shall pass him still
I have a rendezvous with Death
    On some scarred slope of battered hill,

When Spring comes round this year
    And the first meadow-flowers appear.

God knows 'twere better to be deep
    Pillowed in silk and scented down
Where love throbs out in blissful sleep
    Pulse nigh to pulse and breath to breath
Where hushed awakenings are dear …
    But I've a rendezvous with Death
At midnight in some flaming town
    When spring trips north again this year
And I to my pledged word am true
    I shall not fail the rendezvous.

QUESTIONS TO CONSIDER

1. Why would this poem—expressing a soldier" reflections on death, duty, and mortality—have been particularly relevant for people living during the First World War?
2. In what ways is the poet both certain and uncertain about the prospect of death? What role does the idea of knowing or not knowing play in the poem?

---

* Alan Seegar, "I Have a Rendezvous with Death," *The Evening Herald*, May 6, 1919, in *Chronicling America: Historic American Newspapers*, Library of Congress.

21.3 ZITKALA-ŠA (GERTRUDE SIMMONS BONNIN), "EDITORIAL COMMENT" (1919)*

Zitkala-Ša was a Dakota writer and activist who wrote about Native American culture and advocated for greater autonomy and rights for Native peoples. She published several books and essays and also co-wrote the first Native American opera, which opened in 1913. Between 1918 and 1919, she served as editor of *American Indian Magazine*, for which she wrote numerous pieces, including this one.

Here, Zitkala-Ša reflects on the peace conference in Paris set to establish a treaty to formally end the First World War, in which her husband had served as a lieutenant. She reflects on the possibility for self-determination by nations and cultures that had previously been constituent parts of larger empires. Zitkala-Ša expresses hope that the governments of the world will be forced to attend to the demands of their people, noting, "Many classes of men and women are clamoring for a hearing." Despite US president Woodrow Wilson's public commitment to self-determination, the rights of Native Americans were not up for discussion at Paris. Zitkala-Ša calls out this hypocrisy, arguing that now is the time to insist on citizenship for Indigenous peoples in America—to insist that they too be treated as a sovereign people being governed by an empire.

The eyes of the world are upon the Peace Conference sitting at Paris.

Under the sun a new epoch is being staged!

Little peoples are to be granted the right of self determination!

Small nations and remnants of nations are to sit beside their great allies at the Peace Table; and their just claims are to be duly incorporated in the terms of a righteous peace.

Paris, for the moment, has become the center of the world's thought. Divers human petitions daily ascend to its Peace Table through foreign emissaries [sic], people's representatives and the interest's lobbyists. From all parts of the earth, claims for adjustments equitable and otherwise are cabled and wirelessed. What patience and wisdom is needed now to render final decisions upon these highly involved and delicate enigmas reeking with inhumanities! The task may be difficult and the exposures of wrongs innumerable, still we believe,—yes, we know, the world is to be made better as a result of these stirring times.

Immortal justice is the vortex around which swing the whirl of human events!

We are seeking to know, justice, not as a fable but as a living, active, practical force in all that concerns our welfare!

Actions of the wise leaders assembled in Paris may be guided ostensibly by temporary man-made laws and aims, dividing human interests into domestic and international affairs, but even so those leaders cannot forget the eternal fact that humanity is essentially one undivided, closely intertwined, fabric through which spiritual truth will shine with increasing brightness until it is fully understood and its requirements fulfilled. The universal cry for freedom from injustice is the voice of a multitude united by afflictions. To appease this human cry the application of democratic principles must be flexible enough to be universal.

Belgium is leading a historic procession of little peoples seeking freedom!

From the very folds of the great allied nations are many classes of men and women clamoring for

* Gertrude Simmons Bonnin, "Editorial Comment," *American Indian Magazine* 6, no. 4 (Winter 1919): 161–62.

a hearing. Their fathers, sons, brothers and husbands fought and died for democracy. Each is eager to receive the reward for which supreme sacrifice was made. Surely will the blood-soaked fields of No-Man's Land unceasingly cry out until the high principles for which blood spilled itself, are established in the governments of men.

Thus in this vast procession to Paris, we recognize and read their flying banners.

Labor organizations are seeking representation at the Peace Conference. Women of the world, mothers of the human race, are pressing forward for recognition. The Japanese are taking up the perplexing problem of race discrimination.

The Black man of America is offering his urgent petition for representation at the Conference; and already President Wilson has taken some action in his behalf by sending to Paris, Dr. Moton, of Tuskegee Institute accompanied by Dr. DuBois.

A large New York assembly of American men and women wirelessed, it is reported, to President Wilson while he was in mid-ocean, enroute to Paris, requesting his aid in behalf of self-government for the Irish people.

The Red man asks for a very simple thing,—citizenship in the land that was once his own,—America. Who shall represent his cause at the World's Peace Conference? The American Indian, too, made the supreme sacrifice for liberty's sake. He loves democratic ideals. What shall world democracy mean to his race?

There never was a time more opportune than now for America to enfranchise the Red man!

QUESTIONS TO CONSIDER

1. How would you describe Zitkala-Ša's tone? What feelings or actions is she trying to encourage in her reader?
2. Why might President Wilson's stated goal of forcing empires to recognize their people's right to self-determination seem hypocritical to Indigenous Americans?

21.4 VISUAL SOURCE: 302ND AND 92ND REGIMENTS IN ACTION IN FRANCE (1918)*

The 92nd infantry division was a segregated unit in the US Army made up of Black American soldiers. In this photograph, machine-gunners from that division enter trenches in preparation for the Meuse River–Argonne Forest offensive in eastern France. One of the last major battles of the First World War, it took place over the course of six weeks in the autumn of 1918 and ended with the armistice on November 11.

Racial segregation in the military had been US policy since the War of the Rebellion, when 200,000 Black Americans had served throughout the armed forces. Throughout the late nineteenth and early twentieth centuries, the US Army kept only four Black regiments active, including cavalry regiments known as Buffalo Soldiers who were frequently deployed in conflicts with Native Americans. Over 350,000 Black Americans served in the US Armed Forces during the First World War, entirely in segregated units. US Army segregation policy did not begin to change until 1948.

* Courtesy of the Library of Congress

QUESTIONS TO CONSIDER

1. How does this photograph illustrate the US Army's segregation policy?
2. What stands out to you about the environment in which the soldiers are fighting?

21.5 VISUAL SOURCE: KU KLUX KLAN PARADE, WASHINGTON, DC (1926)*

The Ku Klux Klan was a violent white supremacist organization established in 1915 near Atlanta, Georgia. The group borrowed its name and some of its iconography from white supremacist paramilitary organizations that had terrorized Black Americans and Republicans in the Reconstruction era South. The clan not only engaged in racially motivated terrorism but also targeted Jews, immigrants, and Catholics. Members of the Klan believed that white Protestants born in the United States were the only real Americans, and they targeted anyone who did not meet these criteria. Their ideology and tactics were similar to contemporary fascist paramilitary groups in Italy and Germany.

Despite the hate and violence that were central to the organization, Klan members insisted that they were a well-meaning fraternal organization. They borrowed practices from other associations like Elks and Odd Fellows and participated publicly in communal events. They saw no contradiction between their patriotism and violent vigilantism. In this photograph, members of the Klan dressed in their regalia march through Washington, DC, in front of on-lookers, bearing American flags.

* Courtesy of the Library of Congress

QUESTIONS TO CONSIDER

1. What message are Klan members trying to send with their parade? How can you tell?
2. How does a parade like this help the Klan's intended appearance as a fraternal association? Why would maintaining that image be important to Klan members?

CHAPTER 22

LOOKING INTO THE ABYSS, 1920–1934

22.1 ELLIOTT BELL, "CRASH" (1938)*

The onset of the Great Depression is commonly dated to October 24, 1929, so-called "Black Thursday." Many investors had borrowed heavily to continue buying stocks in a market where prices only seemed to go up. When the realities of the slowing economy of the late 1920s—lower consumer demand, shrinking industrial output, declining demand for construction services, etc.—eventually led some stock traders to begin to sell overvalued stocks, investors panicked. As stock prices rapidly declined and imagined wealth in the form of stock prices evaporated, banks called in the loans they had made, only to discover that few could pay. The crisis intensified as traders tried to shed devalued shares to cover their debts, only driving prices down further in their desperate bid to sell.

Elliott Bell (1902–1983), then a new financial reporter for the *New York Times*, describes watching the panic setting in at the New York Stock Exchange on Black Thursday. Already skittish bankers and traders gather and are soon swamped by orders to sell coming in by telegraph from around the country via the ticker service. The panic soon draws crowds, as onlookers are drawn to the scene, and Bell concludes in hindsight that "the panic was on."

October 24, 1929, was not the first day of the big break in stocks, nor was it the last. Nevertheless, it was the most terrifying and unreal day I have ever seen on the Street, and it constitutes an important financial landmark, for that day marked the great decline in the prestige and power of Wall Street over national affairs.

The day was overcast and cool. A light north-west wind blew down the canyons of Wall Street, and the temperature, in the low fifties, made bankers and brokers on their way to work button their topcoats around them. The crowds of market traders in the brokers' board rooms were nervous but hopeful as the ten o'clock hour for the start of trading approached. The general feeling was that the worst was over and a good many speculators who had prudently sold out earlier in the decline were congratulating themselves at having bought back their stocks a good deal cheaper. Seldom had the small trader had better or more uniform advice to go by.

---

* Elliott V. Bell, "Panic and Crash: 1929," *New York Times*, November 11, 1938.

The market opened steady with prices little changed from the previous day, though some rather large blocks, of 20,000 to 25,000 shares, came out at the start. It sagged easily for the first half-hour, and then around eleven o'clock the deluge broke.

It came with a speed and ferocity that left men dazed. The bottom simply fell out of the market. From all over the country a torrent of selling orders poured onto the floor of the Stock Exchange and there were no buying orders to meet it. Quotations of representative active issues, like Steel [U.S. Steel], Telephone [AT&T], and Anaconda, began to fall two, three, five, and even ten points between sales. Less active stocks became unmarketable. Within a few moments the ticker service was hopelessly swamped and from then on no one knew what was really happening. By one-thirty the ticker tape was nearly two hours late; by two-thirty it was 147 minutes late. The last quotation was not printed on the tape until 7:08 ½ p.m., four hours, eight and one-half minutes after the close. In the meantime, Wall Street had lived through an incredible nightmare.

In the strange way that news of a disaster spreads, the word of the market collapse flashed through the city. By noon great crowds had gathered at the corner of Broad and Wall Streets where the Stock Exchange on one corner faces Morgan's across the way. On the steps of the Sub-Treasury Building, opposite Morgan's, a crowd of press photographers and newsreel men took up their stand. Traffic was pushed from the streets of the financial district by the crush.

It was in this wild setting that the leading bankers scurried into conference at Morgan's in a belated effort to save the day. . . .

The news of the bankers' meeting flashed through the streets and over the news tickers—stocks began to rally—but for many it was already too late. Thousands of traders, little and big, had gone "overboard" in that incredible hour between eleven and twelve. Confidence in the financial and political leaders of the country, faith in the "soundness" of economic conditions had received a shattering blow. The panic was on.

QUESTIONS TO CONSIDER

1. Bell's account of this day was published nearly ten years after it took place. How is his narrative influenced by the knowledge in hindsight that this was the beginning of the Great Depression?
2. How does Bell describe the behavior of the people around him as the panic begins? How does the public respond to news of the crash?

22.2 FRANKLIN DELANO ROOSEVELT, BANKING CRISIS FIRESIDE CHAT (1933)*

Franklin Delano Roosevelt (1882–1945) assumed the presidency in early 1933 after a landslide victory in the election the previous fall. Although the previous president, Herbert Hoover (1874–1964), had attempted to pull the US economy out of the depression, he had little success. The Emergency Banking Act, passed in March 1933, was one of Roosevelt's first efforts to curb the economic downturn by propping up the US banking system. The act allowed him to impose a bank holiday, effectively a nationwide closure, so that with the government's help banks could acquire enough

* University of Virginia's Miller Center

currency to respond to requests to withdraw funds. By making sure that banks had the money they needed to meet demands, Roosevelt hoped to increase public confidence in the banking system as a whole.

Roosevelt explained this news to Americans in the first of his "Fireside Chats"—radio addresses aimed at everyday Americans that he used to explain important issues of the day or changes in policy. By speaking directly to the American people in plain language, Roosevelt hoped to demystify his government's policy and encourage Americans to have confidence in him and the newly restored banks.

I want to talk for a few minutes with the people of the United States about banking—with the comparatively few who understand the mechanics of banking but more particularly with the overwhelming majority who use banks for the making of deposits and the drawing of checks. I want to tell you what has been done in the last few days, why it was done, and what the next steps are going to be. I recognize that the many proclamations from State Capitols and from Washington, the legislation, the Treasury regulations, etc., couched for the most part in banking and legal terms should be explained for the benefit of the average citizen. I owe this in particular because of the fortitude and good temper with which everybody has accepted the inconvenience and hardships of the banking holiday. I know that when you understand what we in Washington have been about I shall continue to have your cooperation as fully as I have had your sympathy and help during the past week.

First of all let me state the simple fact that when you deposit money in a bank the bank does not put the money into a safe deposit vault. It invests your money in many different forms of credit-bonds, commercial paper, mortgages and many other kinds of loans. In other words, the bank puts your money to work to keep the wheels of industry and of agriculture turning around. A comparatively small part of the money you put into the bank is kept in currency—an amount which in normal times is wholly sufficient to cover the cash needs of the average citizen. In other words the total amount of all the currency in the country is only a small fraction of the total deposits in all of the banks.

What, then, happened during the last few days of February and the first few days of March? Because of undermined confidence on the part of the public, there was a general rush by a large portion of our population to turn bank deposits into currency or gold. A rush so great that the soundest banks could not get enough currency to meet the demand. The reason for this was that on the spur of the moment it was, of course, impossible to sell perfectly sound assets of a bank and convert them into cash except at panic prices far below their real value.

By the afternoon of March 3 scarcely a bank in the country was open to do business. Proclamations temporarily closing them in whole or in part had been issued by the Governors in almost all the states.

It was then that I issued the proclamation providing for the nation-wide bank holiday, and this was the first step in the Government's reconstruction of our financial and economic fabric. The second step was the legislation promptly and patriotically passed by the Congress confirming my proclamation and broadening my powers so that it became possible in view of the requirement of time to entend (*sic*) the holiday and lift the ban of that holiday gradually. This law also gave authority to develop a program of rehabilitation of our banking facilities. I want to tell our citizens in every part of the Nation that the national Congress—Republicans and Democrats alike—showed by this action a devotion to public welfare and a realization of the emergency and the necessity for speed that it is difficult to match in our history.

The third stage has been the series of regulations permitting the banks to continue their functions to take care of the distribution of food and household necessities and the payment of payrolls.

This bank holiday while resulting in many cases in great inconvenience is affording us the opportunity to supply the currency necessary to meet the situation. No sound bank is a dollar worse off than it was when it closed its doors last Monday. Neither is any bank which may turn out not to be in a position for immediate opening. The new law allows the twelve Federal Reserve banks to issue additional currency on good assets and thus the banks that reopen will be able to meet every legitimate call. The new currency is being sent out by the Bureau of Engraving and Printing in large volume to every part of the country. It is sound currency because it is backed by actual, good assets.

A question you will ask is this—why are all the banks not to be reopened at the same time? The answer is simple. Your Government does not intend that the history of the past few years shall be repeated. WE do not want and will not have another epidemic of bank failures.

As a result we start tomorrow, Monday, with the opening of banks in the twelve Federal Reserve Bank cities—those banks which on first examination by the Treasury have already been found to be all right. This will be followed on Tuesday by the resumption of all their functions by banks already found to be sound in cities where there are recognized clearinghouses. That means about 250 cities of the United States.

On Wednesday and succeeding days banks in smaller places all through the country will resume business, subject, of course, to the Government's physical ability to complete its survey. It is necessary that the reopening of banks be extended over a period in order to permit the banks to make applications for necessary loans, to obtain currency needed to meet their requirements and to enable the Government to make common sense checkups.

Let me make it clear to you that if your bank does not open the first day you are by no means justified in believing that it will not open. A bank that opens on one of the subsequent days is in exactly the same status as the bank that opens tomorrow.

I know that many people are worrying about State banks not members of the Federal Reserve System. These banks can and will receive assistance from member banks and from the Reconstruction Finance Corporation. These state banks are following the same course as the national banks except that they get their licenses to resume business from the state authorities, and these authorities have been asked by the Secretary of the Treasury to permit their good banks to open up on the same schedule as the national banks. I am

confident that the state banking departments will be as careful as the National Government in the policy relating to the opening of banks and will follow the same broad policy.

It is possible that when the banks resume a very few people who have not recovered from their fear may again begin withdrawals. Let me make it clear that the banks will take care of all needs—and it is my belief that hoarding during the past week has become an exceedingly unfashionable pastime. It needs no prophet to tell you that when the people find that they can get their money—that they can get it when they want it for all legitimate purposes—the phantom of fear will soon be laid. People will again be glad to have their money where it will be safely taken care of and where they can use it conveniently at any time. I can assure you that it is safer to keep your money in a reopened bank than under the mattress.

The success of our whole great national program depends, of course, upon the cooperation of the public—on its intelligent support and use of a reliable system.

Remember that the essential accomplishment of the new legislation is that it makes it possible for banks more readily to convert their assets into cash than was the case before. More liberal provision has been made for banks to borrow on these assets at the Reserve Banks and more liberal provision has also been made for issuing currency on the security of those good assets. This currency is not fiat currency. It is issued only on adequate security—and every good bank has an abundance of such security.

One more point before I close. There will be, of course, some banks unable to reopen without being reorganized. The new law allows the Government to assist in making these reorganizations quickly and effectively and even allows the Government to subscribe to at least a part of new capital which may be required.

I hope you can see from this elemental recital of what your government is doing that there is nothing complex, or radical in the process.

We had a bad banking situation. Some of our bankers had shown themselves either incompetent or dishonest in their handling of the people's funds. They had used the money entrusted to them in speculations and unwise loans. This was of course not true in the vast majority of our banks but it was true in enough of them to shock the people for a time into a sense of insecurity and to put them into a frame of mind where they did not differentiate, but seemed to assume that the acts of a comparative few had tainted them all. It was the Government's job to straighten out this situation and do it as quickly as possible—and the job is being performed.

I do not promise you that every bank will be reopened or that individual losses will not be suffered, but there will be no losses that possibly could be avoided; and there would have been more and greater losses had we continued to drift. I can even promise you salvation for some at least of the sorely pressed banks. We shall be engaged not merely in reopening sound banks but in the creation of sound banks through reorganization. It has been wonderful to me to catch the note of confidence from all over the country. I can never be sufficiently grateful to the people for the loyal support they have given me in their acceptance of the judgment that has dictated our course, even though all of our processes may not have seemed clear to them.

After all there is an element in the readjustment of our financial system more important than currency, more important than gold, and that is the confidence of the people. Confidence and courage are the essentials of success in carrying out our plan. You people must have faith; you must not be stampeded by rumors or guesses. Let us unite in banishing fear. We have provided the machinery to restore our financial system; it is up to you to support and make it work.

It is your problem no less than it is mine. Together we cannot fail.

QUESTIONS TO CONSIDER

1. Who is Roosevelt's intended audience for his Fireside Chat? How can you tell?
2. What does Roosevelt want Americans to do? How will this aid the economic recovery?

22.3 "DEFENSA DE LOS NORTEÑOS" (N.D.)*

Mexican Americans had lived in significant numbers in the United States since the annexation of Texas in the mid-nineteenth century, but in the early twentieth century immigration from Mexico increased dramatically. The chaos of the Mexican Revolution, which began in 1910, was an important factor in encouraging Mexicans to seek opportunities elsewhere, and many found work in the agricultural industries in the Southwestern United States.

Not everyone who made the journey to the US stayed permanently—many worked only seasonally or returned to Mexico periodically. The song "Defense of the Emigrants" captures the desperation and privation that encouraged Mexicans to seek work in the United States ("we left the country/ From sheer necessity") and also how some who returned from the US made the trip appealing to others in desperate circumstances ("One succeeds in earning/More than any of our countrymen").

* María Herrera-Sobek, in Herrera-Sobek, *Northward Bound: The Mexican Immigrant Experience in Ballad and Song* (Bloomington: Indiana University Press, 1993), 80–83.

Defensa de los norteños	*Defense of the Emigrants*
Lo que dicen de nosotros	What they say about us
Casi todo es reqalidad;	Is mostly the truth,
Más salimos del terreno	But we left the country
Por pura necesidad.	From sheer necessity
Que muchos vienen facetos	So many come back boasting,
Yo también se los dijera;	I too can tell you that;
Por eso la prensa chica	That is why the local press
Tuvo donde echar tijera.	Speaks harshly about them.
Pero la culpa la tienen	But those who are to blame
Esos ingrates patrones	Are those unking employers
Que no les dan a su gente	Who don't give their people [work]
Ni aun cuando porte chaqueta.	Even when they wear a jacket.
No es porque hable del país	I'm not criticizing the country,
Pero claro se los digo	But I frankly will tell you
Que muchos trabajadores	That many of the laborers
Enseñan hasta el ombligo . . .	Are naked to their navels . . .
Yo no digo que en el norte	I don't say that in the North
Se va uno a estar muy sentado,	One is going to be taking it easy
Ni aun cuando porte chaqueta	Even though one wears a jacket
Lo hacen a uno diputado.	One is not made a congressman.
Allí se va a trabajar	One has to work there,
Macizo, a lo Americano,	Hard, in the American fashion,
Pero alcanza uno a ganar	But one succeeds in earning
Más que cualesquier paisano . . .	More than any of our countrymen . . .
Mucha gente así lo ha dicho:	Many people have said
Dizque no somos patriotas	That we are not patriotic
Porque les vamos a server	Because we go to serve
A los infames patotas.	The accursed big-footed ones.
Pero que se abran trabajos	But let them give us jobs
Y que paguen buen dinero,	And pay us decent wages;

Defensa de los norteños	*Defense of the Emigrants*
Y no queda un Mexicano	Not one Mexican then
Que se vaya al extranjero.	Will go to foreign lands.
Ansia temenos de Volver	We're anxious to return again
A nuestra patria idolatrada,	To our adored country;
Pero qué le hemos de hacer	But what can we do about it
Si está la patria arruinada	If the country is ruined?
Si han hablado de nosotros	If they're talked about us,
Es por muchos fanfarrones	It is because of all the braggarts
Que andan sonando los pesos	Who go jingling their dollars
Cual si trajeran millones . . .	As if they brought back millions . . .
Que no vengan de facetos	"Don't come back boasting,"
Les digo a mis companeros;	I say to my companions;
Amigos, yo no presume	"Friends, I don't put on airs
Porque soy de los rancheros . . .	Because I am just a ranchero." . . .
Yo ya me voy para el norte	Now I am leaving for the North;
Amigos, no se los niego;	Friends, I do not deny it;
Ahí les dejo a sus requites	I leave you with your rich fellows—
A que los toree Juan Diego.	Let who will be bothered with them.
Muchachos, yo los convido	Boys, I invite you
A la Nación extranjera;	To the foreign nation;
No le hace que algunos digan	Don't be bothered if they say
Que somos chucha cuerera.	That we are mercenary.

QUESTIONS TO CONSIDER

1. What is the song "defending" the emigrants against?
2. How would you describe the tone of the song? Hopeful? Mournful? Celebratory?

22.4 THE CARTER FAMILY, "NO DEPRESSION IN HEAVEN" (1936)*

The Carter Family was an influential folk/country group from southwestern Virginia whose songs became some of the first popular country music in the new era of music recording and broadcasting. Known for their innovative guitar technique, the group found rapid success with a series of recordings in the late 1920s and early 1930s. "No Depression in Heaven," released after more than five years of economic crisis in the United States, mourns the scenes of destitution and privation of recent years and hopes for a release from earthly misery in the afterlife. The song includes deliberate apocalyptic imagery that captures a spirit of hopelessness that gripped many Americans after years of hardship. The song continues to be adapted by folk and country acts, including Uncle Tupelo (1990) and Sheryl Crow (2004).

For fear the hearts of men are failing
For these are latter days we know
The Great Depression now is spreading
God's word declared it would be so

I'm going where there's no depression
To the lovely land that's free from care
I'll leave this world of toil and trouble
My home's in Heaven, I'm going there

In that bright land, there'll be no hunger
No orphan children crying for bread
No weeping widows, toil or struggle
No shrouds, no coffins and no death

I'm going where there's no depression
To the lovely land that's free from care
I'll leave this world of toil and trouble
My home's in Heaven, I'm going there

This dark hour of midnight nearing
Tribulation time will come
This storm will hurl in midnight fear
And sweep lost millions to their doom

I'm going where there's no depression
To the lovely land that's free from care
I'll leave this world of toil and trouble
My home's in Heaven, I'm going there

QUESTIONS TO CONSIDER

1. What about this song might have resonated with Americans in the mid-1930s?
2. While the song expresses an abiding hope in the goodness of heaven, it paints a bleak picture of the mortal world. Is the mood of the song hopeful or dispiriting, and what makes you think so?

---

* The Carter Family, "No Depression in Heaven," *Can the Circle Be Unbroken* (Vocalion Records, 1936), LP.

22.5 VISUAL SOURCE: DOROTHEA LANGE, *FAMILY WHO TRAVELED BY FREIGHT TRAIN (1939)**

Dorothea Lange (1895–1965) was an innovative photojournalist known for capturing humanizing images of the victims of the Great Depression. Years of unemployment following the stock market crash of 1929 combined with an agricultural crisis known as the Dust Bowl in the Midwest and Southwest. This led many rural Americans to turn to migrant labor, moving from place to place with their families to gain temporary employment picking crops. Derogatorily termed "Okies," these destitute and displaced Americans were frequently greeted with hostility. Working for government agencies tasked with reducing rural poverty, Lange documented the lives of many of these transient families, producing images that helped drive home the human cost of the Great Depression.

In this photograph Lange captured a family resting in a train yard in the Yakima Valley of southern Washington. With few personal possessions, two children accompanying them, and no mode of transportation beyond the freight trains they rest next to, the desperation of Lange's subjects is clear.

---

* Courtesy of the Library of Congress

QUESTIONS TO CONSIDER

1. How does the way Lange's shot is framed—its angle and setting, for example—tell the viewer that the family is in desperate circumstances?
2. What about the photograph gives it a quality of realism? How can you tell it is not a staged portrait?

CHAPTER 23

BIRTH PANGS OF SOCIAL DEMOCRACY, 1933–1940

23.1 CAROLINE HENDERSON, LETTER TO A FRIEND IN MARYLAND "FROM THE DUST BOWL" (1935)*

Published in *The Atlantic* magazine in the mid-1930s, this letter from farmer Caroline Henderson (1877–1966) to an acquaintance in Maryland captures the struggles of those who continued to try to eke out a living even as the Dust Bowl ravaged their farms. Years of plow farming on the Great Plains removed native grasses that had previously trapped moisture and prevented erosion. When drought conditions then combined with high winds, communities in the southern Great Plains began to suffer from massive dust storms. With little hope of change while the drought persisted, many families left to become migrant agricultural laborers. Caroline Henderson and her husband, however, farmers for nearly thirty years, tried to stick it out.

Henderson's letter captures the desperation of life on the Great Plains in the 1930s. She tells of the dwindling population of nearby farms and of efforts to retain moisture in the field despite the lack of rain. She is proud of her community for continuing to work hard, but it is clear that she and her neighbors are at the mercy of the weather.

August 11, 1935
MY DEAR Evelyn: —
On this blistering Sunday afternoon, I am, like Alexander Selkirk,

Monarch of all I survey;
My right there is none to dispute.

There is no one within a mile and a half, and all day I've seen just one person pass by in an old stripped-down Ford.

Will and Eleanor went early this morning with a family of neighbors to visit the dinosaur pit in the next county to the westward—about seventy miles from here where the State University is engaged in excavating the bones of some of these ancient monsters, reminders of a time when there was plenty of water even in the Panhandle.

It seemed impossible for us all to leave home at once, so I stayed here to care for a new Shorthorn brother, to keep the chickens' pails filled with fresh

* Caroline A. Henderson, "Letters from the Dust Bowl," *The Atlantic*, May 1936.

90

water, to turn the cattle and horses in to water at noon, and to keep them from straying to the extremely poisonous drouth-stricken cane. We spent the better part of a night during the week trying to save two of the best young cows from the effects of the prussic acid which develops in the stunted sorghum. We thought they would die and I am not sure yet whether they recovered because of the liberal doses of melted lard and molasses or whether the poison was not quite strong enough to be fatal. It produces a paralysis of the respiratory system, and when death occurs, as it frequently does, it is due to suffocation from lack of oxygen.

Ever since your letter came, I have been thinking how different are the causes of our personal difficulties. It is hard for us prodigals in this far country, in our scarcity of all things, not to feel envious of the Del Mar Va pigs luxuriating in potatoes, peaches (and cream?), and the delicious Youngerberries. But, as I started to say, our own problems are of a quite different sort. We cannot complain of laziness on the part of our citizens. Oklahoma is one of the first states to get away from direct relief. Official reports of the administrators here emphasize the eagerness with which people accept any sort of work to help themselves and to make unnecessary the acceptance of public aid. In our county the FERA force is being cut down. Three case workers and two from the office force have been dismissed during the past week.

This progress toward more nearly normal conditions of employment occurs in the face of the most critical farm situation that we have ever encountered. For over a month we have had no rain, and the two light local showers early in July had only a slight and temporary effect. All hope of an adequate forage crop has now followed into oblivion the earlier hopes of wheat and maize production. We have no native or cultivated hay crops. The cattle stay alive thus far on weeds, but the pastures are destitute of grass. Many think it can never be restored. The heat is intense and the drying winds are practically continuous, with a real "duster" occurring every few days to keep us humble. After the government erosion control project was carried through there was, for a time, a partial cessation of the dust blowing. But as the freshly upturned earth is pulverizing under the influence of continued heat and wind and entire lack of moisture, it too is ready to

blow. A recently established Oklahoma law permits the County Commissioners to require the working of kind that is being allowed to blow to the detriment of other farms, and I note that one such order has recently been issued in our county.

You asked about the soil erosion control programme and what could be done with an allowance of ten cents per acre. That amount just about covers actual expense of fuel and oil for listing with a large tractor. Possibly it leaves a slight margin if listing is done with a lighter outfit. In no case was any allowance made for a man's labor or the use of his farming equipment. The plan was proposed to encourage widespread and practically simultaneous working of the blowing fields, with a reasonable proportion on contour lines, Undoubtedly it has been of great benefit, and had rains followed, as everyone hoped, we should feel that we were approaching the turn in the long road. As a matter of fact, the complete absence of rain has given us no chance to test the effectiveness of the contour listing. A few people signed up for terracing as a more permanent method of conserving and distributing the longed for moisture—if it ever comes! Will has been working early and late with one of the county terracing machines, laying up ridges on contour lines for every foot of fall. He hopes to be ready to-morrow to turn the machine over to a neighbor who will also make the experiment. Later on he would like to run the terrace lines across the pasture lands, but the future for us is most uncertain.

Everything now depends on whether a definite change of moisture conditions occurs in time for people to sow wheat for 1936. The "suitcase farmers" that is, insurance agents, preachers, real-estate men, and so forth, from cities near or far—have bet thousands of dollars upon rain, or, in other words, have hired the preparation of large areas of land all around us which no longer represent the idea of homes at all, but just parts of a potential factory for the low-cost production of wheat if it rains. A short time ago a big tractor, working for one of these absentee farmers across the road from our home, accidentally hooked on to the cornerstone of the original survey and dragged it off up the road. All these many years that stone has marked the corner of our homestead. I have walked past it hundreds of times as I have taken the cows to their pasture or brought them home again. Always it has suggested the beauty of the untouched prairie as it was when the surveyors set the stone, the luxuriant thick turf of native grasses,—grama grass, buffalo, and curly mesquite, the pincushion cactuses, straw-color and rose, the other wild flowers which in their season fulfilled the thought of Shakespeare:—

> The summer's flower is to the summer sweet, Though to itself it only live and die.

The cornerstone has also suggested the preparation for human occupation—the little homes that were so hopefully established here, of which so very few remain. After twenty-nine years, eight places in our township, out of the possible 136 (excluding the two school sections), are still occupied by those who made the original homestead entry. And now the stone is gone and the manner of its removal seemed almost symbolic of the changes that appear inevitable.

We can't see why your wheat prices should be so hopelessly low. You may judge now a little of how we felt in 1931, with wheat at less than "two bits" per bushel! The price here has recently been about a dollar a bushel, several cents above the Kansas City price. I suppose the idea is to discourage shipment, as there is not enough wheat in this area now to provide for fall sowing—if it rains—and seed wheat must be shipped in.

One morning at the store, being in a reckless mood, I invested a dime in five small tomatoes and wished you might be getting something like that price for your surplus. Potatoes cost us around thirty cents a peck. I hope the protest of the Maryland growers has been successful in giving them some return for their work. Peaches are priced at four pounds for a quarter, but are not for us. So count your mercies, lady. It may surprise you to see how numerous they are.

The last sack of flour cost $1.69, and twelve-ounce loaves of good bread are still to be had for a nickel, considerably less than the price we paid during the dear old days of reputed prosperity—before processing taxes were a subject for political debate and court consideration. We feel rather proud that the proprietor of the Elkhart flour mill which we have patronized for many years has withdrawn from the group of Kansas millers suing the government for recovery of the processing tax. He explained his position by stating that, as the benefits derived from these taxes had been an actual lifesaver for farming and general business interests in this section, he would not seek to embarrass the government in its attempt to collect the tax. His independent action in refusing to join in the raid seems worth mentioning in these days when individualism is supposed to be dead.

It's time to do the evening work, put the guinea pig to bed, and begin to watch for the return of our explorers. I do hope weather conditions are favoring the growth of your crops.

QUESTIONS TO CONSIDER

1. How has the drought impacted Henderson and her community? How are they trying to mitigate the drought?
2. What parts of Henderson's letter indicate that life has gotten considerably harder? How have Henderson's life and the world around her changed as a result?

23.2 FRANKLIN DELANO ROOSEVELT, CAMPAIGN ADDRESS AT MADISON SQUARE GARDEN (1936)*

Running for re-election in 1936, President Franklin Roosevelt (1882–1945) chose to emphasize the leftward shift in his administration. He appealed to voters by highlighting what he had done to help curb predatory practices of capitalism like child labor, and to provide wage-earning Americans with more financial stability, such as unemployment insurance. He also supported workers' and farmers' collective organizations such as unions and cooperative farms. He portrayed his critics as self-interested businessmen who twisted the truth to make the policies of Roosevelt's New Deal sound like more of a hindrance to wage earners than a help.

When Roosevelt won handily in 1936, it did much to solidify the New Deal coalition of Democrats as the governing party in the United States. Supporting an activist central government that would try to intervene in the lives of citizens to provide aid and prevent destitution, the New Deal coalition added industrial workers and ethnic and religious groups such as Black, Jewish, and Italian Americans to its traditional base of Southern farmers and urban wage-earners. Although the Depression was ongoing, voters responded positively to Roosevelt's many initiatives to ease the hardships of everyday Americans.

Senator Wagner, Governor Lehman, ladies and gentlemen:

On the eve of a national election, it is well for us to stop for a moment and analyze calmly and without prejudice the effect on our Nation of a victory by either of the major political parties.

The problem of the electorate is far deeper, far more vital than the continuance in the Presidency of any individual. For the greater issue goes beyond units of humanity—it goes to humanity itself.

In 1932 the issue was the restoration of American democracy; and the American people were in a mood to win. They did win. In 1936 the issue is the preservation of their victory. Again they are in a mood to win. Again they will win.

More than four years ago in accepting the Democratic nomination in Chicago, I said: "Give me your help not to win votes alone, but to win in this crusade to restore America to its own people."

The banners of that crusade still fly in the van of a Nation that is on the march.

It is needless to repeat the details of the program which this Administration has been hammering out on the anvils of experience. No amount of misrepresentation or statistical contortion can conceal or blur or smear that record. Neither the attacks of unscrupulous enemies nor the exaggerations of over-zealous friends will serve to mislead the American people.

What was our hope in 1932? Above all other things the American people wanted peace. They wanted peace of mind instead of gnawing fear.

First, they sought escape from the personal terror which had stalked them for three years. They wanted the peace that comes from security in their homes: safety for their savings, permanence in their jobs, a fair profit from their enterprise.

Next, they wanted peace in the community, the peace that springs from the ability to meet the needs of community life: schools, playgrounds, parks, sanitation, highways—those things which are expected of solvent local government. They sought escape from disintegration and bankruptcy in local and state affairs.

---

* University of Virginia's Miller Center

They also sought peace within the Nation: protection of their currency, fairer wages, the ending of long hours of toil, the abolition of child labor, the elimination of wild-cat speculation, the safety of their children from kidnappers.

And, finally, they sought peace with other Nations—peace in a world of unrest. The Nation knows that I hate war, and I know that the Nation hates war.

I submit to you a record of peace; and on that record a well-founded expectation for future peace— peace for the individual, peace for the community, peace for the Nation, and peace with the world.

Tonight I call the roll—the roll of honor of those who stood with us in 1932 and still stand with us today.

Written on it are the names of millions who never had a chance—men at starvation wages, women in sweatshops, children at looms.

Written on it are the names of those who despaired, young men and young women for whom opportunity had become a will-o'-the-wisp.

Written on it are the names of farmers whose acres yielded only bitterness, business men whose books were portents of disaster, home owners who were faced with eviction, frugal citizens whose savings were insecure.

Written there in large letters are the names of countless other Americans of all parties and all faiths, Americans who had eyes to see and hearts to understand, whose consciences were burdened because too many of their fellows were burdened, who looked on these things four years ago and said, "This can be changed. We will change it."

We still lead that army in 1936. They stood with us then because in 1932 they believed. They stand with us today because in 1936 they know. And with them stand millions of new recruits who have come to know.

Their hopes have become our record.

We have not come this far without a struggle and I assure you we cannot go further without a struggle.

For twelve years this Nation was afflicted with hear-nothing, see-nothing, do-nothing Government. The Nation looked to Government but the Government looked away. Nine mocking years with the golden calf and three long years of the scourge! Nine crazy years at the ticker and three long years in the breadlines! Nine mad years of mirage and three long years of despair! Powerful influences strive today to restore that kind of government with its doctrine that that Government is best which is most indifferent.

For nearly four years you have had an Administration which instead of twirling its thumbs has rolled up its sleeves. We will keep our sleeves rolled up.

We had to struggle with the old enemies of peace— business and financial monopoly, speculation, reckless banking, class antagonism, sectionalism, war profiteering.

They had begun to consider the Government of the United States as a mere appendage to their own affairs. We know now that Government by organized money is just as dangerous as Government by organized mob.

Never before in all our history have these forces been so united against one candidate as they stand today. They are unanimous in their hate for me—and I welcome their hatred.

I should like to have it said of my first Administration that in it the forces of selfishness and of lust for power met their match. I should like to have it said of my second Administration that in it these forces met their master.

The American people know from a four-year record that today there is only one entrance to the White House—by the front door. Since March 4, 1933, there has been only one pass-key to the White House. I have carried that key in my pocket. It is there tonight. So long as I am President, it will remain in my pocket.

Those who used to have pass-keys are not happy. Some of them are desperate. Only desperate men with their backs to the wall would descend so far below the level of decent citizenship as to foster the current pay-envelope campaign against America's working people. Only reckless men, heedless of consequences, would risk the disruption of the hope for a new peace between worker and employer by returning to the tactics of the labor spy.

Here is an amazing paradox! The very employers and politicians and publishers who talk most loudly of class antagonism and the destruction of the American system now undermine that system by this attempt to coerce the votes of the wage earners of this country. It is the 1936 version of the old threat to close down the factory or the office if a particular candidate does not win. It is an old strategy of tyrants to delude their victims into fighting their battles for them.

Every message in a pay envelope, even if it is the truth, is a command to vote according to the will of the employer. But this propaganda is worse—it is deceit.

They tell the worker his wage will be reduced by a contribution to some vague form of old-age insurance. They carefully conceal from him the fact that for every dollar of premium he pays for that insurance, the employer pays another dollar. That omission is deceit.

They carefully conceal from him the fact that under the federal law, he receives another insurance policy to help him if he loses his job, and that the premium of that policy is paid 100 percent by the employer and not one cent by the worker. They do not tell him that the insurance policy that is bought for him is far more favorable to him than any policy that any private insurance company could afford to issue. That omission is deceit.

They imply to him that he pays all the cost of both forms of insurance. They carefully conceal from him the fact that for every dollar put up by him his employer puts up three dollars three for one. And that omission is deceit.

But they are guilty of more than deceit. When they imply that the reserves thus created against both these policies will be stolen by some future Congress, diverted to some wholly foreign purpose, they attack the integrity and honor of American Government itself. Those who suggest that, are already aliens to the spirit of American democracy. Let them emigrate and try their lot under some foreign flag in which they have more confidence.

The fraudulent nature of this attempt is well shown by the record of votes on the passage of the Social Security Act. In addition to an overwhelming majority of Democrats in both Houses, seventy-seven Republican Representatives voted for it and only eighteen against it and fifteen Republican Senators voted for it and only five against it. Where does this last-minute drive of the Republican leadership leave these Republican Representatives and Senators who helped enact this law?

I am sure the vast majority of law-abiding businessmen who are not parties to this propaganda fully appreciate the extent of the threat to honest business contained in this coercion.

I have expressed indignation at this form of campaigning and I am confident that the overwhelming majority of employers, workers and the general public share that indignation and will show it at the polls on Tuesday next.

Aside from this phase of it, I prefer to remember this campaign not as bitter but only as hard-fought. There should be no bitterness or hate where the sole thought is the welfare of the United States of America. No man can occupy the office of President without realizing that he is President of all the people.

It is because I have sought to think in terms of the whole Nation that I am confident that today, just as four years ago, the people want more than promises.

Our vision for the future contains more than promises.

This is our answer to those who, silent about their own plans, ask us to state our objectives.

Of course we will continue to seek to improve working conditions for the workers of America—to reduce hours over-long, to increase wages that spell starvation, to end the labor of children, to wipe out sweatshops. Of course we will continue every effort to end monopoly in business, to support collective bargaining, to stop unfair competition, to abolish dishonorable trade practices. For all these we have only just begun to fight.

Of course we will continue to work for cheaper electricity in the homes and on the farms of America, for better and cheaper transportation, for low interest rates, for sounder home financing, for better banking, for the regulation of security issues, for reciprocal trade among nations, for the wiping out of slums. For all these we have only just begun to fight.

Of course we will continue our efforts in behalf of the farmers of America. With their continued cooperation we will do all in our power to end the piling up of huge surpluses which spelled ruinous prices for their crops. We will persist in successful action for better land use, for reforestation, for the conservation of water all the way from its source to the sea, for drought and flood control, for better marketing facilities for farm commodities, for a definite reduction of farm tenancy, for encouragement of farmer cooperatives, for crop insurance and a stable food supply. For all these we have only just begun to fight.

Of course we will provide useful work for the needy unemployed; we prefer useful work to the pauperism of a dole.

Here and now I want to make myself clear about those who disparage their fellow citizens on the relief rolls. They say that those on relief are not merely jobless—that they are worthless. Their solution for the relief problem is to end relief—to purge the rolls by starvation. To use the language of the stock broker, our needy unemployed would be cared for when, as, and if some fairy godmother should happen on the scene.

You and I will continue to refuse to accept that estimate of our unemployed fellow Americans. Your Government is still on the same side of the street with the Good Samaritan and not with those who pass by on the other side.

Again—what of our objectives?

Of course we will continue our efforts for young men and women so that they may obtain an education and an opportunity to put it to use. Of course we will continue our help for the crippled, for the blind, for the mothers, our insurance for the unemployed, our security for the aged. Of course we will continue to protect the consumer against unnecessary price spreads, against the costs that are added by monopoly and speculation. We will continue our successful efforts to increase his purchasing power and to keep it constant.

For these things, too, and for a multitude of others like them, we have only just begun to fight.

All this—all these objectives—spell peace at home. All our actions, all our ideals, spell also peace with other nations.

Today there is war and rumor of war. We want none of it. But while we guard our shores against threats of war, we will continue to remove the causes of unrest and antagonism at home which might make our people easier victims to those for whom foreign war is profitable. You know well that those who stand to profit by war are not on our side in this campaign.

"Peace on earth, good will toward men"—democracy must cling to that message. For it is my deep conviction that democracy cannot live without that true religion which gives a nation a sense of justice and of moral purpose. Above our political forums, above our market places stand the altars of our faith—altars on which burn the fires of devotion that maintain all that is best in us and all that is best in our Nation.

We have need of that devotion today. It is that which makes it possible for government to persuade those who are mentally prepared to fight each other to go on instead, to work for and to sacrifice for each other. That is why we need to say with the Prophet: "What doth the Lord require of thee—but to do justly, to love mercy and to walk humbly with thy God." That is why the recovery we seek, the recovery we are winning, is more than economic. In it are included justice and love and humility, not for ourselves as individuals alone, but for our Nation.

That is the road to peace.

QUESTIONS TO CONSIDER

1. How would you describe Roosevelt's goals for his next term? Do any of them surprise you?
2. How does Roosevelt characterize the opponents of his policies?

23.3 VISUAL SOURCE: PETER STACKPOLE, *BAY BRIDGE WORKERS AT QUITTING TIME* (1935)*

In this image by photographer Peter Stackpole (1913–1997), workers on the Golden Gate Bridge in San Francisco Bay return home by boat. Begun in 1933, the Golden Gate Bridge was a marvel of modern engineering at its completion. Almost a mile long, it was the longest suspension bridge in the world when it opened in 1937. Connecting the north and south sides of the populous San Francisco Bay, the bridge was a significant improvement over the previous ferry service and stands as one of the most impressive feats of American infrastructure.

The bridge was also incredibly dangerous to build. At least ten men belonged to an informal "Half-Way to Hell Club" of those who had fallen from the bridge during construction but had been saved by safety nets below. In total, eleven men lost their lives working on the bridge, ten of them in an accident three months before the bridge opened when the scaffold they were on fell and broke through the safety net.

QUESTIONS TO CONSIDER

1. How does the photographer frame the workers relative to the bridge? What connections is he trying to draw between the men and the unfinished structure?
2. What is the demeanor of the men? How do you think they feel? Is this photo posed or true to life, and how can you tell?

---

* Peter Stackpole Archive/Gift of the Stackpole Family

23.4 VISUAL SOURCE: RUSSELL LEE, FRONT OF SPANISH LANGUAGE MOVIE THEATER, SAN ANTONIO, TX (1939)*

In the early twentieth century, white Americans imposed social segregation by race and ethnicity across many American cities, including Austin, Texas. Austin's growing population of Mexican Americans frequented their own businesses and cultural institutions, like the movie theater in this photograph. The marquee advertises an Italian film, *Castles in the Air*, which may have been dubbed in Spanish.

Photographer Russell Lee (1903–1986) was a renowned photojournalist of the Great Depression Era. Along with other photographers like Dorothea Lange, Lee worked for the Farm Security Administration, an agency established by the Roosevelt administration to combat rural poverty. Lee created iconic documentary photographs in Texas and New Mexico and later documented the internment of Japanese Americans during the Second World War.

QUESTIONS TO CONSIDER

1. What stands out to you about this theater? How does it compare to modern cinemas?
2. Film was still a relatively new entertainment medium in 1939. Why might a cinema like this have been an important cultural institution?

---

* Courtesy of the Library of Congress

23.5 VISUAL SOURCE: BORIS DEUTSCH, *CULTURAL CONTRIBUTIONS OF NORTH, SOUTH AND CENTRAL AMERICA* (1939–1944)*

This mural was commissioned by the US Treasury Department and now appears in the Los Angeles Terminal Annex post office. It was painted by Boris Deutsch (1892–1978), a Jewish artist born in what is now Lithuania, in the Russian Empire. After deserting the Russian army during the First World War, he made his way to the western United States, where he worked as an art teacher and received several notable commissions. Deutsch was allowed to choose the subject of his composition for the post office and chose "Culture of the Americas."

The mural consists of eleven parts, with six featuring Native Americans in a pre-contact world and five others representing modern science, technology, and industry. Deutsch drew from Indigenous cultures from throughout the Americas to inspire his mural; in this segment Pueblo architecture and pottery, commonly associated with the American Southwest, are prominently featured. While Deutsch's work emphasizes the role of Native peoples in the history of the Americas, the blending of Indigenous cultures and their juxtaposition to images of modern technology unfortunately also portray Native Americans as an undifferentiated culture relegated to the past.

* Alpha Stock / Alamy Stock Photo

QUESTIONS TO CONSIDER

1. What activities and crafts are displayed in the mural and why might they be important?
2. How does Deutsch portray the faces and bodies of the Native Americans in his mural? Does his composition humanize his subjects?

CHAPTER 24

FLAMES OF GLOBAL WAR, VISIONS OF GLOBAL PEACE, 1940–1945

24.1 FRANKLIN DELANO ROOSEVELT, ANNUAL MESSAGE TO CONGRESS AND "FOUR FREEDOMS" (1941)*

President Franklin D. Roosevelt (1882–1945) used his State of the Union Address in early 1941 to call attention to military invasions by fascist powers and to convince Americans that the United States must be involved in resisting them. In the previous eighteen months, Nazi Germany had invaded Poland, Belgium, France, Denmark, Norway, and the Netherlands, and was bombing the British Isles. The Japanese Empire was engaged in an invasion and occupation of China that had already been lasting for several years.

Roosevelt argued that the United States could not afford to stand by while this aggression continued—that the US could not safely isolate itself from the problems of the world. Although he did not call for American soldiers to join the fray, he encouraged Congress to approve the production of weapons to be supplied to those fighting fascist powers—a policy that eventually became known as the Lend–Lease Program. As he called for America to become involved in this new world war, he also outlined the aims that they would hope to secure, commonly referred to as the four freedoms: freedom of speech, freedom of worship, freedom from want, and freedom from fear.

Mr. President, Mr. Speaker, Members of the Seventy-seventh Congress:

I address you, the Members of the Seventy-seventh Congress, at a moment unprecedented in the history of the Union. I use the word "unprecedented," because at no previous time has American security been as seriously threatened from without as it is today.

Since the permanent formation of our Government under the Constitution, in 1789, most of the periods of crisis in our history have related to our domestic affairs. Fortunately, only one of these—the four-year War Between the States—ever threatened our national unity. Today, thank God, one hundred and thirty million Americans, in forty-eight States,

* National Archives

have forgotten points of the compass in our national unity.

It is true that prior to 1914 the United States often had been disturbed by events in other Continents. We had even engaged in two wars with European nations and in a number of undeclared wars in the West Indies, in the Mediterranean and in the Pacific for the maintenance of American rights and for the principles of peaceful commerce. But in no case had a serious threat been raised against our national safety or our continued independence.

What I seek to convey is the historic truth that the United States as a nation has at all times maintained clear, definite opposition, to any attempt to lock us in behind an ancient Chinese wall while the procession of civilization went past. Today, thinking of our children and of their children, we oppose enforced isolation for ourselves or for any other part of the Americas.

That determination of ours, extending over all these years, was proved, for example, during the quarter century of wars following the French Revolution.

While the Napoleonic struggles did threaten interests of the United States because of the French foothold in the West Indies and in Louisiana, and while we engaged in the War of 1812 to vindicate our right to peaceful trade, it is nevertheless clear that neither France nor Great Britain, nor any other nation, was aiming at domination of the whole world.

In like fashion from 1815 to 1914—ninety-nine years—no single war in Europe or in Asia constituted a real threat against our future or against the future of any other American nation.

Except in the Maximilian interlude in Mexico, no foreign power sought to establish itself in this Hemisphere; and the strength of the British fleet in the Atlantic has been a friendly strength. It is still a friendly strength.

Even when the World War broke out in 1914, it seemed to contain only small threat of danger to our own American future. But, as time went on, the American people began to visualize what the downfall of democratic nations might mean to our own democracy.

We need not overemphasize imperfections in the Peace of Versailles. We need not harp on failure of the democracies to deal with problems of world reconstruction. We should remember that the Peace of 1919

was far less unjust than the kind of "pacification" which began even before Munich, and which is being carried on under the new order of tyranny that seeks to spread over every continent today. The American people have unalterably set their faces against that tyranny.

Every realist knows that the democratic way of life is at this moment being directly assailed in every part of the world—assailed either by arms, or by secret spreading of poisonous propaganda by those who seek to destroy unity and promote discord in nations that are still at peace.

During sixteen long months this assault has blotted out the whole pattern of democratic life in an appalling number of independent nations, great and small. The assailants are still on the march, threatening other nations, great and small.

Therefore, as your President, performing my constitutional duty to "give to the Congress information of the state of the Union," I find it, unhappily, necessary to report that the future and the safety of our country and of our democracy are overwhelmingly involved in events far beyond our borders.

Armed defense of democratic existence is now being gallantly waged in four continents. If that defense fails, all the population and all the resources of Europe, Asia, Africa and Australasia will be dominated by the conquerors. Let us remember that the total of those populations and their resources in those four continents greatly exceeds the sum total of the population and the resources of the whole of the Western Hemisphere—many times over.

In times like these it is immature—and incidentally, untrue—for anybody to brag that an unprepared America, single-handed, and with one hand tied behind its back, can hold off the whole world.

No realistic American can expect from a dictator's peace international generosity, or return of true independence, or world disarmament, or freedom of expression, or freedom of religion—or even good business.

Such a peace would bring no security for us or for our neighbors. "Those, who would give up essential liberty to purchase a little temporary safety, deserve neither liberty nor safety."

As a nation, we may take pride in the fact that we are softhearted; but we cannot afford to be softheaded.

We must always be wary of those who with sounding brass and a tinkling cymbal preach the "ism" of appeasement.

We must especially beware of that small group of selfish men who would clip the wings of the American eagle in order to feather their own nests.

I have recently pointed out how quickly the tempo of modern warfare could bring into our very midst the physical attack which we must eventually expect if the dictator nations win this war.

There is much loose talk of our immunity from immediate and direct invasion from across the seas. Obviously, as long as the British Navy retains its power, no such danger exists. Even if there were no British Navy, it is not probable that any enemy would be stupid enough to attack us by landing troops in the United States from across thousands of miles of ocean, until it had acquired strategic bases from which to operate.

But we learn much from the lessons of the past years in Europe—particularly the lesson of Norway, whose essential seaports were captured by treachery and surprise built up over a series of years.

The first phase of the invasion of this Hemisphere would not be the landing of regular troops. The necessary strategic points would be occupied by secret agents and their dupes—and great numbers of them are already here, and in Latin America.

As long as the aggressor nations maintain the offensive, they—not we—will choose the time and the place and the method of their attack.

That is why the future of all the American Republics is today in serious danger.

That is why this Annual Message to the Congress is unique in our history.

That is why every member of the Executive Branch of the Government and every member of the Congress faces great responsibility and great accountability.

The need of the moment is that our actions and our policy should be devoted primarily—almost exclusively—to meeting this foreign peril. For all our domestic problems are now a part of the great emergency.

Just as our national policy in internal affairs has been based upon a decent respect for the rights and the dignity of all our fellow men within our gates, so our national policy in foreign affairs has been based on a decent respect for the rights and dignity of all nations, large and small. And the justice of morality must and will win in the end.

Our national policy is this:

First, by an impressive expression of the public will and without regard to partisanship, we are committed to all-inclusive national defense.

Second, by an impressive expression of the public will and without regard to partisanship, we are committed to full support of all those resolute peoples, everywhere, who are resisting aggression and are thereby keeping war away from our Hemisphere. By this support, we express our determination that the democratic cause shall prevail; and we strengthen the defense and the security of our own nation.

Third, by an impressive expression of the public will and without regard to partisanship, we are committed to the proposition that principles of morality and considerations for our own security will never permit us to acquiesce in a peace dictated by aggressors and sponsored by appeasers. We know that enduring peace cannot be bought at the cost of other people's freedom.

In the recent national election there was no substantial difference between the two great parties in respect to that national policy. No issue was fought out on this line before the American electorate. Today it is abundantly evident that American citizens everywhere are demanding and supporting speedy and complete action in recognition of obvious danger.

Therefore, the immediate need is a swift and driving increase in our armament production.

Leaders of industry and labor have responded to our summons. Goals of speed have been set. In some cases these goals are being reached ahead of time; in some cases we are on schedule; in other cases there are slight but not serious delays; and in some cases—and I am sorry to say very important cases—we are all concerned by the slowness of the accomplishment of our plans.

The Army and Navy, however, have made substantial progress during the past year. Actual experience is improving and speeding up our methods of production with every passing day. And today's best is not good enough for tomorrow.

I am not satisfied with the progress thus far made. The men in charge of the program represent the best in

training, in ability, and in patriotism. They are not satisfied with the progress thus far made. None of us will
be satisfied until the job is done.

No matter whether the original goal was set too
high or too low, our objective is quicker and better results. To give you two illustrations:

We are behind schedule in turning out finished airplanes; we are working day and night to solve the innumerable problems and to catch up.

We are ahead of schedule in building warships but
we are working to get even further ahead of that
schedule.

To change a whole nation from a basis of peacetime production of implements of peace to a basis of
wartime production of implements of war is no small
task. And the greatest difficulty comes at the beginning
of the program, when new tools, new plant facilities,
new assembly lines, and new ship ways must first be
constructed before the actual materiel begins to flow
steadily and speedily from them.

The Congress, of course, must rightly keep itself informed at all times of the progress of the program.
However, there is certain information, as the Congress
itself will readily recognize, which, in the interests of
our own security and those of the nations that we are
supporting, must of needs be kept in confidence.

New circumstances are constantly begetting new
needs for our safety. I shall ask this Congress for greatly
increased new appropriations and authorizations to
carry on what we have begun.

I also ask this Congress for authority and for funds
sufficient to manufacture additional munitions and
war supplies of many kinds, to be turned over to those
nations which are now in actual war with aggressor
nations.

Our most useful and immediate role is to act as an
arsenal for them as well as for ourselves. They do not
need man power, but they do need billions of dollars
worth of the weapons of defense.

The time is near when they will not be able to pay
for them all in ready cash. We cannot, and we will not,
tell them that they must surrender, merely because of
present inability to pay for the weapons which we
know they must have.

I do not recommend that we make them a loan of
dollars with which to pay for these weapons—a loan to
be repaid in dollars.

I recommend that we make it possible for those
nations to continue to obtain war materials in the
United States, fitting their orders into our own program. Nearly all their materiel would, if the time ever
came, be useful for our own defense.

Taking counsel of expert military and naval authorities, considering what is best for our own security, we
are free to decide how much should be kept here and
how much should be sent abroad to our friends who
by their determined and heroic resistance are giving us
time in which to make ready our own defense.

For what we send abroad, we shall be repaid within
a reasonable time following the close of hostilities, in
similar materials, or, at our option, in other goods of
many kinds, which they can produce and which we
need.

Let us say to the democracies: "We Americans are
vitally concerned in your defense of freedom. We are
putting forth our energies, our resources and our organizing powers to give you the strength to regain and
maintain a free world. We shall send you, in ever-
increasing numbers, ships, planes, tanks, guns. This is
our purpose and our pledge."

In fulfillment of this purpose we will not be intimidated by the threats of dictators that they will
regard as a breach of international law or as an act of
war our aid to the democracies which dare to resist
their aggression. Such aid is not an act of war, even if a
dictator should unilaterally proclaim it so to be.

When the dictators, if the dictators, are ready to
make war upon us, they will not wait for an act of war
on our part. They did not wait for Norway or Belgium
or the Netherlands to commit an act of war.

Their only interest is in a new one-way international law, which lacks mutuality in its observance,
and, therefore, becomes an instrument of oppression.

The happiness of future generations of Americans
may well depend upon how effective and how immediate we can make our aid felt. No one can tell the
exact character of the emergency situations that we
may be called upon to meet. The Nation's hands must
not be tied when the Nation's life is in danger.

We must all prepare to make the sacrifices that the
emergency—almost as serious as war itself—demands.
Whatever stands in the way of speed and efficiency in
defense preparations must give way to the national
need.

A free nation has the right to expect full cooperation from all groups. A free nation has the right to look to the leaders of business, of labor, and of agriculture to take the lead in stimulating effort, not among other groups but within their own groups.

The best way of dealing with the few slackers or trouble makers in our midst is, first, to shame them by patriotic example, and, if that fails, to use the sovereignty of Government to save Government.

As men do not live by bread alone, they do not fight by armaments alone. Those who man our defenses, and those behind them who build our defenses, must have the stamina and the courage which come from unshakable belief in the manner of life which they are defending. The mighty action that we are calling for cannot be based on a disregard of all things worth fighting for.

The Nation takes great satisfaction and much strength from the things which have been done to make its people conscious of their individual stake in the preservation of democratic life in America. Those things have toughened the fibre of our people, have renewed their faith and strengthened their devotion to the institutions we make ready to protect.

Certainly this is no time for any of us to stop thinking about the social and economic problems which are the root cause of the social revolution which is today a supreme factor in the world.

For there is nothing mysterious about the foundations of a healthy and strong democracy. The basic things expected by our people of their political and economic systems are simple. They are:

Equality of opportunity for youth and for others.
Jobs for those who can work.
Security for those who need it.
The ending of special privilege for the few.
The preservation of civil liberties for all.
The enjoyment of the fruits of scientific progress in a wider and constantly rising standard of living.

These are the simple, basic things that must never be lost sight of in the turmoil and unbelievable complexity of our modern world. The inner and abiding strength of our economic and political systems is dependent upon the degree to which they fulfill these expectations.

Many subjects connected with our social economy call for immediate improvement.
As examples:

We should bring more citizens under the coverage of old-age pensions and unemployment insurance.
We should widen the opportunities for adequate medical care.
We should plan a better system by which persons deserving or needing gainful employment may obtain it.

I have called for personal sacrifice. I am assured of the willingness of almost all Americans to respond to that call.

A part of the sacrifice means the payment of more money in taxes. In my Budget Message I shall recommend that a greater portion of this great defense program be paid for from taxation than we are paying today. No person should try, or be allowed, to get rich out of this program; and the principle of tax payments in accordance with ability to pay should be constantly before our eyes to guide our legislation.

If the Congress maintains these principles, the voters, putting patriotism ahead of pocketbooks, will give you their applause.

In the future days, which we seek to make secure, we look forward to a world founded upon four essential human freedoms.

The first is freedom of speech and expression—everywhere in the world.

The second is freedom of every person to worship God in his own way—everywhere in the world.

The third is freedom from want—which, translated into world terms, means economic understandings which will secure to every nation a healthy peacetime life for its inhabitants—everywhere in the world.

The fourth is freedom from fear—which, translated into world terms, means a world-wide reduction of armaments to such a point and in such a thorough fashion that no nation will be in a position to commit an act of physical aggression against any neighbor—anywhere in the world.

That is no vision of a distant millennium. It is a definite basis for a kind of world attainable in our own time and generation. That kind of world is the very antithesis of the so-called new order of tyranny which the dictators seek to create with the crash of a bomb.

To that new order we oppose the greater conception—the moral order. A good society is able to face schemes of world domination and foreign revolutions alike without fear.

Since the beginning of our American history, we have been engaged in change—in a perpetual peaceful revolution—a revolution which goes on steadily, quietly adjusting itself to changing conditions—without the concentration camp or the quick-lime in the ditch. The world order which we seek is the cooperation of free countries, working together in a friendly, civilized society.

This nation has placed its destiny in the hands and heads and hearts of its millions of free men and women; and its faith in freedom under the guidance of God. Freedom means the supremacy of human rights everywhere. Our support goes to those who struggle to gain those rights or keep them. Our strength is our unity of purpose. To that high concept there can be no end save victory.

QUESTIONS TO CONSIDER

1. How does Roosevelt frame this new world war? What is the conflict about and what are the sides, according to the president?
2. How was Roosevelt's goal of securing the four freedoms expressed in his domestic policy as well?

24.2 A. PHILIP RANDOLPH, PROGRAM OF THE MARCH ON WASHINGTON MOVEMENT (1941)*

The March on Washington was a planned protest initiated by Black labor activists A. Philip Randolph (1889–1979) and Bayard Rustin (1912–1987) to protest employment discrimination against Black Americans by the federal government. After a decade of economic malaise, new spending on munitions and war material by the federal government created many new jobs. Black activists worried that, if Black workers were denied an opportunity to work these jobs, whether because of Jim Crow laws or personal discrimination, Black Americans would be left in poverty while others experienced an economic recovery.

Randolph met with Roosevelt to encourage him to order desegregation within the armed forces and defense industries. When Roosevelt did not do so, Randolph and Bayard began planning a mass march on Washington by Black workers to highlight the importance of this issue. Days before the planned march in early July 1941, President Roosevelt issued Executive Order 8802, which barred employment discrimination in the defense industry and established a Fair Employment Practice Committee to ensure compliance. Having secured this goal, Randolph canceled the march but continued his activism.

* *Survey Graphic* vol. 31 (November 1942), 488–89.

FELLOW MARCHERS and delegates to the Policy Conference of the March on Washington Movement and Friends:

We have met at an hour when the sinister shadows of war are lengthening and becoming more threatening. As one of the sections of the oppressed darker races, and representing a part of the exploited millions of the workers of the world, we are deeply concerned that the totalitarian legions of Hitler, Hirohito, and Mussolini do not batter the bastions of democracy. We know that our fate is tied up with the fate of the democratic way of life. And so, out of the depth of our hearts, a cry goes up for the triumph of the United Nations. But we would not be honest with ourselves were we to stop for a victory of arms alone. We know this is not enough. We fight that the democratic faiths, values, heritages and ideals may prevail.

Unless this war sound the death knell to the old Anglo-American empire systems, the hapless story of which is one of exploitation for the profit and power of a monopoly-capitalist economy, it will have been fought in vain. Our aim then must not only be to defeat Nazism, fascism, and militarism on the battlefield but to win the peace, for democracy, for freedom and the Brotherhood of Man without regard to his pigmentation, land of his birth or the God of his fathers.

We therefore sharply score the Atlantic Charter as expressing a vile and hateful racism and a manifestation of the tragic and utter collapse of an old, decadent democratic political liberalism which worshiped at the shrine of a world-conquering monopoly-capitalism. This system grew fat and waxed powerful off the sweat and tears of the tireless toilers of the human race and the sons and daughters of color in the underdeveloped lands of the world.

When this war ends, the people want something more than the dispersal of equality and power among individual citizens in a liberal, political democratic system. They demand with striking comparability the dispersal of equality and power among the citizen-workers in an economic-democracy that will make certain the assurance of the good life—the more abundant-life—in a warless world.

But, withal this condition of freedom, equality and democracy is not the gift of the gods. It is, the task of men, yes, men, brave men, honest men, determined men.

This is why we have met in Detroit in this Policy Conference of the March on Washington Movement. We have come to set forth our goals, declare our principles, formulate our policies, plan our program and discuss our methods, strategy, and tactics.

This is the job of every movement which seeks to map out clearly the direction in which it is going as well as build up and strengthen the motivations.

Now our goals are what we hope to attain. They are near and remote, immediate and ultimate. This requires the long and short range program.

Thus our feet are set in the path toward equality—economic, political and social and racial. Equality is the heart and, essence of democracy, freedom and justice. Without equality of opportunity in industry, in labor unions, schools and colleges, government, politics and before the law, without equality in social relations and in all phases of human endeavor, the Negro is certain to be consigned to an inferior status. There must be no dual standards of justice, no dual rights, privileges, duties or responsibilities of citizenship. No dual forms of freedom.

If Negroes are not the equal of white citizens, then they are unequal, either above. Or below them. But if they are to set the standards, Negroes will be below them. And if Negroes are considered unequal on a substandard basis, then they will receive unequal or inferior treatment.

Justice for the slave is not the same justice for the freeman. Treatment of thoroughbred is not the same as the treatment of a workhorse.

But our nearer goals include the abolition of discrimination, segregation, and Jim Crow in the Government, the Army, Navy, Air Corps, U.S. Marine, Coast Guard, Women's Auxiliary Army Corps and the Waves, and defense industries; the elimination of discriminations in hotels, restaurants, on public transportation conveyances, in educational, recreational, cultural, and amusement and entertainment places such as theatres, beaches, and so forth.

We want the full works of citizenship with no reservations. We will accept nothing less.

But goals must be achieved. They are not secured because it is just and right that they be possessed; by Negro or white people. Slavery was not abolished because it was bad and unjust. It was abolished because men fought, bled and died on the battlefield in the

Union Army and conquered the Confederate forces in the Civil War. Of course slavery was uneconomic, and would have disappeared in time, but this economic axiom involves no moral judgment.

Therefore, if Negroes secure their goals, immediate and remote, they must win them and to win them they must fight, sacrifice, suffer, go to jail, and if need be die for them. These rights will not be given. They must be taken.

Democracy was fought for and taken from political royalists—the kings. Industrial democracy, the rights of the workers to organize and designate the representatives of their own choosing to bargain collectively is being won and taken from the economic royalists—big business.

Now the realization of goals and rights by a nation, race or class requires belief in and loyalty to principles and policies. Principles represent the basic and deep human and social convictions of a man or a people such as democracy, equality, freedom of conscience, the deification of the state, protestantism. Policies rest upon principles. Concretely a policy sets forth one's position on vital public questions such as political affiliations, religious alliances. The March on Washington Movement must be opposed to partisan-political commitments, religious or denominational alliances. We cannot sup with the Communists, for they rule or ruin any movement. This is their policy. Our policy must be to shun them. This does not mean that Negro Communists may not join the March on Washington Movement.

As to the compositions of our movement. Our policy is that it be all-Negro, and pro-Negro but not anti-white, or anti-Semitic or anti-labor or anti-Catholic. The reason for this policy is that all oppressed people must assume the responsibility and take the initiative to free themselves. Jews must wage their battle to abolish anti-semitism. Catholics must wage their battle to abolish anti-catholicism. The workers must wage their battle to advance and protect their interests and rights.

But this does not mean that because Jews must take the responsibility and initiatives to solve their own problems that they should not seek the cooperation and support of Gentiles, or that Catholics should not seek the support of Negroes, or that the workers

should not attempt to enlist the backing of Jews, Catholics, and Negroes in their fight to win a strike; but the main reliance must be upon the workers themselves. By the same token because Negroes build an all-Negro movement such as the March, it does not follow that our movement should not call for the collaboration of Jews, Catholics, trade unions and white liberals to help restore the President's Fair Employment Practice Committee to its original status of independence, with responsibility to the President. That was done. William Green, President of the A. F. of L. and Philip Murray, President of C. I. o. were called upon to send telegrams to the President to restore the Committee to its independence. Both responded. Their cooperation had its effects. Workers have formed citizens committees to back them while on strike, but this does not mean that they take those citizens into their unions as members. No, not at all.

And while the March on Washington Movement may find it advisable to form a citizens committee of friendly white citizens to give moral support to a fight against the poll tax or white primaries, it does not imply that these white citizens or citizens of any racial group should be taken into the March on Washington Movement as members. The essential value of an all-Negro movement such as the March on Washington is that it helps to create faith by Negroes in Negroes. It develops a sense of self-reliance with Negroes depending on Negroes in vital matters. It helps to break down the slave psychology and inferiority complex in Negroes which comes and is nourished with Negroes relying on white people for direction and support. This inevitably happens in mixed organizations that are supposed to be in the Negro.

Now, in every community there are many and varied problems. Some are specialized and others are generalized. For instance the problem of anti-Semitism is a specialized one and must be attacked by the Jews through a Jewish organization which considers this question its major interest. The organization of the unorganized workers and the winning of wage increases, shorter hours, and better working conditions, is a specialized problem of workers which must be handled through a trade union composed of workers, not lawyers, doctors, preachers, or business men or by an organizations of Catholics or Negroes.

The problem of lynching is a specialized one and Negroes must take the responsibility and initiative to solve it, because Negroes are the chief victims of it just as the workers are the victims of low wages and must act to change and raise them.

But the problems of taxation, sanitation, health, a proper school system, an efficient fire department, and crime are generalized problems. They don't only concern the workers or Jews or Negroes or Catholics but everybody and hence it is sound and proper social strategy, and policy for all of these groups in the community to form a generalized or composite movement, financed by all, to handle these problems that are definitely general in nature. Neither group can depend upon the other in dealing with a general social problem. No one group can handle it properly. But this same general organization could not be depended upon to fight for the abolition of segregation of Negroes in the government, or to abolish company unionism in the interest of the workers, or to fight anti-semitism. Its structure is too general to qualify it to attempt to solve a special problem. And, by the same logic, the Zionist Movement, or the Knights of Columbus, or the Longshoremen's Union is too special in structure and purpose to be qualified to deal with such a general problem as crime or health or education in a community.

Therefore, while the March on Washington Movement is interested in the general problems of every community and will lend its aid to help solve them, it has as its major interest and task the liberation of the Negro people, and this is sound social economy. It is in conformity with the principle of the division of labor. No organization can do everything. Every organization can do something, and each organization is charged with the social responsibility to do that which it can do, it is built to do.

I have given quite some time to the discussion of this question of organizational structure and function and composition, because the March on Washington Movement is a mass movement of Negroes which is being built to achieve a definite objective, and is a departure from the usual pattern of Negro efforts and thinking. As a rule, Negroes do not choose to be to themselves in anything, they are only to themselves as a result of compulsive segregation. Negroes are

together voluntarily for the same reason workers join voluntarily into a trade union. But because workers only join trade unions, does not mean that the very same workers may not join organizations composed of some non-workers, such as art museums or churches or fraternal lodges that have varying purposes. This same thing is true of Negroes. Because Negroes only can join the March on Washington Movement, does not indicate that Negroes in the M.O.W.M. may not join an inter-racial golf club or church or Elks Lodge or, debating society or trade union.

No one would claim that a society of Filipinos is undemocratic because it does not take in Japanese members, or that Catholics are anti-Jewish because the Jesuits won't accept Jews as members or that trade unions are not liberal because they deny membership to employers. Neither is the March on Washington Movement undemocratic because it confines its members to Negroes. Now this reasoning would not apply to a public school or a Pullman car because these agencies are a service which is necessary to all people of a community.

Now, the question of which I have been discussing involves, for example, the March on Washington Movement's position on the war. We say that the Negro must fight for his democratic rights now for after the war it may be too late. This is our policy on the Negro and the war. But this policy raises the question of method, programs, strategy, and tactics; namely, how is this to be done. It is not sufficient to say that Negroes must fight for their rights now, during the war. Some methods must be devised, program set up, and strategy outlined.

This Policy Conference is designed to do this very thing. The first requirement to executing the policies of the March on Washington Movement is to have something to execute them with. This brings me to the consideration of organization. Organization supplies the power. The formulation of policies and the planning process furnish direction. Now there is organization and organization. Some people say, for instance, Negroes are already organized and they cite, The Sisters of the Mysterious Ten, The Sons and Daughters of I Will Arise, The Holy Rollers, the social clubs, and so forth. But these organizations are about the individual interest of helping the sick and funeralizing the dead or providing amusement and recreation.

They deal with no social or racial problem which concerns of the entire people. The Negro people as a whole is not interested in whether Miss A. plays Contract Bridge on Friday or not, whether the deacon of the Methodist Church has a 200 or 500 dollar casket when he dies. These are personal questions. But the Negro race is concerned about Negroes being refused jobs in defense plants, or whether a Negro can purchase a lower in a Pullman Car, or whether the U. S. Treasury segregates Negro girls. Thus, while it is true Negroes are highly organized, the organizations are not built to deal with and manipulate the mechanics of power. Nobody cares how many Whist Clubs or churches or secret lodges Negroes establish because they are not compulsive or coercive. They don't seek to transform the socioeconomic racial milieu. They accept and do not challenge conditions with an action program.

Hence, it is apparent that the Negro needs more than organization. He needs mass organization with an action program, aggressive, bold and challenging in spirit. Such a movement is our March on Washington.

Our first job then is to actually organize millions of Negroes, and build them into block systems with captains to that they may be summoned into physical motion. Without this type of organization, Negroes will never develop mass power which is the most effective weapon a minority people can wield. Witness the strategy and maneuver of the people of India with mass civil disobedience and non-cooperation and the marches to the sea to make salt. It may be said that the Indian people have not won their freedom. This is so, but they will win it …

We must develop huge demonstrations because the world is used to big dramatic affairs. They think in terms of hundreds of thousands and millions and billions. Millions of Germans and Russians clash on the Eastern front. Billions of dollars are appropriated at the twinkling of an eye. Nothing little counts.

Besides, the unusual attracts. We must develop a series marches of Negroes at a given time in a hundred or more cities throughout the country, or stage a big march of a hundred thousand Negroes on Washington to put our cause into the main stream of public opinion and focus the attention of world interests. This is why India is in the news.

Therefore, our program is in part as follows:

1. A national conference for, the integration and expression of the integration and expression of the collective mind and will of the Negro masses.

2. The mobilization and proclamation of a nation-wide series of mass marches on the City Halls and City Councils to awaken the Negro masses and center attention upon the grievances and goals of the Negro people and to serve as training and discipline for the Negro masses for the more strenuous struggle of a March on Washington, if, as and when an affirmative decision is made thereon by the Negro masses of the country through our national conference.

3. A march on Washington as evidence to white America that black America is on a march for its rights and means business.

4. The picketing of the White House following the March on Washington and maintain the said picket line until the country and the world recognize the Negro has come of age and will sacrifice his all to counted as men, free men.

This program is drastic and exacting. It will test our best mettle and stamina and courage. Let me warn you that in these times of storm and stress, this program will be opposed. Our Movement therefore must be well-knit together. It must have moral and spiritual vision, understanding, and wisdom.

PROGRAM OF THE MARCH ON WASHINGTON MOVEMENT

1. We demand, in the interest of national unity, the abrogation of every law which makes a distinction in treatment between citizens based on religion, creed, color, or national origin. This means an end to Jim Crow in education, in housing, in transportation and in every other social, economic, and political privilege. Especially, we demand, in the capital of the nation, an end to all segregation in public places and in public institutions.

2. We demand legislation to enforce the Fifth and Fourteenth Amendments guaranteeing that no person shall be deprived of life, liberty or property without due process of law, so that the full weight of the national government may be used for the protection of life and thereby may end the disgrace of lynching.

3. We demand the enforcement of the Fourteenth and Fifteenth Amendments and the enactment of the Pepper Poll Tax bill so that all barriers in the exercise of suffrage are eliminated.

4. We demand the abolition of segregation and discrimination in the army, navy, marine corps, air corps, and all other branches of national defense.

5. We demand an end to discrimination in jobs and job training. Further, we demand that the F.E.P.C. be made a permanent administrative agency of the U.S. Government and that it be given power to enforce its decisions based on its findings.

6. We demand that federal funds be withheld from any agency which practices discrimination in the use of such funds.

7. We demand colored and minority group representation on all administrative agencies so that these groups may have recognition of their democratic right to participate in formulating policies.

8. We demand representation for the colored and minority racial groups on all missions, political and technical, which will be sent to the peace conference so that the interests of all people everywhere may be fully recognized and justly provided for in the post-war settlement.

QUESTIONS TO CONSIDER

1. What is Randolph's position on forming alliances with other "oppressed people"? Why is it important to him that the March be an "all-Negro movement"?

2. Why does Randolph believe a large march will be an effective demonstration?

24.3 JANET MATSUDA, "HOPE OUT OF GLOOM" (1944/45)*

Two months after the surprise attack on Pearl Harbor, President Roosevelt issued Executive Order 9066, which ordered the secretary of war to establish camps where Japanese immigrants and American citizens of Japanese descent would be held. Over a hundred thousand Japanese Americans, mostly in California, were forced to abandon their homes and businesses and relocate to isolated camps throughout the United States. Over a quarter of those incarcerated in these camps were children, mostly *nisei*—that is, second-generation Japanese Americans who were born in the United States with American citizenship.

Many Japanese American families spent years in these camps, and during that time, children attended woefully inadequate schools, taught entirely in English with few books or other educational supplies. This poem appeared in the 1944 yearbook of the high school at the Tule Lake Internment Camp on the California–Oregon border. Student Janet Matsuda describes the setting and rising of the sun to capture both the despair of being trapped in the camp and her remaining hope for the future.

---

* "Janet Matsuda poem" in "Aquila" [yearbook], 1944/45, Guy & Marguerite Cook Nisei Collection, Box 2, Folder 13, University of the Pacific, Stockton, CA.

Day is done; the sun is dying
In the west; where all is lying
Beneath a sky adorned with gold
Which shines like the halos of angels of old.

Then overhead the sky grows dark,
And purple clouds mass to an arc;
The stars begin to twinkle and glow
The sun has sunk to a place below

An om'nous place, forever unseen,
A reminder of things as they have been.

The world has settled into a gloom,
The flower of hope refuses to bloom,
'Til life is renewed by the kindly light,
Which out of the darkness shines so bright,
And spreads its rays o'er all the earth,
To signify another day's birth.

QUESTIONS TO CONSIDER

1. Why does Matsuda set her poem in dusk and night?
2. How might children like Matsuda, who had lived their whole childhoods in the United States before internment, have felt about being incarcerated by their own government for suspected disloyalty?

24.4 VISUAL SOURCE: RUSSELL LEE, CHILD WAITING AT LOS ANGELES EVACUATION CENTER (1942)*

Russell Lee (1903–1986) was a photographer known for documenting Americans during the Great Depression and the exodus of Japanese Americans to internment camps. Bowing to fears that Japanese Americans could not be trusted while the United States was at war with Japan, President Roosevelt issued Executive Order 9066 in February 1944. He ordered the secretary of war to establish internment camps that would eventually hold over a hundred thousand Japanese Americans, most of them US citizens. Japanese Americans were given little time to pack what they could and abandon their homes and businesses to relocate to their assigned camps throughout the western United States.

Over a quarter of those interned were children like the toddler in this photograph. Many remained in the camps for four years, spending a significant portion of their childhood under guard and far from home.

* Courtesy of the Library of Congress

QUESTIONS TO CONSIDER

1. How does Lee frame this photograph to make the viewer feel the same disorientation and confusion as the child in the picture?
2. Why do you think Lee chose a child as his subject? What was he trying to communicate about internment?

24.5 VISUAL SOURCE: *THIS MAN IS YOUR FRIEND: CHINESE—HE FIGHTS FOR FREEDOM* (1942)*

The Japanese Empire invaded the Republic of China in 1937, sparking an eight-year war throughout Asia that eventually became considered part of the Second World War. Early in the war, the Japanese army captured several major cities, including Beijing, Shanghai, and Nanjing, which was the capital of China at the time. Following the capture of Nanjing, the Japanese army committed a massacre, killing hundreds of thousands of Chinese civilians over the course of six weeks. Although Chinese forces continued to resist, they relied heavily on American arms and material, as much of China's industrial capacity was occupied by Japan.

* United States. Office of Facts and Figures. This man is your friend: Chinese: he fights for freedom., poster, 1942; [Washington D.C.]. (https://digital.library.unt.edu/ark:/67531/metadc233/ accessed August 17, 2022), University of North Texas Libraries, UNT Digital Library, https://digital.library.unt.edu; crediting UNT Libraries Government Documents Department.

This poster was one of several made for US audiences to encourage solidarity with other nationalities fighting against fascism throughout the world. The Chinese forces were a major beneficiary of the US Lend–Lease program that offered war materials to other combatants, and China was the primary nation fighting against the Japanese Empire along with the United States. Posters like this one reinforced the war aims President Roosevelt had articulated in his Four Freedoms speech, framing the United States and other democracies as allies in a fight for freedom against tyranny.

QUESTIONS TO CONSIDER

1. This poster is straightforward and to the point with no extraneous words or details. Do you think this made it more effective? Why or why not?
2. What is the vision of the war that is articulated in this poster? Who are the combatants and what are they fighting for?

CHAPTER 25

COLD WAR AMERICA, 1945–1957

25.1 SENATE RESOLUTION 301: CENSURE OF SENATOR JOSEPH McCARTHY (1954)*

Joseph McCarthy (1908–1957) was a US senator from Wisconsin who launched a series of crusades against supposed communists in American public life. American fears about communism increased in the late 1940s, in part because of international events such as a communist regime taking power in China and the Soviet Union developing a nuclear weapon. When McCarthy began alleging in 1950 that there were hundreds of communist sympathizers within the US government, his charges gained traction because Americans had been primed to view communists as dangerous outsiders. Over the course of the early 1950s, McCarthy's investigations of government officials, and the "witch hunts" those investigations encouraged, led to the harassment and ostracizing of thousands of Americans from all walks of life.

By the mid-1950s, however, McCarthy's confrontational tactics caught up with him. McCarthy was rarely able to offer any proof of his accusations, many of which relied on hyperbole and innuendo. As McCarthy began to target supposed communist sympathizers in the US military, he lost the support of other anti-communist lawmakers. He was formally censured by the Senate in late 1954 for abusing and insulting his fellow senators and he died less than three years later.

S. RES 301

IN THE SENATE OF THE UNITED STATES

Resolved, That the Senator from Wisconsin, Mr. McCarthy, failed to cooperate with the Subcommittee on Privileges and Elections of the Senate Committee on Rules and Administration in clearing up matters referred to that subcommittee which concerned his conduct as a Senator and affected the honor of the Senate and, instead, repeatedly abused the subcommittee and its members who were trying to carry out assigned duties, thereby obstructing the constitutional processes of the Senate, and that this conduct of the Senator from Wisconsin, Mr. McCarthy, is contrary to senatorial traditions and is hereby condemned.

Sec 2. The Senator from Wisconsin, Mr. McCarthy, in writing to the chairman of the Select Committee to Study Censure Charges (Mr. Watkins) after the Select Committee had issued its report and before the report

* National Archives

was presented to the Senate charging three members of the Select Committee with "deliberate deception" and "fraud" for failure to disqualify themselves; in stating to the press on November 4, 1954, that the special Senate session that was to begin November 8, 1954, was a "lynch-party"; in repeatedly describing this special Senate session as a "lynch bee" in a nationwide television and radio show on November 7, 1954; in stating to the public press on November 13, 1954, that the chairman of the Select Committee (Mr. Watkins) was guilty of "the most unusual, most cowardly things I've ever heard of" and stating further: "I expected he would be afraid to answer the questions, but didn't think he'd be stupid enough to make a public statement;" and in

characterizing the said committee as the "unwitting handmaiden," "involuntary agent" and "attorneys-in-fact" of the Communist Party and in charging that the said committee in writing its report "imitated Communist methods—that it distorted, misrepresented, and omitted in its effort to manufacture a plausible rationalization" in support of its recommendations to the Senate, which characterizations and charges were contained in a statement released to the press and inserted in the Congressional Record of November 10, 1954, acted contrary to senatorial ethics and tended to bring the Senate into dishonor and disrepute, to obstruct the constitutional processes of the Senate, and to impair its dignity; and such conduct is hereby condemned.

QUESTIONS TO CONSIDER

1. What is the behavior that got McCarthy censured? Why do you think his colleagues found these actions in particular to be worthy of condemnation?
2. What sort of language and accusations did McCarthy use to condemn his opponents? How was this indicative of Cold War culture?

25.2 STUDENT NONVIOLENT COORDINATING COMMITTEE (SNCC), STATEMENT OF PURPOSE (1960, REVISED 1962)*

The Student Nonviolent Coordinating Committee (SNCC) was a group founded in 1960 to organize young people for nonviolent protest for civil rights. The group drew inspiration from recent sit-in protests in Greensboro, North Carolina, and Nashville, Tennessee, in which Black activists took seats at segregated lunch counters and refused to move. SNCC members favored similar "direct action" tactics meant to challenge an unjust law, policy, or regulation intentionally and openly without violence. Authorities would be forced to either leave the law or regulation unenforced, or to instigate violent force in order to execute it. The SNCC had perhaps its most significant impact on the civil rights movement by organizing students for freedom rides in which activists rode interstate buses to challenge local authorities to respect a recent Supreme Court decision declaring segregation on interstate transport unconstitutional.

* Constitution of the Student Nonviolent Coordinating Committee, originally adopted spring 1960, Raleigh, NC, revised April 29, 1962, published in *Nonviolence in America: A Documentary History*, ed., Staughton Lynd (New York: Bobbs-Merrill Co., 1995), 398–99.

The document that eventually became the SNCC Statement of Purpose was drafted by theology student and activist James Lawson in early 1960. It reflects the impact of Gandhi's nonviolent antico-lonial protest in British-ruled India, a recent example of successful protest that influenced many leaders in the civil rights movement.

We affirm the philosophical or religious ideal of nonviolence as the foundation of our purpose, the presupposition of our faith, and the manner of our action. Nonviolence as it grows from the Judaeo-Christian tradition seeks a social order of justice permeated by love. Integration of human endeavor represents the crucial first step towards such a society.

Through nonviolence, courage displaces fear; love transforms hate. Acceptance dissipates prejudice; hope ends despair. Peace dominates war; faith reconciles doubt. Mutual regard cancels enmity. Justice for all overcomes injustice. The redemptive community supersedes systems of gross social immorality.

Love is the central motif of nonviolence. Love is the force by which God binds man to himself and man to man. Such love goes to the extreme; it remains loving and forgiving even in the midst of hostility. It matches the capacity of evil to inflict suffering with an even more enduring capacity to absorb evil, all the while persisting in love.

By appealing to conscience and standing on the moral nature of human existence, nonviolence nurtures the atmosphere in which reconciliation and justice become actual possibilities.

QUESTIONS TO CONSIDER

1. This short statement uses the word "love" six times. What was the importance of love to the SNCC according to this statement?
2. How does the SNCC understand justice according to this document? How is this different from how a state or political authority might understand justice?

25.3 US GOVERNMENT AMICUS CURIAE BRIEF FOR *BROWN V. BOARD OF EDUCATION* (1952)*

Brown v. Board of Education was a landmark Supreme Court decision in which the Court unanimously declared racial segregation unconstitutional. The case originated as a class-action suit by several Black families of Topeka, Kansas, who were required to send their children to a more distant segregated school rather than more accessible nearby public schools. National Association for the Advancement of Colored People (NAACP) chief counsel Thurgood Marshall (1908–1993) represented the Topeka families, who eventually secured a decision in their favor after three years of litigation.

---

* James P. McGranery, Attorney General, "Brief for the United States as Amicus Curiae: *Oliver Brown, et. al. v. Board of Education of Topeka*, 347 U.S. 483 (1954)."

The accompanying document is an *amicus curiae,* or amicus brief, from the US attorney general James P. McGranery (1895–1962). In an amicus brief, a party who is not involved in the legal dispute offers their own insight or expertise for the benefit of the court. Because a decision that invalidated racial discrimination would have wide-ranging consequences throughout the United States, where segregationist laws and practices were common, the US government offered its opinion on the impact of segregation for the consideration of the Court.

In recent years the Federal Government has increasingly recognized its special responsibility for assuring vindication of the fundamental civil rights guaranteed by the Constitution. The President has stated: "We shall not . . . finally achieve the ideals for which this Nation was founded so long as any American suffers discrimination as a result of his race, or religion, or color, or the land of origin of his forefathers. . . . The Federal Government has a clear duty to see that constitutional guarantees of individual liberties and of equal protection under the laws are not denied or abridged anywhere in our Union."

Recognition of the responsibility of the Federal Government with regard to civil rights is not a matter of partisan controversy, even though differences of opinion may exist as to the need for particular legislative or executive action. Few Americans believe that government should pursue a *laissez-faire* policy in the field of civil rights, or that it adequately discharges its duty to the people so long as it does not itself intrude on their civil liberties. Instead, there is general acceptance of an affirmative government obligation to insure respect for fundamental human rights.

The shamefulness and absurdity of Washington's treatment of Negro Americans is highlighted by the presence of many dark-skinned foreign visitors. Capital custom not only humiliates colored citizens, but is a source of considerable embarrassment to these visitors. . . . Foreign officials are often mistaken for American Negroes and refused food, lodging and entertainment. However, once it is established that they are not Americans, they are accommodated.

It is in the context of the present world struggle between freedom and tyranny that the problem of racial discrimination must be viewed. The United States is trying to prove to the people of the world, of every nationality, race, and color, that a free democracy is the most civilized and most secure form of government yet devised by man. We must set an example for others by showing firm determination to remove existing flaws in our democracy.

The existence of discrimination against minority groups in the United States has an adverse effect upon our relations with other countries. Racial discrimination furnishes grist for the Communist propaganda mills, and it raises doubts even among friendly nations as to the intensity of our devotion to the democratic faith. In response to the request of the Attorney General for an authoritative statement of the effects of racial discrimination in the United States upon the conduct of foreign relations, the Secretary of State has written as follows:

. . . I wrote the Chairman of the Fair Employment Practices Committee on May 8, 1946, that the existence of discrimination against minority groups was having an adverse effect upon our relations with other countries. At that time I pointed out that discrimination against such groups in the United States created suspicion and resentment in other countries, and that we would have better international relations were these reasons for suspicion and resentment to be removed.

During the past six years, the damage to our foreign relations attributable to this source has become progressively greater. The United States is under constant attack in the foreign press, over the foreign radio, and in such international bodies as the United Nations because of various practices of discrimination against minority groups in this country. As might be expected, Soviet spokesmen regularly exploit this situation in propaganda against the United States, both within the United Nations and through radio broadcasts and the press, which reaches all corners of the world. Some of these attacks against us are based on falsehood or distortion; but the undeniable existence of racial discrimination gives unfriendly governments the most effective kind of ammunition for their propaganda warfare. The hostile reaction among normally friendly peoples, many of whom are particularly sensitive in regard to the status of non-European races, is growing in alarming proportions. In such countries the view is expressed more and more vocally that the United States is hypocritical in claiming to be the champion of democracy while permitting practices of racial discrimination here in this country.

QUESTIONS TO CONSIDER

1. What reasons does Attorney General James McGranery offer to explain why segregation is undesirable? What arguments against segregation does he avoid?
2. How do you think Cold War culture influenced McGranery's brief?

25.4 VISUAL SOURCE: LINDA CHRISTIAN AS "ANATOMIC BOMB" (1945)*

The attacks on Hiroshima and Nagasaki in early August 1945 were the first most Americans knew of atomic bombs, but they quickly entered pop culture and the national lexicon. The "Atomic Age" that followed this first successful deployment of nuclear technology was at first welcomed as a golden era in which atomic power and weapons would provide electric power and deter conflict. As tensions quickly developed between the United States and the USSR, however, the threat of military conflict between nuclear-armed powers gave the atomic power a more ominous reputation, not yet present in this issue of *Life* magazine.

Life was a popular magazine devoted to photography and light articles that published frequently during the Second World War. Here *Life* describes model and actress Linda Christian (1923–2011) as an "Anatomic Bomb" and heralds the "Atomic Age of Hollywood," exhibiting the hope and promise that were synonymous with nuclear power in the late 1940s. Linda Christian went on to appear in dozens of films across a forty-year career as an actress.

SPRAWLED GRACEFULLY ON THE CURVING EDGE OF A SWIMMING POOL, STARLET LINDA CHRISTIANS, HOLLYWOOD'S ANATOMIC BOMB, SOAKS UP SOLAR ENERGY

ANATOMIC BOMB

Starlet Linda Christians brings
the new atomic age to Hollywood

Almost before ink was dry on headlines announc-ing the crash of the first atomic bomb, Holly-wood had turned the event to good publicity. At the Metro-Goldwyn-Mayer studio Miss Linda Christ-ians, a hitherto obscure starlet, was solemnly pro-claimed the Anatomic Bomb. Half-Mexican, half-Dutch, Linda was born in Tampico, Mexico, thinks it was 22 years ago. Her real name is Blanca Rosa Welter. Her father, an oil executive, traveled widely,

taking his family with him. They were in Palestine in 1941 during a bomb scare. Linda was evacuated to Mexico with a bad case of malaria, recovered, went to Hollywood to join her brother, got a job model-ing hats, was seen and signed by M-G-M. So far she has been in no pictures, the publicity role of the Ana-tomic Bomb being her first important assignment. With long residence in Holland, Italy, France and Switzerland, Linda thinks Hollywood is wonderful.

CONTINUED ON NEXT PAGE   53

QUESTIONS TO CONSIDER

1. What does this page from *Life* tell you about American attitudes toward nuclear technology when it was first made public?
2. What was *Life* trying to convey with the choice of Christian for this photograph? What is she meant to represent and why?

25.5 VISUAL SOURCE: U.S. STEEL'S "BRIDE'S HOUSE" ADVERTISEMENT (1956)*

In the years following the Second World War, many Americans, especially white Americans of the middle and professional classes, experienced a period of relative stability and material wealth that sharply contrasted with the preceding decade-and-a-half. The years of the Great Depression, followed by the Second World War, had left Americans dealing with little savings, underemployment, rationing, and scarcity. Even as the economy improved during the war, many consumer goods had been unavailable as corporations shifted production to meet the needs of the war rather than domestic consumption.

With the end of the war, many Americans had the opportunity to purchase numerous new essentials and luxuries that were now available. This included single-family homes that began to dot the American landscape as the suburban population grew exponentially. Most Americans had long lived in multi-generational dwellings that included older parents, extended relatives, or (among the wealthy) servants or staff, as well as children. New suburban homes predicated on the idea of housing only a couple and their children were an innovation that became increasingly popular as the expanding interstate highway system made it feasible to commute to work from beyond city limits.

---

* U.S. Steel's "Bride House" Advertisement, *Life*, April 23 (1956), p. 96.

NOW! See how U. S. Steel's **bride's house** can give you new freedom to live as you please

AS FEATURED IN THE SUMMER ISSUE OF HOUSE BEAUTIFUL'S "GUIDE FOR THE BRIDE"

QUESTIONS TO CONSIDER

1. What is the sales pitch for the "Bride's House"? What does it purport to offer and what might this tell us about Americans in the mid-1950s?
2. Who is the target of this advertisement? How can you tell?

CHAPTER 26

REBELLION ON THE LEFT, RESURGENCE ON THE RIGHT, 1957–1968

26.1 JOHN LEWIS, "WAKE UP AMERICA" (1963)*

In the spring and summer of 1963, the civil rights movement, led by Dr. Martin Luther King Jr. and the Southern Christian Leadership Council, engaged in numerous high-profile protests. Nonviolent civil rights protestors faced assault and arrest in Alabama, prompting President John F. Kennedy to announce in June that he would propose new sweeping civil rights legislation. That August, King and his allies, including labor organizer A. Philip Randolph, held a massive rally in Washington where over two hundred thousand mostly Black activists turned out for the "March for Jobs and Freedom."

Although the march is best remembered today as the site of King's "I Have a Dream" speech, other leaders who spoke at the protest included John Lewis (1940–2020), who represented the Student Nonviolent Coordinating Committee (SNCC), an interracial group of young activists who had participated in major protest initiatives such as the freedom rides. Although only twenty-three at the time of this speech, Lewis was already a veteran activist, having been assaulted and arrested during the original freedom rides. Lewis would go on to serve over thirty years as a congressman for Atlanta, Georgia.

We march today for jobs and freedom, but we have nothing to be proud of. For hundreds and thousands of our brothers are not here. For they are receiving starvation wages, or no wages at all. While we stand here, there are sharecroppers in the Delta of Mississippi who are out in the fields working for less than three dollars a day, twelve hours a day. While we stand here there are students in jail on trumped-up charges. Our brother James Farmer, along with many others, is also in jail. We come here today with a great sense of misgiving.

It is true that we support the administration's civil rights bill. We support it with great reservations, however. Unless Title III is put in this bill, there is nothing to protect the young children and old women who must face police dogs and fire hoses in the South while they engage in peaceful demonstrations. In its present form, this bill will not protect the citizens of Danville,

---

* John Lewis, "Text of Speech to be Delivered at Lincoln Memorial," August 28, 1963. Student Nonviolent Coordinating Committee Papers, Martin Luther King, Jr., Library and Archives.

Virginia, who must live in constant fear of a police state. It will not protect the hundreds and thousands of people that have been arrested on trumped charges. What about the three young men, SNCC field secretaries in Americus, Georgia, who face the death penalty for engaging in peaceful protest?

As it stands now, the voting section of this bill will not help the thousands of black people who want to vote. It will not help the citizens of Mississippi, of Alabama and Georgia, who are qualified to vote, but lack a sixth-grade education. "One man, one vote" is the African cry. It is ours too. It must be ours!

We must have legislation that will protect the Mississippi sharecropper who is put off of his farm because he dares to register to vote. We need a bill that will provide for the homeless and starving people of this nation. We need a bill that will ensure the equality of a maid who earns five dollars a week in a home of a family whose total income is $100,000 a year. We must have a good FEPC bill.

My friends, let us not forget that we are involved in a serious social revolution. By and large, American politics is dominated by politicians who build their careers on immoral compromises and ally themselves with open forms of political, economic, and social exploitation. There are exceptions, of course. We salute those. But what political leader can stand up and say, "My party is the party of principles"? For the party of Kennedy is also the party of Eastland. The party of Javits is also the party of Goldwater. Where is our party? Where is the political party that will make it unnecessary to march on Washington?

Where is the political party that will make it unnecessary to march in the streets of Birmingham? Where is the political party that will protect the citizens of Albany, Georgia? Do you know that in Albany, Georgia, nine of our leaders have been indicted, not by the Dixiecrats, but by the federal government for peaceful protest? But what did the federal government do when Albany's deputy sheriff beat Attorney C.B.

King and left him half-dead? What did the federal government do when local police officials kicked and assaulted the pregnant wife of Slater King, and she lost her baby?

To those who have said, "Be patient and wait," we have long said that we cannot be patient. We do not want our freedom gradually, but we want to be free now! We are tired. We are tired of being beaten by policemen. We are tired of seeing our people locked up in jail over and over again. And then you holler, "Be patient." How long can we be patient? We want our freedom and we want it now. We do not want to go to jail. But we will go to jail if this is the price we must pay for love, brotherhood, and true peace.

I appeal to all of you to get into this great revolution that is sweeping this nation. Get in and stay in the streets of every city, every village and hamlet of this nation until true freedom comes, until the revolution of 1776 is complete. We must get in this revolution and complete the revolution. For in the Delta in Mississippi, in southwest Georgia, in the Black Belt of Alabama, in Harlem, in Chicago, Detroit, Philadelphia, and all over this nation, the black masses are on the march for jobs and freedom.

They're talking about slow down and stop. We will not stop. All of the forces of Eastland, Barnett, Wallace, and Thurmond will not stop this revolution. If we do not get meaningful legislation out of this Congress, the time will come when we will not confine our marching to Washington. We will march through the South; through the streets of Jackson, through the streets of Danville, through the streets of Cambridge, through the streets of Birmingham. But we will march with the spirit of love and with the spirit of dignity that we have shown here today. By the force of our demands, our determination, and our numbers, we shall splinter the segregated South into a thousand pieces and put them together in the image of God and democracy. We must say: "Wake up America! Wake up!" For we cannot stop, and we will not and cannot be patient.

QUESTIONS TO CONSIDER

1. What policies or protections does Lewis want included in any civil rights legislation?
2. Lewis ends his speech by declaring that "we will not and cannot be patient." Why is this an urgent campaign for Lewis? What is the cost as he sees it of being "patient"?

26.2 BARRY GOLDWATER, SPEECH TO CONGRESS EXPLAINING VOTE AGAINST 1964 CIVIL RIGHTS ACT (1964)*

Following years of protests and activism by civil rights leaders, including headline-grabbing protests in Birmingham, Alabama, President John F. Kennedy proposed a major civil rights bill in the summer of 1963. After he was assassinated later that year, his successor, Lyndon B. Johnson, made the bill a legislative priority, leading to the passage of the Civil Rights Act of 1964. The new law was very broad in scope, barring discrimination based upon race, gender, or national origin in many areas of American public life such as employment, public accommodation (e.g., hotels, restaurants), and education. Although the law passed with over two thirds of the vote in both houses, prominent conservatives vocally opposed it.

Barry Goldwater (1909–1998) was a US senator from Arizona and a presidential hopeful in the spring of 1964. A bestselling author and prominent conservative, Goldwater was popular within the Republican Party despite worries among many that his views were too extreme to enjoy national popularity. In this speech he justified his decision to vote against the Civil Rights Act, arguing that the sections dealing with public accommodations (Title II) and employment (Title VII) represented an unconstitutional overreach by the federal government.

There have been few, if any, occasions when the searching of my conscience and the re-examination of my views of our constitutional system have played a greater part in the determination of my vote than they have on this occasion.

I am unalterably opposed to discrimination or segregation on the basis of race, color or creed, or on any other basis; not only my words, but more importantly my actions through the years have repeatedly demonstrated the sincerity of my feeling in this regard.

This is fundamentally a matter of the heart. The problems of discrimination can never be cured by laws alone; but I would be the first to agree that laws can help—laws carefully considered and weighed in an atmosphere of dispassion, in the absence of political demagoguery, and in the light of fundamental constitutional principles.

For example, throughout my 12 years as a member of the Senate Labor and Public Welfare Committee, I have repeatedly offered amendments to bills pertaining to labor that would end discrimination in unions, and repeatedly those amendments have been turned down by the very members of both parties who now so vociferously support the present approach to the solution of our problem. Talk is one thing, action is another, and until the members of this body and the people of this country realize this, there will be no real solution to the problem we face.

To be sure, a calm environment for the consideration of any law dealing with human relationships is not easily attained—emotions run high, political pressures become great, and objectivity is at a premium. Nevertheless, deliberation and calmness are indispensable to success.

It was in this context that I maintained high hopes for this current legislation—high hopes that, notwithstanding the glaring defects of the measure as it reached us from the other body and the sledgehammer

* Barry Goldwater, "Text of Goldwater Speech on Rights," *New York Times,* June 19, 1964, 18.

political tactics which produced it, this legislation, through the actions of what was once considered to be the greatest deliberative body on earth, would emerge in a form both effective for its lofty purposes and acceptable to all freedom-loving people.

It is with great sadness that I realize the nonfulfillment of these high hopes. My hopes were shattered when it became apparent that emotion and political pressure, not persuasion, not common sense, not deliberation, had become the rule of the day and of the processes of this great body.

One has only to review the defeat of common-sense amendments to this bill—amendments that would in no way harm it but would, in fact, improve it—to realize that political pressure, not persuasion or common sense, has come to rule the consideration of this measure.

I realize fully that the Federal Government has a responsibility in the field of civil rights. I supported the civil rights bills which were enacted in 1957 and 1960, and my public utterances during the debates on those measures and since reveal clearly the areas in which I feel that Federal responsibility lies and Federal legislation on this subject can be both effective and appropriate. Many of those areas are encompassed in this bill, and, to that extent, I favor it.

I wish to make myself perfectly clear. The two portions of this bill to which I have constantly and consistently voiced objections, and which are of such overriding significance that they are determinative of my vote on the entire measure, are those which would embark the Federal Government on a regulatory course of action with regard to private enterprise in the area of so-called "public accommodations" and in the area of employment—to be more specific, Titles II and VII of the bill.

I find no constitutional basis for the exercise of Federal regulatory authority in either of these areas; and I believe the attempted usurpation of such power to be a grave threat to the very essence of our basic system of government, namely, that of a constitutional republic in which 50 sovereign states have reserved to themselves and to the people those powers not specifically granted to the central or Federal Government.

If it is the wish of the American people that the Federal Government should be granted the power to regulate in these two areas and in the manner contemplated by this bill, then I say that the Constitution should be so amended by the people as to authorize such action in accordance with the procedures for amending the Constitution, which the great document itself prescribes.

I say further that for this great legislative body to ignore the Constitution and the fundamental concepts of our governmental system is to act in a manner which could ultimately destroy the freedom of all American citizens, including the freedoms of the very persons whose feelings and whose liberties are the major subject of this legislation.

My basic objection to this measure is, therefore, constitutional. But in addition, I would like to point out to my colleagues in the Senate and to the people of America, regardless of their race, color or creed, the implications involved in the enforcement of regulatory legislation of this sort.

To give genuine effect to the prohibitions of this bill will require the creation of a Federal police force of mammoth proportions. It also bids fair to result in the development of an "informer" psychology in great areas of our national life—neighbors spying on neighbors, worker spying on workers, businessmen spying on businessmen, where those who would harass their fellow citizens for selfish and narrow purposes will have ample inducement to do so. These the Federal police force and an "informer" psychology, are the hallmarks of the police state and landmarks in the destruction of a free society.

I repeat again: I am unalterably opposed to discrimination of any sort and I believe that though the problem is fundamentally one of the heart, some law can help—but not law that embodies features like these, provisions which fly in the face of the Constitution and which require for their effective execution the creation of a police state. And so, because I am unalterably opposed to any threats to our great system of government and the loss of our God-given liberties, I shall vote "no" on this bill.

This vote will be reluctantly cast, because I had hoped to be able to vote "yea" on this measure as I have on the civil rights bills which have preceded it; but I cannot, in good conscience to the oath that I took when assuming office, cast my vote in the affirmative.

With the exception of Titles II and VII, I could whole-heartedly support this bill; but with their inclusion, not measurably improved by the compromise version we have been working on, my vote must be "no."

If my vote is misconstrued, let it be, and let me suffer its consequences. Just let me be judged in this by the real concern I have voiced here and not by words that others may speak or by what others may say about what I think.

My concern extends beyond this single legislative moment. My concern extends beyond any single group in our society. My concern is for the entire nation, for the freedom of all who live in it and for all who will be born into it.

It is the general welfare that must be considered now, not just the special appeals for special welfare. This is the time to attend to the liberties of all.

This is my concern. And this is where I stand.

QUESTIONS TO CONSIDER

1. What does Goldwater say worries him most about the bill? How are his fears informed by Cold War culture?
2. Why would the sections on employment and public accommodation have been so important? What problems were the bill's authors trying to solve?

26.3 LYNDON B. JOHNSON, SPECIAL MESSAGE TO CONGRESS (1965)*

Following the assassination of President John F. Kennedy in late 1963, Lyndon B. Johnson (1908–1973) took office determined to pass the civil rights legislation that Kennedy had introduced. Soon Johnson announced his intention to go even further, proposing new social programs to combat poverty as part of a push toward a "Great Society." As part of his program to expand and improve American social programs, Johnson sought to ensure voting access with a voting rights act that would enforce the Fifteenth Amendment of the Constitution and ensure that all eligible Americans could vote, regardless of race.

At the time, many Southern states imposed taxes or used intentionally difficult and opaque tests to prevent Black Americans from registering to vote or casting ballots. Because these laws were enforced at the local level, they could be applied selectively by white supremacist officials to target potential Black voters and make it difficult or impossible for them to participate in elections. The Voting Rights Act, passed in 1965, banned these practices and established special federal oversight of states with a history of discriminatory voting practices.

* National Archives

Mr. Speaker, Mr. President, Members of the Congress, My Fellow Americans:

I speak tonight for the dignity of man and the destiny of democracy.

I urge every member of both parties, Americans of all religions and of all colors, from every section of this country, to join me in that cause.

At times history and fate meet at a single time in a single place to shape a turning point in man's unending search for freedom. So it was at Lexington and Concord. So it was a century ago at Appomattox. So it was last week in Selma, Alabama.

There, long-suffering men and women peacefully protested the denial of their rights as Americans. Many were brutally assaulted. One good man, a man of God, was killed.

There is no cause for pride in what has happened in Selma.

There is no cause for self-satisfaction in the long denial of equal rights of millions of Americans.

But there is cause for hope and for faith in our democracy in what is happening here tonight.

For the cries of pain and the hymns and protests of oppressed people have summoned into convocation all the majesty of this great government—the government of the greatest nation on earth.

Our mission is at once the oldest and the most basic of this country: to right wrong, to do justice, to serve man.

In our time we have come to live with moments of great crisis. Our lives have been marked with debate about great issues; issues of war and peace, issues of prosperity and depression. But rarely in any time does an issue lay bare the secret heart of America itself. Rarely are we met with a challenge, not to our growth or abundance, our welfare or our security, but rather to the values and the purposes and the meaning of our beloved Nation.

The issue of equal rights for American Negroes is such an issue. And should we defeat every enemy, should we double our wealth and conquer the stars, and still be unequal to this issue, then we will have failed as a people and as a nation.

For with a country as with a person, "What is a man profited, if he shall gain the whole world, and lose his own soul?"

There is no Negro problem. There is no Southern problem. There is no Northern problem. There is only an American problem.

And we are met here tonight as Americans—not as Democrats or Republicans—we are met here as Americans to solve that problem.

This was the first nation in the history of the world to be founded with a purpose. The great phrases of that purpose still sound in every American heart, North and South: "All men are created equal"—"government by consent of the governed"—"give me liberty or give me death." Well, those are not just clever words, or those are not just empty theories. In their name Americans have fought and died for two centuries, and tonight around the world they stand there as guardians of our liberty, risking their lives.

Those words are a promise to every citizen that he shall share in the dignity of man. This dignity cannot be found in a man's possessions; it cannot be found in his power, or in his position. It really rests on his right to be treated as a man equal in opportunity to all others. It says that he shall share in freedom, he shall choose his leaders, educate his children, and provide for his family according to his ability and his merits as a human being.

To apply any other test—to deny a man his hopes because of his color or race, his religion or the place of his birth—is not only to do injustice, it is to deny America and to dishonor the dead who gave their lives for American freedom.

Our fathers believed that if this noble view of the rights of man was to flourish, it must be rooted in democracy. The most basic right of all was the right to choose your own leaders. The history of this country, in large measure, is the history of the expansion of that right to all of our people.

Many of the issues of civil rights are very complex and most difficult. But about this there can and should be no argument. Every American citizen must have an equal right to vote. There is no reason which can excuse the denial of that right. There is no duty which weighs more heavily on us than the duty we have to ensure that right.

Yet the harsh fact is that in many places in this country men and women are kept from voting simply because they are Negroes.

Every device of which human ingenuity is capable has been used to deny this right. The Negro citizen may go to register only to be told that the day is wrong, or the hour is late, or the official in charge is absent.

If he persists, and if he manages to present himself to the registrar, he may be disqualified because he did not spell out his middle name or because he abbreviated a word on the application.

If he manages to fill out an application he is given a test. The registrar is the sole judge of whether he passes this test. He may be asked to recite the entire Constitution, or explain the most complex provisions of State law. And even a college degree cannot be used to prove that he can read and write.

For the fact is that the only way to pass these barriers is to show a white skin.

Experience has clearly shown that the existing process of law cannot overcome systematic and ingenious discrimination. No law that we now have on the books—and I have helped to put three of them there—can ensure the right to vote when local officials are determined to deny it.

In such a case our duty must be clear to all of us. The Constitution says that no person shall be kept from voting because of his race or his color. We have all sworn an oath before God to support and to defend that Constitution. We must now act in obedience to that oath.

Wednesday I will send to Congress a law designed to eliminate illegal barriers to the right to vote.

The broad principles of that bill will be in the hands of the Democratic and Republican leaders tomorrow. After they have reviewed it, it will come here formally as a bill. I am grateful for this opportunity to come here tonight at the invitation of the leadership to reason with my friends, to give them my views, and to visit with my former colleagues.

I have had prepared a more comprehensive analysis of the legislation which I had intended to transmit to the clerk tomorrow but which I will submit to the clerks tonight. But I want to really discuss with you now briefly the main proposals of this legislation,

This bill will strike down restrictions to voting in all elections—Federal, State, and local—which have been used to deny Negroes the right to vote.

This bill will establish a simple, uniform standard which cannot be used, however ingenious the effort, to flout our Constitution.

It will provide for citizens to be registered by officials of the United States Government if the State officials refuse to register them.

It will eliminate tedious, unnecessary lawsuits which delay the right to vote.

Finally, this legislation will ensure that properly registered individuals are not prohibited from voting.

I will welcome the suggestions from all of the Members of Congress—I have no doubt that I will get some—on ways and means to strengthen this law and to make it effective. But experience has plainly shown that this is the only path to carry out the command of the Constitution.

To those who seek to avoid action by their National Government in their own communities; who want to and who seek to maintain purely local control over elections, the answer is simple:

Open your polling places to all your people.

Allow men and women to register and vote whatever the color of their skin.

Extend the rights of citizenship to every citizen of this land.

There is no constitutional issue here. The command of the Constitution is plain.

There is no moral issue. It is wrong—deadly wrong—to deny any of your fellow Americans the right to vote in this country.

There is no issue of States fights or national rights. There is only the struggle for human rights.

I have not the slightest doubt what will be your answer.

The last time a President sent a civil rights bill to the Congress it contained a provision to protect voting rights in Federal elections. That civil rights bill was passed after eight long months of debate. And when that bill came to my desk from the Congress for my signature, the heart of the voting provision had been eliminated.

This time, on this issue, there must be no delay, no hesitation and no compromise with our purpose.

We cannot, we must not, refuse to protect the right of every American to vote in every election that he may desire to participate in. And we ought not and we cannot and we must not wait another eight months before we get a bill. We have already waited a hundred years and more, and the time for waiting is gone.

So I ask you to join me in working long hours—nights and weekends, if necessary—to pass this bill. And I don't make that request lightly. For outside this chamber is the outraged conscience of a nation, the grave concern of many nations, and the harsh judgment of history on our acts.

But even if we pass this bill, the battle will not be over. What happened in Selma is part of a far larger movement which reaches into every section and State of America. It is the effort of American Negroes to secure for themselves the full blessings of American life.

Their cause must be our cause too. Because it is not just Negroes, but really it is all of us, who must overcome the crippling legacy of bigotry and injustice. And we shall overcome.

As a man whose roots go deeply into Southern soil I know how agonizing racial feelings are. I know how difficult it is to reshape the attitudes and the structure of our society.

But a century has passed, more than a hundred years, since the Negro was freed. And he is not fully free tonight.

It was more than a hundred years ago that Abraham Lincoln, a great President of another party, signed the Emancipation Proclamation, but emancipation is a proclamation and not a fact.

A century has passed, more than a hundred years, since equality was promised. And yet the Negro is not equal.

A century has passed since the day of promise. And the promise is unkept.

The time of justice has now come. I tell you that I believe sincerely that no force can hold it back. It is right in the eyes of man and God that it should come. And when it does, I think that day will brighten the lives of every American.

For Negroes are not the only victims. How many white children have gone uneducated, how many white families have lived in stark poverty, how many white lives have been scarred by fear, because we have wasted our energy and our substance to maintain the barriers of hatred and terror?

So I say to all of you here, and to all in the Nation tonight, that those who appeal to you to hold on to the past do so at the cost of denying you your future.

This great, rich, restless country can offer opportunity and education and hope to all: black and white, North and South, sharecropper and city dweller. These are the enemies: poverty, ignorance, disease. They are the enemies and not our fellow man, not our neighbor. And these enemies too, poverty, disease and ignorance, we shall overcome.

Now let none of us in any sections look with prideful righteousness on the troubles in another section, or on the problems of our neighbors. There is really no part of America where the promise of equality has been fully kept. In Buffalo as well as in Birmingham, in Philadelphia as well as in Selma, Americans are struggling for the fruits of freedom.

This is one nation. What happens in Selma or in Cincinnati is a matter of legitimate concern to every American. But let each of us look within our own hearts and our own communities, and let each of us put our shoulder to the wheel to root out injustice wherever it exists.

As we meet here in this peaceful, historic chamber tonight, men from the South, some of whom were at Iwo Jima, men from the North who have carried Old Glory to far corners of the world and brought it back without a stain on it, men from the East and from the West, are all fighting together without regard to religion, or color, or region, in Vietnam. Men from every region fought for us across the world 20 years ago.

And in these common dangers and these common sacrifices the South made its contribution of honor and gallantry no less than any other region of the great Republic—and in some instances, a great many of them, more. And I have not the slightest doubt that good men from everywhere in this country, from the Great Lakes to the Gulf of Mexico, from the Golden Gate to the harbors along the Atlantic, will rally together now in this cause to vindicate the freedom of all Americans. For all of us owe this duty; and I believe that all of us will respond to it.

Your President makes that request of every American.

The real hero of this struggle is the American Negro. His actions and protests, his courage to risk safety and even to risk his life, have awakened the conscience of this Nation. His demonstrations have been designed to call attention to injustice, designed to provoke change, designed to stir reform. He has called upon us to make good the promise of America. And who among us can say that we would have made the same progress were it not for his persistent bravery, and his faith in American democracy.

For at the real heart of battle for equality is a deep-seated belief in the democratic process. Equality depends not on the force of arms or tear gas but upon the force of moral right; not on recourse to violence but on respect for law and order.

There have been many pressures upon your President and there will be others as the days come and go. But I pledge you tonight that we intend to fight this battle where it should be fought: in the courts, and in the Congress, and in the hearts of men.

We must preserve the right of free speech and the right of free assembly. But the right of free speech does not carry with it, as has been said, the right to holier fire in a crowded theater. We must preserve the right to free assembly, but free assembly does not carry with it the right to block public thoroughfares to traffic.

We do have a right to protest, and a right to march under conditions that do not infringe the constitutional rights of our neighbors. And I intend to protect all those rights as long as I am permitted to serve in this office.

We will guard against violence, knowing it strikes from our hands the very weapons which we seek—progress, obedience to law, and belief in American values.

In Selma as elsewhere we seek and pray for peace. We seek order. We seek unity. But we will not accept the peace of stifled rights, or the order imposed by fear, or the unity that stifles protest. For peace cannot be purchased at the cost of liberty.

In Selma tonight, as in every—and we had a good day there—as in every city, we are working for just and peaceful settlement. We must all remember that after this speech I am making tonight, after the police and the FBI and the Marshals have all gone, and after you have promptly passed this bill, the people of Selma and the other cities of the Nation must still live and work together. And when the attention of the Nation has gone elsewhere they must try to heal the wounds and to build a new community. This cannot be easily done on a battleground of violence, as the history of

the South itself shows. It is in recognition of this that men of both races have shown such an outstandingly impressive responsibility in recent days—last Tuesday, again today.

The bill that I am presenting to you will be known as a civil rights bill. But, in a larger sense, most of the program I am recommending is a civil rights program. Its object is to open the city of hope to all people of all races.

Because all Americans just must have the right to vote. And we are going to give them that right.

All Americans must have the privileges of citizenship regardless of race. And they are going to have those privileges of citizenship regardless of race.

But I would like to caution you and remind you that to exercise these privileges takes much more than just legal right. It requires a trained mind and a healthy body. It requires a decent home, and the chance to find a job, and the opportunity to escape from the clutches of poverty.

Of course, people cannot contribute to the Nation if they are never taught to read or write, if their bodies are stunted from hunger, if their sickness goes untended, if their life is spent in hopeless poverty just drawing a welfare check.

So we want to open the gates to opportunity. But we are also going to give all our people, black and white, the help that they need to walk through those gates.

My first job after college was as a teacher in Cotulla, Texas, in a small Mexican-American school. Few of them could speak English, and I couldn't speak much Spanish. My students were poor and they often came to class without breakfast, hungry. They knew even in their youth the pain of prejudice. They never seemed to know why people disliked them. But they knew it was so, because I saw it in their eyes.

I often walked home late in the afternoon, after the classes were finished, wishing there was more that I could do. But all I knew was to teach them the little that I knew, hoping that it might help them against the hardships that lay ahead.

Somehow you never forget what poverty and hatred can do when you see its scars on the hopeful face of a young child.

I never thought then, in 1928, that I would be standing here in 1965. It never even occurred to me in my fondest dreams that I might have the chance to help the sons and daughters of those students and to help people like them all over this country.

But now I do have that chance—and I'll let you in on a secret—I mean to use it. And I hope that you will use it with me.

This is the richest and most powerful country which ever occupied the globe. The might of past empires is little compared to ours. But I do not want to be the President who built empires, or sought grandeur, or extended dominion.

I want to be the President who educated young children to the wonders of their world. I want to be the President who helped to feed the hungry and to prepare them to be taxpayers instead of taxeaters.

I want to be the President who helped the poor to find their own way and who protected the right of every citizen to vote in every election.

I want to be the President who helped to end hatred among his fellow men and who promoted love among the people of all races and all regions and all parties.

I want to be the President who helped to end war among the brothers of this earth.

And so at the request of your beloved Speaker and the Senator from Montana; the majority leader, the Senator from Illinois; the minority leader, Mr. McCulloch, and other Members of both parties, I came here tonight—not as President Roosevelt came down one time in person to veto a bonus bill, not as President Truman came down one time to urge the passage of a railroad bill—but I came down here to ask you to share this task with me and to share it with the people that we both work for. I want this to be the Congress, Republicans and Democrats alike, which did all these things for all these people.

Beyond this great chamber, out yonder in 50 States, are the people that we serve. Who can tell what deep and unspoken hopes are in their hearts tonight as they sit there and listen. We all can guess, from our own lives, how difficult they often find their own pursuit of happiness, how many problems each little family has. They look most of all to themselves for their futures. But I think that they also look to each of us.

Above the pyramid on the great seal of the United States it says—in Latin—"God has favored our undertaking."

God will not favor everything that we do. It is rather our duty to divine His will. But I cannot help believing that He truly understands and that He really favors the undertaking that we begin here tonight.

QUESTIONS TO CONSIDER

1. What role does American history play in Johnson's speech? How does he frame American history to support his legislative initiative?
2. How does ensuring voting rights support Johnson's vision of a future "Great Society" for America?

26.4 PAUL POTTER, ON THE VIETNAM WAR (1965)*

The Students for a Democratic Society (SDS) were an organization of left-wing college students established in 1964 as a critique of what they saw as the manifold failings of modern American culture and the state. They criticized American capitalism, racism, and imperialism as well as the emerging military-industrial complex. They envisioned a more participatory democratic process where citizens' involvement in politics did not begin and end with voting in elections every two to four years. They were particularly critical of the Vietnam War, a conflict that the United States had been involved in since the late 1950s, but which had increased in intensity throughout the 1960s.

The SDS was part of a larger movement known as the New Left, which emerged in the 1960s. Less concerned with the traditional issues of labor and class associated with left-wing politics and opposed to liberals who participated in the capitalist and imperialist projects of the United States, New Left activists were motivated by what they saw as the failings of modern American society. The below speech was delivered by Paul Potter, who was then president of SDS, at a protest against the Vietnam War in Washington, DC.

MOST OF US grew up thinking that the United States was a strong but humble nation, that involved itself in world affairs only reluctantly, that respected the integrity of other nations and other systems, and that engaged in wars only as a last resort. This was a nation with no large standing army, with no design for external conquest, that sought primarily the opportunity to develop its own resources and its own mode of living. If at some point we began to hear vague and disturbing things about what this country had done in Latin America, China, Spain and other places, we somehow remained confident about the basic integrity of this nation's foreign policy. The Cold War with all of its neat categories and black and white descriptions did much to assure us that what we had been taught to believe was true.

But in recent years, the withdrawal from the hysteria of the Cold War era and the development of a more aggressive, activist foreign policy have done much to force many of us to rethink attitudes that were deep and basic sentiments about our country. The incredible war in Vietnam has provided the razor, the terrifying sharp cutting edge that has finally severed the last vestige of illusion that morality and democracy are the guiding principles of American foreign policy. The saccharine self-righteous moralism that promises the Vietnamese a billion dollars of economic aid at the very moment we are delivering billions for economic and social destruction and political repression is rapidly losing what power it might ever have had to reassure us about the decency of our foreign policy. The further we explore the reality of what this country is doing and planning in Vietnam the more we are driven toward the conclusion of Senator Morse that the United States may well be the greatest threat to peace in the world today. That is a terrible and bitter insight for people who grew up as we did—and our revulsion at that insight, our refusal to accept it as inevitable or necessary, is one of the reasons that so many people have come here today.

The President says that we are defending freedom in Vietnam. Whose freedom? Not the freedom of the Vietnamese. The first act of the first dictator, Diem, the United States installed in Vietnam, was to

* Paul Potter, "The Incredible War," Speech at the Washington Antiwar March, April 17, 1965, in Massimo Teodori, ed., *The New Left: A Documentary History* (New York: Bobbs-Merrill, 1968), 246–48.

systematically begin the persecution of all political op-position, non-Communist as well as Communist. The first American military supplies were not used to fight Communist insurgents; they were used to control, imprison or kill any who sought something better for Vietnam than the personal aggrandizement, political corruption and the profiteering of the Diem regime. The elite of the forces that we have trained and equipped are still used to control political unrest in Saigon and defend the latest dictator from the people.

And yet in a world where dictatorships are so commonplace and popular control of government so rare, people become callous to the misery that is implied by dictatorial power. The rationalizations that are used to defend political despotism have been drummed into us so long that we have somehow become numb to the possibility that some-thing else might exist. And it is only the kind of terror we see now in Vietnam that awakens conscience and reminds us that there is something deep in us that cries out against dictatorial suppression.

The pattern of repression and destruction that we have developed and justified in the war is so thorough that it can only be called cultural genocide. I am not simply talking about napalm or gas or crop destruction or torture, hurled indiscriminately on women and children, insurgent and neutral, upon the first suspicion of rebel activity. That in itself is horrendous and incredible beyond belief. But it is only part of a larger pattern of destruction to the very fabric of the country. We have uprooted the people from the land and imprisoned them in concentration camps called "sunrise villages." Through conscription and direct political intervention and control, we have destroyed local customs and traditions, trampled upon those things of value which give dignity and purpose to life.

What is left to the people of Vietnam after 20 years of war? What part of themselves and their own lives will those who survive be able to salvage from the wreckage of their country or build on the "peace" and "security" our Great Society offers them in reward for their allegiance? How can anyone be surprised that people who have had total war waged on themselves and their culture rebel in increasing numbers against that tyranny? What other course is available? And still our only response to rebellion is more vigorous repression, more merciless opposition to the social and cultural institutions which sustain dignity and the will to resist.

Not even the President can say that this is a war to defend the freedom of the Vietnamese people. Perhaps what the President means when he speaks of freedom is the freedom of the American people.

WHAT IN FACT has the war done for freedom in America? It has led to even more vigorous governmental efforts to control information, manipulate the press and pressure and persuade the public through distorted or downright dishonest documents such as the White Paper on Vietnam. It has led to the confiscation of films and other anti-war material and the vigorous harassment by the FBI of some of the people who have been most outspokenly active in their criticism of the war. As the war escalates and the administration seeks more actively to gain support for any initiative it may choose to take, there has been the beginnings of a war psychology unlike anything that has burdened this country since the 1950s. How much more of Mr. Johnson's freedom can we stand? How much freedom will be left in this country if there is a major war in Asia? By what weird logic can it be said that the freedom of one people can only be maintained by crushing another?

In many ways this is an unusual march because the large majority of people here are not involved in a peace movement as their primary basis of concern. What is exciting about the participants in this march is that so many of us view ourselves consciously as participants as well in a movement to build a more. decent society. There are students here who have been involved in protests over the quality and kind of education they are receiving in growingly bureaucratized, depersonalized institutions called universities; there are Negroes from Mississippi and Alabama who are struggling against the tyranny and repression of those states; there are poor people here—Negro and white—from Northern urban areas who are attempting to build movements that abolish poverty and secure democracy; there are faculty who are beginning to question the relevance of their institutions to the critical problems facing the society. Where will these people and the movements they are a part of be if the President is allowed to expand the war in Asia? What happens to the hopeful beginnings of expressed discontent that are trying to shift American attention to long-neglected internal priorities of shared abundance, democracy and decency at home when those priorities have to compete with the all-consuming priorities and psychology of a war against an enemy thousands of miles away?

The President mocks freedom if he insists that the war in Vietnam is a defense of American freedom. Perhaps the only freedom that this war protects is the freedom of the warhawks in the Pentagon and the State Department to experiment with counter-insurgency and guerilla warfare in Vietnam.

Vietnam, we may say, is a laboratory ran by a new breed of gamesmen who approach war as a kind of rational exercise in international power politics. It is the testing ground and staging area for a new American response to the social revolution that is sweeping through the impoverished downtrodden areas of the world. It is the beginning of the American counter-revolution, and so far no one—none of us—not the N.Y. Times, nor 17 Neutral Nations, nor dozens of worried allies, nor the United States Congress have been able to interfere with the freedom of the President and the Pentagon to carry out that experiment.

THUS FAR the war in Vietnam has only dramatized the demand of ordinary people to have some opportunity to make their own lives, and of their unwillingness, even under incredible odds, to give up the struggle against external domination. We are told, however, that the struggle can be legitimately suppressed since it might lead to the development of a Communist system, and before that ultimate menace all criticism is supposed to melt.

This is a critical point and there are several things that must be said here—not by way of celebration, but because I think they are the truth. First, if this country were serious about giving the people of Vietnam some alternative to a Communist social revolution, that opportunity was sacrificed in 1954 when we helped to install Diem and his repression of non-Communist movements. There is no indication that we were serious about that goal—that we were ever willing to contemplate the risks of allowing the Vietnamese to choose their own destinies. Second, those people who insist now that Vietnam can be neutralized are for the most part looking for a sugar coating to cover the bitter

bill. We must accept the consequences that calling for an end of the war in Vietnam is in fact allowing for the likelihood that a Vietnam without war will be a self-styled Communist Vietnam. Third, this country must come to understand that creation of a Communist country in the world today is not an ultimate defeat. If people are given the opportunity to choose their own lives it is likely that some Of them will choose what we have called "Communist systems." We are not powerless in that situation. Recent years have finally and indisputably broken the myth that the Communist world is monolithic and have conclusively shown that American power can be significant in aiding countries dominated by greater powers to become more independent and self-determined. And yet the war that we are creating and escalating in Southeast Asia is rapidly eroding the base of independence of North Vietnam as it is forced to turn to China and the Soviet Union, involving them in the war and involving itself in the compromises that that implies. Fourth, I must say to you that I would rather see Vietnam Communist than see it under continuous subjugation of the ruin that American domination has brought.

But the war goes on; the freedom to conduct that war depends on the dehumanization not only of Vietnamese people but of Americans as well; it depends on the construction of a system of premises and thinking that insulates the President and his advisors thoroughly and completely from the human consequences of the decisions they make. I do not believe that the President or Mr. Rusk or Mr. McNamara or even McGeorge Bundy are particularly evil men. If asked to throw napalm on the back of a ten-year-old child they would shrink in horror—but their decisions have led to mutilation and death of thousands and thousands of people.

What kind of system is it that allows good men to make those kinds of decisions? What kind of system is it that justifies the United States or any country seizing the destinies of the Vietnamese people and using them callously for its own purpose? What kind of system is it that disenfranchises people in the South, leaves millions upon millions of people throughout the country impoverished and excluded from the mainstream and promise of American society, that creates faceless and terrible bureaucracies and makes those the place where people spend their lives and do their work, that consistently puts material values before human values—and still persists in calling itself free and still persists in finding itself fit to police the world? What place is there for ordinary men in that system and how are they to control it, make it bend itself to their wills rather than bending them to its?

We must name that system. We must name it, describe it, analyze it, understand it and change it. For it is only when that system is changed and brought under control that there can be any hope for stopping the forces that create a war in Vietnam today or a murder in the South tomorrow or all the incalculable, innumerable more subtle atrocities that are worked on people all over—all the time.

How do you stop a war then? If the war has its roots deep in the institutions of American society, how do you stop it? Do you march to Washington? Is that enough? Who will hear us? How can you make the decision makers hear us, insulated as they are, if they cannot hear the screams of a little girl burnt by napalm?

I believe that the administration is serious about expanding the war in Asia. The question is whether the people here are as serious about ending it. I wonder what it means for each of us to say we want to end the war in Vietnam—whether, if we accept the full meaning of that statement and the gravity of the situation, we can simply leave the march and go back to the routines of a society that acts as if it were not in the midst of a grave crisis. Maybe we, like the President, are insulated from the consequences of our own decision to end the war. Maybe we have yet really to listen to the screams of a burning child and decide that we cannot go back to whatever it is we did before today until that war has ended.

There is no simple plan, no scheme or gimmick that can be proposed here. There is no simple way to attack something that is deeply rooted in the society. If the people of this country are to end the war in Vietnam, and to change the institutions which create it, then the people of this country must create a massive social movement—and if that can be built around the issue of Vietnam then that is what we must do.

By a social movement I mean more than petitions or letters of protest, or tacit support of dissident Congressmen; I mean people who are willing to change their lives, who are willing to challenge the system, to take the problem of change seriously. By a social movement I mean an effort that is powerful enough to make the country understand that our problems are not in Vietnam, or China or Brazil or outer space or at the bottom of the ocean, but are here in the United States. What we must do is begin to build a democratic and humane society in which Vietnams are unthinkable, in which human life and initiative are precious. The reason there are twenty thousand people here today and not a hundred or none at all is because five years ago in the South students began to build a social movement to change the system. The reason there are poor people, Negro and white, housewives, faculty members, and many others here in Washington is because that movement has grown and spread and changed and reached out as an expression of the broad concerns of people throughout the society. The reason the war and the system it represents will be stopped, if it is stopped before it destroys all of us, will be because the movement has become strong enough to exact change in the society. Twenty thousand people, the people here, if they were serious, if they were willing to break out of their isolation and to accept the consequences of a decision to end the war and commit themselves to building a movement wherever they are and in whatever way they effectively can, would be, I'm convinced, enough.

To build a movement rather than a protest or some series of protests, to break out of our insulations and accept the consequences of our decisions, in effect to change our lives, means that we can open ourselves to the reactions of a society that believes that it is moral and just, that we open ourselves to libeling and persecution, that we dare to be really seen as wrong in a society that doesn't tolerate fundamental challenges.

It means that we desert the security of our riches and reach out to people who are tied to the mythology of American power and make them part of our movement. We must reach out to every organization and individual in the country and make them part of our movement.

But that means that we build a movement that works not simply in Washington but in communities and with the problems that face people throughout the society. That means that we build a movement that understands Vietnam in all its horror as but a symptom of a deeper malaise, that we build a movement that makes possible the implementation of the values that would have prevented Vietnam, a movement based on the integrity of man and a belief in man's capacity to tolerate all the weird formulations of society that men may choose to strive for; a movement that will build on the new and creative forms of protest that are beginning to emerge, such as the teach-in, and extend their efforts and intensify them; that we will build a movement that will find ways to support the increasing numbers of young men who are unwilling to and will not fight in Vietnam; a movement that will not tolerate the escalation or prolongation of this war but will, if necessary, respond to the administration war effort with massive civil disobedience all over the country, that will wrench the country into a confrontation with the issues of the war; a movement that must of necessity reach out to all these people in Vietnam or elsewhere who are struggling to find decency and control for their lives.

For in a strange way the people of Vietnam and the people on this demonstration are united in much more than a common concern that the war be ended. In both countries there are people struggling to build a movement that has the power to change their condition. The system that frustrates these movements is the same. All our lives, our destinies, our very hopes to live, depend on our ability to overcome that system.

QUESTIONS TO CONSIDER

1. Disillusionment is a central theme in Potter's speech. What does Potter feel betrayed by and how does this inform his politics?
2. What does the Vietnam War represent to the SDS? What aspects of American society does the SDS take issue with and how does the war represent these?

26.5 VISUAL SOURCE: POLICE ARRESTING BLACK MEN DURING THE WATTS UPRISING, LOS ANGELES (1965)*

In August 1965, Los Angeles police officers violently arrested a young Black man in the Watts neighborhood of southern Los Angeles. The struggle drew a crowd and sparked nearly a week of civil unrest, alternatively termed a "riot" or an "uprising," throughout Watts. The unrest and subsequent response from Los Angeles police and the California national guard led to thirty-four deaths and over a thousand injuries.

Because of discriminatory housing practices such as redlining and housing covenants, mid-twentieth-century Watts was an overwhelmingly Black neighborhood. The unrest there is generally attributed to longstanding resentment over racial discrimination against Black Los Angeles residents in general, and racially targeted police violence in particular. The two men in this photograph were some of the over three thousand residents who were arrested by Los Angeles police during the six days of violence.

* Courtesy of the Library of Congress, World-Telegram photo

QUESTIONS TO CONSIDER

1. Who are the sympathetic figures in this photograph? Why?
2. How does the context of this photograph, coming at the end of the violence, change the meaning of this image?

CHAPTER 27

DESTABILIZATIONS, 1969–1979

27.1 BLACK PANTHER PARTY FOR SELF DEFENSE, "TEN-POINT PROGRAM" (1966)*

The Black Panther Party was a political organization founded by activist Huey P. Newton (1942–1989) in 1966 to defend and advocate for Black Americans. Newton and other leaders believed that American governments did not adequately protect or support Black communities and that Black Americans should organize for their own mutual aid and protection. Members of the Black Panther Party famously openly carried firearms to deter violence from police officers and to assert their Second Amendment rights, but the party organized a variety of social programs as well. Initiatives like the Black Panther–run Free Breakfast for Children program reflected Newton's beliefs that the basics of human life ought to be provided for all, regardless of wealth, as well as the Panthers' commitment to mutual aid among Black Americans.

The Black Panther Party was one of the primary targets of the federal Counterintelligence Program (COINTELPRO), which President Richard Nixon used to infiltrate, harass, and disrupt left-wing organizations. Nearly thirty Black Panthers were killed as a result, including Chicago leader Fred Hampton (1948–1969), who was killed in his home by the FBI.

1. We Want Freedom. We Want Power to Determine the Destiny of Our Black Community.

   We believe that Black people will not be free until we are able to determine our destiny.

2. We Want Full Employment for Our People.

   We believe that the federal government is responsible and obligated to give every man employment or a guaranteed income. We believe that if the White American businessmen will not give full employment, then the means of production should be taken from the businessmen and placed in the community so that the people of the community can organize and employ all of its people and give a high standard of living.

3. We Want An End to the Robbery By the Capitalists of Our Black Community.

   We believe that this racist government has robbed us, and now we are demanding the overdue debt of

* "The Black Panther Party Ten-Point Program," in Huey P. Newton, *War Against the Panthers: A Study of Repression in America* (Santa Cruz: University of California, Santa Cruz, 1980), reprinted at blackpast.org.

forty acres and two mules. Forty acres and two mules were promised 100 years ago as restitution for slave labor and mass murder of Black people. We will accept the payment in currency which will be distributed to our many communities. The Germans are now aiding the Jews in Israel for the genocide of the Jewish people. The Germans murdered six million Jews. The American racist has taken part in the slaughter of over fifty million Black people; therefore, we feel that this is a modest demand that we make.

4. We Want Decent Housing Fit For The Shelter of Human Beings.

We believe that if the White Landlords will not give decent housing to our Black community, then the housing and the land should be made into cooperatives so that our community, with government aid, can build and make decent housing for its people.

5. We Want Education for Our People That Exposes The True Nature Of This Decadent American Society. We Want Education That Teaches Us Our True History And Our Role in the Present-Day Society.

We believe in an educational system that will give to our people a knowledge of self. If a man does not have knowledge of himself and his position in society and the world then he has little chance to relate to anything else.

6. We Want All Black Men To Be Exempt From Military Service.

We believe that Black people should not be forced to fight in the military service to defend a racist government that does not protect us. We will not fight and kill other people of color in the world who, like Black people, are being victimized by the White racist government of America. We will protect ourselves from the force and violence of the racist police and the racist military by whatever means necessary.

7. We Want An Immediate End to Police Brutality and the Murder of Black People.

We believe we can end police brutality in our Black community by organizing Black self-defense groups that are dedicated to defending our Black community from racist police oppression and brutality. The Second Amendment to the Constitution of the United States gives a right to bear arms. We therefore believe that all Black people should arm themselves for self-defense.

8. We Want Freedom For All Black Men Held in Federal, State, County and City Prisons and Jails.

We believe that all Black People should be released from the many jails and prisons because they have not received a fair and impartial trial.

9. We Want All Black People When Brought to Trial To Be Tried In Court By A Jury Of Their Peer Group Or People From Their Black Communities, As Defined By the Constitution of the United States.

We believe that the courts should follow the United States Constitution so that Black people will receive fair trials. The Fourteenth Amendment of the U.S. Constitution gives a man a right to be tried by his peer group. A peer is a person from a similar economic, social, religious, geographical, environmental, historical, and racial background. To do this the court will be forced to select a jury from the Black community from which the Black defendant came. We have been, and we are being, tried by all-White juries that have no understanding of the "average reasoning man" of the Black community.

10. We Want Land, Bread, Housing, Education, Clothing, Justice And Peace.

When, in the course of human events, it becomes necessary for one people to dissolve the political bands which have connected them with another, and to assume, among the powers of the earth, the separate and equal station to which the laws of nature and nature's God entitle them, a decent respect of the opinions of mankind requires that they should declare the causes which impel them to the separation.

We hold these truths to be self-evident, that all men are created equal; that they are endowed by their Creator with certain inalienable rights; that among these are life, liberty, and the pursuit of happiness. That, to secure these rights, governments are instituted among men, deriving their just powers from the consent of the governed; that, whenever any form of government becomes destructive of these ends, it is the right of the people to alter or abolish it, and to institute a new government, laying its foundation on such principles, and organizing its powers in such form, as to them shall seem most likely to effect their safety and happiness. Prudence, indeed, will dictate that governments long established should not be changed for light and transient causes; and, accordingly, all experience hath shown that mankind are more disposed to suffer, while evils are sufferable, than to right themselves by abolishing the forms to which they are accustomed. But, when a long train of abuses and usurpations, pursing invariably the same object, evinces a design to reduce them under absolute despotism, it is their right, it is their duty, to throw off such government, and to provide new guards for their future security.

QUESTIONS TO CONSIDER

1. In the Black Panthers' view, how do imperialism, capitalism, and racism harm Black Americans? What solutions do they propose?
2. The Black Panthers end their Ten Point Program with a lengthy quotation from the Declaration of Independence. How does quoting from this American founding document support their list of demands?

27.2 THIRD WORLD GAY REVOLUTION, "SIXTEEN POINT PLATFORM AND PROGRAM" (1970)*

The Third World Gay Revolution was a group of Black and Latinx Gay Liberation Front (GLF) activists who formed their own group to address the difficulties they faced as gay people of color. Members of the Third World Gay Revolution felt that they suffered oppression not only from homophobia, sexism, and capitalism, but from racism as well. Their platform outlining their beliefs and demands drew inspiration from Huey Newton's program for the Black Panther Party (see Source 27.1).

GLF groups were founded following the Stonewall Riot of 1969, in which an attempt by New York police to harass and arrest the gay patrons of the Stonewall Inn in Lower Manhattan sparked immediate resistance by hundreds of gay New Yorkers over the course of several days. The GLF resembled other left-wing groups of the 1960s and 1970s in that they rejected capitalism and imperialism, but what set them apart was that they focused particularly on challenging norms of heterosexuality and gender. Along with women's liberation groups, the GLF challenged the bounds of conventional sexuality and advocated for individuals' freedom to live in whatever way they felt right.

* Third World Gay Revolution, "Sixteen Point Platform and Program," November 11, 1970, reprinted in *Pinko* #1, October 15, 2019. Courtesy of Pinko Magazine; https://pinko.online/.

Our straight sisters and brothers must recognize and support that we, third world gay women and men, are equal in every way within the revolutionary ranks.

We each organize our people about different issues; but our struggles are the same against oppression, and we will defeat it together—Once we understand these struggles, and gain a love for our sisters and brothers involved in these struggles, we must learn how best to become involved in them.

The struggles of the peoples of the world are our fight as well; their victories are our victories and our victories are theirs. Our freedom will come only with their freedom.

Together, not alone, we must explore how we view ourselves, and analyze the assumptions behind our self-identity—We can then begin to crack the barriers of our varying illnesses, our passivity, sexual chauvinism, in essence, our inability to unabashedly love each other, to live, fight, and if necessary, die for the people of the earth.

As we begin to understand our place in the international revolution, and join with others in this understanding, we must develop the skills necessary to destroy the forces of repression and exploitation, so as to make it possible for a new woman and man to evolve in a society based on communal love.

While we understand that in the United States our main enemy is the socio-economic-political system of capitalism and the people who make profits off our sufferings, fights and divisions, we also recognize that we must struggle against any totalitarian, authoritarian, sex-controlled, repressive, irrational, reactionary, fascist government or government machine.

WHAT WE WANT, WHAT WE BELIEVE:

1. We want the right of self-determination for all third world and gay people, as well as control of the destinies of our communities.

   We believe that third world and gay people cannot be free until we are able to determine our own destinies. The system must be changed. Socialism is the answer.

2. We want the right of self-determination over the use of our bodies: The right to be gay, anytime, anyplace; The right to free physiological change

and modification of sex on demand; The right to free dress and adornment.

We believe that these are human rights which must be defended with our bodies being put on the line. The system as it now exists denies these basic human rights by implementing forced heterosexuality. The system must be changed. Socialism is the answer.

3. We want liberation for all women: We want free and safe birth control information and devices on demand. We want free 24 hour child care centers controlled by those who need and use them. We want a redefinition of education and motivation (especially for third world women) towards broader educational opportunities without limitations because of sex. We want truthful teaching of women's history. We want an end to hiring practices which make women and national minorities a readily available source of cheap labor confined to mind-rotting jobs under the worst conditions.

   We believe that the struggles of all oppressed groups under any form of government which does not meet the true needs of its people will eventually result in the overthrow of that government. The struggle for liberation of women is a struggle to be waged by all peoples. We must also struggle within ourselves and within our various movements to end this oldest form of oppression and its foundation—male chauvinism. We cannot develop a truly liberating form of socialism unless we fight these tendencies. The system must be changed. Socialism is the answer.

4. We want full protection of the law and social sanction for all human sexual self-expression and pleasure between consenting persons, including youth. We believe that present laws are oppressive to third world people, gay people, and the masses. Such laws expose the inequalities of capitalism, which can only exist in a state where there are oppressed people or groups. This must end. The system must be changed. Socialism is the answer.

5. We want the abolition of the institution of the bourgeois nuclear family.

   We believe that the bourgeois nuclear family perpetuates the false, categories of homosexuality and heterosexuality by creating sex roles, sex definitions and sexual exploitation. The bourgeois nuclear family as the basic unit of capitalism creates oppressive roles of homosexuality and heterosexuality. All oppressions originate within the nuclear family structure. Homosexuality is a threat to this family structure and therefore to capitalism. The mother is an instrument of reproduction and teaches the necessary values of capitalist society, i.e., racism, sexism, etc. from infancy on. The father physically enforces (upon the mother and children) the behavior necessary in a capitalist system, intelligence and competitiveness in young boys and passivity in young girls. Further, it is every child's right to develop in a non-sexist, non-racist, non-possessive atmosphere which is the responsibility of all people, including gays, to create. Therefore, the system must be changed. Socialism is the answer.

6. We want a free non-compulsory education system that teaches us our true identity and history, and presents the entire range of human sexuality without advocating any one form or style; that sex roles and determination of skills according to sex be eliminated from the school system; that language be modified so that no gender takes priority; and that gay people must share the responsibilities of education.

We believe that we have been taught to compete with our sisters and brothers for power, and from that competitive attitude grows sexism, racism, male and national chauvinism and distrust of our sisters and brothers. As we begin to understand these things within ourselves, we attempt to free ourselves of them and are moved toward a revolutionary consciousness. The system must be changed. Socialism is the answer.

7. We want guaranteed full equal employment for third world and gay people at all levels of production.

We believe that any system of government is responsible for giving every woman and man a guaranteed income or employment, regardless of sex or sexual preference. Being interested only in profits, capitalism cannot meet the needs of the people. The system must be changed. Socialism is the answer.

8. We want decent and free housing, fit shelter for human beings.

We believe that free shelter is a basic need and right which must not be denied on any grounds.

Landlords are capitalists, and, like all capitalists, are motivated only by the accumulation of profits, as opposed to the welfare of the people. Therefore, the system must be changed. Socialism is the answer.

9. We want to abolish the existing judicial system. We want all third world and gay people when brought to trial, to be tried by a people's court with a jury of their peers. A peer is a person from similar social, economic, geographical, racial, historical, environmental, and sexual background. We believe that the function of the judicial system under capitalism is to uphold the ruling class and keep the masses under control. The system must be changed. Socialism is the answer.

10. We want the reparation for and release of all third world, gay and all political prisoners from jails and mental institutions.

We believe that these people should be released because they have not received a fair and impartial trial. The system must be changed. Socialism is the answer.

11. We want the abolition of capital punishment, all forms of institutional punishment, and the penal system.

We want the establishment of psychiatric institutions for the humane treatment and rehabilitation of criminal persons as decided by the people's court. We want the establishment of a sufficient number of free and non-compulsory clinics for the treatment of sexual disturbances, as defined by the individual. We believe that the system must be changed. Socialism is the answer.

12. We want an immediate end to the fascist police force. We believe that the only way this can be accomplished is by putting the defense of the people in the hands of the people. The system must be changed. Socialism is the answer.

13. We want all third world and gay men to be exempt from compulsory military service, in the imperialist army. We want an end to military oppression both at home and abroad.

We believe that the only true army for oppressed people is the people's army and third world, gay people, and women should have full participation in the People's Revolutionary Army. The system must be changed. Socialism is the answer.

14. We want an end to all institutional religions because they aid in genocide by teaching superstition and hatred of third world people, homosexuals and women. We want a guarantee of freedom to express natural spirituality.

    We believe that institutionalized religions are an instrument of capitalism, therefore an enemy of the People. The system must be changed. Socialism is the answer.

15. We demand immediate non-discriminatory open admission/membership for radical homosexuals into all left-wing revolutionary groups and organizations and the right to caucus.

    We believe that so-called comrades who call themselves "revolutionaries" have failed to deal with their sexist attitudes. Instead they cling to male supremacy and therefore to the conditioned role of oppressors. Men still fight for the privileged position of man-on-the-top. Women quickly fall in line behind-their-men. By their counterrevolutionary struggle to maintain and to force heterosexuality and the nuclear family, they perpetuate decadent remnants of capitalism. To gain their anti-homosexual stance, they have used the weapons of the oppressor, thereby becoming the agent of the oppressor.

    It is up to men to realistically define masculinity, because it is they who, throughout their lives, have struggled to gain the unrealistic roles of "men." Men have always tried to reach this precarious position by climbing on the backs of women and homosexuals. "Masculinity" has been defined by capitalist society as the amount of possessions (including women) a man collects, and the amount of physical power gained over other men. Third world men have been denied even these false standards of "masculinity." Anti-homosexuality fosters sexual repressions, male-supremacy, weakness in revolutionary drive, and results in an inaccurate non-objective political perspective. Therefore, we believe that all left-wing revolutionary groups and organizations must immediately establish non-discriminatory, open admission/membership policies. The system must be changed. Socialism is the answer.

16. We want a new society—a revolutionary socialist society. We want liberation of humanity, free food, free shelter, free clothing, free transportation, free healthcare, free utilities, free education, free art for all. We want a society where the needs of the people come first. We believe that all people should share the labor and products of society, according to each one's needs and abilities, regardless of race, sex, age, or sexual preferences. We believe the land, technology, and the means of production belong to the people, and must be shared by the people collectively for the liberation of all.

REVOLUTIONARY SOCIALISM IS THE ANSWER. ALL POWER TO THE PEOPLE!

QUESTIONS TO CONSIDER

1. In what ways do the ideas and demands of the Third World Gay Revolution resemble those of other left-wing organizations from this era? What are some significant differences?

2. What does the Third World Gay Revolution hope to change about how Americans understand and practice sexuality? Why do they find existing norms oppressive?

27.3 YOUNG LORDS PARTY, "THIRTEEN POINTS PROGRAM AND PLATFORM" (1969)*

The Young Lords Party is a political and civil rights organization founded in 1968 to advocate for the self-determination of Puerto Rico and Latinx. Puerto Rico has been a territory of the United States since 1898, and Puerto Ricans have had American citizenship since 1917, but the island has no voting representatives in the US federal government and its residents cannot vote for any national office. Founded in Chicago, the Young Lords spread to multiple American cities including New York, which has a significant Puerto Rican population. Like other left-wing organizations of the 1960s and 1970s, the Young Lords opposed US imperialism and capitalism and attributed many challenges facing their communities to racist practices of the US government. Like the Black Panther Party, the Young Lords were targeted by the federal Counterintelligence Program (COINTELPRO), which attempted to disrupt their activism.

THE YOUNG LORDS PARTY IS A REVOLUTIONARY POLITICAL PARTY FIGHTING FOR THE LIBERATION OF ALL OPPRESSED PEOPLE

1. WE WANT SELF-DETERMINATION FOR PUERTO RICANS, LIBERATION OF THE ISLAND AND INSIDE THE UNITED STATES.

   For 500 years, first spain and then united states have colonized our country. Billions of dollars in profits leave our country for the united states every year. In every way we are slaves of the gringo. We want liberation and the Power in the hands of the People, not Puerto Rican exploiters. QUE VIVA PUERTO RICO LIBRE!

2. WE WANT SELF-DETERMINATION FOR ALL LATINOS.

   Our Latin Brothers and Sisters, inside and outside the united states, are oppressed by amerikkkan business. The Chicano people built the Southwest, and we support their right to control their lives and their land. The people of Santo Domingo continue to fight against gringo domination and its puppet generals. The armed liberation struggles in Latin America are part of the war of Latinos against imperialism. QUE VIVA LA RAZA!

3. WE WANT LIBERATION OF ALL THIRD WORLD PEOPLE.

   Just as Latins first slaved under spain and the yanquis, Black people, Indians, and Asians slaved to build the wealth of this country. For 400 years they have fought for freedom and dignity against racist Babylon. Third World people have led the fight for freedom. All the colored and oppressed peoples of the world are one nation under oppression. NO PUERTO RICAN IS FREE UNTIL ALL PEOPLE ARE FREE!

4. WE ARE REVOLUTIONARY NATIONALISTS AND OPPOSE RACISM.

   The Latin, Black, Indian and Asian people inside the u.s. are colonies fighting for liberation. We know that washington, wall street and city hall will try to make our nationalism into racism; but Puerto Ricans are of all colors and we resist racism. Millions of poor white people are rising up to demand freedom and we support them. These are the ones in the u.s. that are stepped on by the rules

* The Young Lords Party, "Young Lords Party: 13 Points Program and Platform," in *Caribe: The Young Lords Party 1969–1975* (New York, 1983), 17. Courtesy of Caribbean Cultural Center African Diaspora Institute (CCCADI), New York, NY.

and the government. We each organize our people, but our fights are against the same oppression and we will defeat it together. **POWER TO ALL OPPRESSED PEOPLE!**

5. **WE WANT EQUALITY FOR WOMEN. DOWN WITH MACHISMO AND MALE CHAUVINISM.**
Under capitalism, our women have been oppressed by both the society and our own men. The doctrine of machismo has been used by our men to take out their frustrations against their wives, sisters, mothers, and children. Men fight along with their sisters in the struggle for economic and social equality, and must recognize that sisters make up over half of the revolutionary army: sisters and brothers are equals fighting for people. **FORWARD SISTERS IN THE STRUGGLE!**

6. **WE WANT COMMUNITY CONTROL OF OUR INSTITUTIONS AND LAND.**
We want control of our communities by our people and programs to guarantee that all institutions serve the needs of our people. People's control of police, health services, churches, schools, housing, transportation and welfare are needed. We want an end to attacks on our land by urban removal, highway destruction, universities and corporations. **LAND BELONGS TO ALL THE PEOPLE!**

7. **WE WANT A TRUE EDUCATION OF OUR AFRO-INDIO CULTURE AND SPANISH LANGUAGE.**
We must learn our history of fighting against cultural, as well as economic genocide by the spaniards and now the yanqui. Revolutionary culture, culture of our people, is the only true teaching. **JIBARI SI, YANQUI NO!**

8. **WE OPPOSE CAPITALISTS AND ALLIANCES WITH TRAITORS.**
Puerto Rican rulers, or puppets of the oppressor, do not help our people. They are paid by the system to lead our people down blind alleys, just like the thousands of poverty pimps who keep our communities peaceful for business, or the street workers who keep gangs divided and blowing each other away. We want a society where the people socialistically control their labor. **VENCEREMOS!**

9. **WE OPPOSE THE AMERIKKKAN MILITARY.**
We demand immediate withdrawal of u.s. military forces and bases from Puerto Rico, VietNam and all oppressed communities inside and outside the u.s. No Puerto Rican should serve in the u.s. army against his Brothers and Sisters, for the only true army of oppressed people is the People's Liberation Army to fight all rulers. **U.S. OUT OF VIETNAM, FREE PUERTO RICO NOW!**

10. **WE WANT FREEDOM FOR ALL POLITICAL PRISONERS.**
No Puerto Rican should be in jail or prison, first because we are a nation, and amerikkka has no claims on us; second, because we have not been tried by our own people (peers). We also want all freedom fighters out of jail, since they are prisoners of the war for liberation. **FREE ALL POLITICAL PRISONERS AND PRISONERS OF WAR!**

11. **WE ARE INTERNATIONALISTS.**
Our people are brainwashed by television, radio, newspapers, schools, and books to oppose people in other countries fighting for their freedom. No longer will we believe these lies, because we have learned who the real enemy is and who are real friends are. We will defend our sisters and brothers around the world who fight for justice and are against the rich rulers of this country. **QUE VIVA CHE GUEVARA!**

12. **WE BELIEVE ARMED SELF-DEFENSE AND ARMED STRUGGLE ARE THE ONLY MEANS TO LIBERATION.**
We are opposed to violence—the violence of hungry children, illiterate adults, diseased old people, and the violence of poverty and profit. We have asked, petitioned, gone to courts, demonstrated peacefully, and voted for politicians full of empty promises. But we still ain't free. The time has come to defend the lives of our people against repression and for revolutionary war against the businessmen, politicians, and police. When a government oppresses our people, we have the right to abolish it and create a new one. **ARM OURSELVES TO DEFEND OURSELVES!**

13. **WE WANT A SOCIALIST SOCIETY.**
We want liberation, clothing, free food, education, health care, transportation, full employment and peace. We want a society where the needs of the people come first, and where we give solidarity and aid to the peoples of the world, not oppression and racism. **HASTA LA VICTORIA SIEMPRE!**

QUESTIONS TO CONSIDER

1. How does the legacy of colonialism inform the Young Lords' program and platform?
2. Why do the Young Lords oppose the American military in particular?

27.4 VISUAL SOURCE: COVER OF
MS. MAGAZINE (1972)*

Ms. was a monthly magazine co-founded by feminist activist Gloria Steinem (b. 1934) in 1971. The magazine published articles by women on topics that did not get attention in mainstream news media, with the goal of expanding the women's liberation movement by offering a space for women to read and write about issues that affected their lives. The cover of the magazine's first issue, pictured here, shows a tearful pregnant woman stylized as the Hindu god Kali and using her many arms to hold items symbolizing the responsibilities of an American housewife. The choice of a Hindu deity may have been influenced by the growing popularity of Hindu-inspired philosophy and religion in the United States during the 1960s and 1970s. Like other liberation movements of this era, *Ms.* represented an effort by a community to offer mutual aid and support by creating their own institutions that mainstream American society did not provide. The cover features articles discussing the value of "sisterhood" or mutual support among women, as well as the experiences of women who had chosen to have an abortion.

* GRANGER

QUESTIONS TO CONSIDER

1. What did the artist try to depict in this illustration about the experience of American women? Why would Steinem and the other editors have chosen this image for their first issue?

2. What does this magazine cover, both the illustration and the featured articles, tell us about the women's liberation movement in the early 1970s?

27.5 VISUAL SOURCE: HERBLOCK, *HOSTAGE* (1979)*

Throughout the 1970s gas prices rose considerably in the United States, primarily as a result of oil-producing nations responding to American foreign policy. In 1973 the Organization of the Petroleum Exporting Countries (OPEC) imposed an oil embargo on the US in response to American support for Israel, a country several OPEC nations were at war with. In 1979 revolutionaries in Iran captured over fifty Americans at the embassy in Tehran, holding them hostage to demand that the US government extradite the Shah Mohammed Pahlavi, while banning oil exports to the US. In this illustration published in the *Washington Post*, cartoon artist Herbert Block (1909–2001), also known as Herblock, parodies this crisis by depicting the United States as a frustrated driver taken hostage by rising gas prices. Because the US imported much of the oil Americans used for driving, the source of the gas hose binding the United States is its dependence on foreign oil. Like the American hostages in Tehran, Block argues, the US has been taken captive by high gas prices as a result of the country's dependence on oil imports from other nations.

QUESTIONS TO CONSIDER

1. What is the attitude of the American man in this cartoon? What does his posture convey about the American response to the gas crisis?
2. Why was dependence on foreign oil so concerning? Why did the United States seem to Block to be a hostage?

CHAPTER 28

A NEW CONSERVATISM AND ITS DISCONTENTS, 1980–1989

28.1 RONALD REAGAN, CAMPAIGN SPEECH AT THE COW PALACE IN SAN FRANCISCO (1966)*

Gubernatorial candidate Ronald Reagan (1911–2004) delivered this speech denouncing student activism while campaigning for governor in 1966. In the preceding years, the Berkeley campus of the University of California had become famous nationwide as a hotbed of left-leaning student activism. A series of mass protests over the course of 1964 and 1965 as part of the free speech movement had challenged university rules barring political activism on campus, and asserted students' rights to promote and organize for political causes. Reagan, a former New Deal Democrat, had become a rising star in the Republican Party following his vocal support of Barry Goldwater in 1964. He opposed a number of social welfare programs that he saw as an infringement on Americans' freedom and worried that civil rights legislation made the federal government too powerful. Reagan went on to win the election and served two terms as governor of California before being elected president in 1980.

There is a leadership gap and a morality and decency gap in Sacramento.

And there is no better illustration of that than what has been perpetrated on the Berkeley campus at the University of California at Berkeley where a small minority of beatniks, radicals and filthy speech advocates have brought such shame to and such a loss of confidence in a great University that applications for enrollment were down 21% this year 1967 and are expected to decline even further next years.

You have read about the report of the Senate Subcommittee on Un-American Activities – its charges that the campus has become a rallying point for Communists and a center of sexual misconduct.

Now I have not seen that report—it has not yet been made public—but I do have information that

---

* Ronald Reagan, "The Morality Gap at Berkeley," speech at Cow Palace, May 12, 1966, in *The Creative Society* (Devin-Adair Co., 1968), 125–29.

verifies at least part of that report. Some incidents in this report are so bad, so contrary to our standards of decent human behavior that I cannot recite them to you in detail.

But there is clear evidence of the sort of things that should not be permitted on a university campus.

The report tells us that many of those attending were clearly of high-school age. The hall was entirely dark except for the light from two movie screens. On these screens the nude torsos of men and women were portrayed from time to time in suggestive positions and movements.

Three rock and roll bands played simultaneously. The smell of marijuana was thick throughout the hall. There were signs that some of those present had taken dope. There were indications of other happenings that cannot be mentioned here.

How could this happen on the campus of a great University? It happened because those responsible abdicated their responsibilities.

The dance was only called to a halt when janitors finally cut off the power in the gymnasium forcing those attending to leave.

And this certainly is not the only sign of a leadership gap on the campus.

It began when so-called "free-speech advocates," who in truth have no appreciation of freedom, were allowed to assault and humiliate an officer of the law. This was the moment when the ringleaders should have been taken by the scruff of the neck and thrown off of the campus—permanently.

It continued through the filthy speech movement, through activities of the Vietnam Day Committee and all this has been allowed to go on in the name of academic freedom.

What in Heaven's name does academic freedom have to do with rioting, with anarchy, with attempts to destroy the primary purpose of the University which is to educate our young people?

This is why I know there must be some substance to the Committee's report. This is why I am also convinced that just the issuance of that report is not enough, not enough for the people of California and not enough for those involved.

These charges made by the Committee are the results of private investigations. They must not be

brought out in public hearings at which those involved must be forced to testify.

Otherwise there is a real danger that the charges will be swept under the rug.

These charges must neither be swept away under the rug by a timid administration or by public apologists for the University. The public has a right to know from open hearings whether the situation at Berkeley is as the report says.

The citizens who pay the taxes that support the University also have a right to know that, if the situation is as the report says, that those responsible will be fired, that the University will be cleaned up and restored to its position as a major institution of learning and research.

The Governor has abdicated his responsibility in this area. His only answer has been to ask the Board of Regents to investigate. This is a straight coverup. What kind of political nonsense is it to ask the Board of Regents to investigate a situation in which it may be involved?

For this reason I today have called on the State Legislature to hold public hearings into the charges of Communism and blatant sexual misbehavior on the campus. I have sent personal wires to Senator Hugh Burns, the President Pro Tern of the Senate and to Assembly Speaker Jesse Unruh urging that they hold joint public hearings.

Only in this way can we get at the facts. Only this way can we find who is responsible for the degradation of a great University.

Only this way can we determine what steps must be taken to restore the University to its position, steps that might go even beyond what I have already suggested.

Yes, there are things that can be done at the University even if a hearing is never held. This administration could make changes. It could demand that the faculty jurisdictions be limited to academic matters.

It could demand that the administrators be told that it is their job to administer the University properly and if you don't we will find someone who will.

The faculty could also be given a code of conduct that would force them to serve as examples of good behavior and decency for the young people in their charge.

When those who advocate an open mind keep it open at both ends with no thought process in the middle, the open mind becomes a hose for any idea that comes along. If scholars are to be recognized as having a right to press their particular value judgments, perhaps the time has come also for institutions of higher learning to assert themselves as positive forces in the battles for men's minds.

This could mean they would insist upon mature, responsible conduct and respect for the individual from their faculty members and might even call on them to be proponents of those ethical and moral standards demanded by the great majority of our society.

These things could be done and should be done. The people not only have a right to know what is going on at their universities, they have a right to expect the best from those responsible for it.

QUESTIONS TO CONSIDER

1. What sort of misbehavior does Reagan believe is occurring at the University of California at Berkeley? Why does this bother him?
2. What values does Reagan claim to hold? How does he want those values to be reflected in public institutions?

28.2 PHYLLIS SCHLAFLY, "WHAT'S WRONG WITH 'EQUAL RIGHTS' FOR WOMEN?" (1972)*

Phyllis Schlafly (1924–2016) was a conservative political activist and newsletter editor who campaigned on a variety of issues, especially those related to social and gender norms. Schlafly was best known as a leader in the opposition to the Equal Rights Amendment (ERA), a proposed constitutional amendment guaranteeing equal rights regardless of gender. Schlafly spoke and wrote frequently in favor of the nuclear family and traditional gender roles and opposed feminism and abortion rights. Schlafly viewed the ERA as an attempt to degrade women by stripping them of what she saw as a privileged position in American law and society.

Of all the classes of people who ever lived, the American woman is the most privileged. We have the most rights and rewards, and the fewest duties. Our unique status is the result of a fortunate combination of circumstances.

1. We have the immense good fortune to live in a civilization which respects the family as the basic unit of society. This respect is part and parcel of our laws and our customs. It is based on the fact of life—which no legislation or agitation can erase—that women have babies and men don't.

If you don't like this fundamental difference, you will have to take up your complaint with God because He created us this way. The fact that women, not men, have babies is not the fault of selfish and domineering men, or of the establishment, or of any clique of conspirators who want to oppress women. It's simply the way God made us.

---

* Phyllis Schlafly, "What's Wrong with 'Equal Rights' for Women?" *The Phyllis Schlafly Report* 5, no. 7 (February 1972): 1–4.

Our Judeo-Christian civilization has developed the law and custom that, since women must bear the physical consequences of the sex act, men must be required to bear the *other* consequences and pay in other ways. These laws and customs decree that a man must carry his share by physical protection and financial support of his children and of the woman who bears his children, and also by a code of behavior which benefits and protects both the woman and the children.

THE GREATEST ACHIEVEMENT OF WOMEN'S RIGHTS

This is accomplished by the institution of the family. Our respect for the family as the basic unit of society, which is ingrained in the laws and customs of our Judeo-Christian civilization, is the greatest single achievement in the entire history of women's rights. It assures a woman the most precious and important right of all—the right to keep her own baby and to be supported and protected in the enjoyment of watching her baby grow and develop.

The institution of the family is advantageous for women for many reasons. After all, what do we want out of life? To love and be loved? Mankind has not discovered a better nest for a lifetime of reciprocal love. A sense of achievement? A man may search 30 to 40 years for accomplishment in his profession. A woman can enjoy real achievement when she is young—by having a baby. She can have the satisfaction of doing a job well—and being recognized for it.

Do we want financial security? We are fortunate to have the great legacy of Moses, the Ten Commandments, especially this one: "Honor thy father and thy mother that thy days may be long upon the land." Children are a woman's best social security—her best guarantee of social benefits such as old age pension, unemployment compensation, workman's compensation, and sick leave. The family gives a woman the physical, financial and emotional security of the home—for all her life.

THE FINANCIAL BENEFITS OF CHIVALRY

2. The second reason why American women are a privileged group is that we are the beneficiaries of a tradition of special respect for women which

dates from the Christian Age of Chivalry. The honor and respect paid to Mary, the Mother of Christ, resulted in all women, in effect, being put on a pedestal.

This respect for women is not just the lip service that politicians pay to "God, Motherhood, and the Flag." It is not—as some youthful agitators seem to think – just a matter of opening doors for women, seeing that they are seated first, carrying their bundles, and helping them in and out of automobiles. Such good manners are merely the superficial evidences of a total attitude toward women which expresses itself in many more tangible ways, such as money.

In other civilizations, such as the African and the American Indian, the men strut around wearing feathers and beads and hunting and fishing (great sport for men!), while the women do all the hard, tiresome drudgery including the tilling of the soil (if any is done), the hewing of wood, the making of fires, the carrying of water, as well as the cooking, sewing and caring for babies.

This is not the American way because we were lucky enough to inherit the traditions of the Age of Chivalry. In America, a man's first significant purchase is a diamond for his bride, and the largest financial investment of his life is a home for her to live in. American husbands work hours of overtime to buy a fur piece or other finery to keep their wives in fashion, and to pay premiums on their life insurance policies to provide for her comfort when she is a widow (benefits in which he can never share).

In the states which follow the English common law, a wife has a dower right in her husband's real estate which he cannot take away from her during life or by his will. A man cannot dispose of his real estate without his wife's signature. Any sale is subject to her ⅓ interest.

Women fare even better in the states which follow the Spanish and French community-property laws, such as California, Arizona, Texas and Louisiana. The basic philosophy of the Spanish/French law is that a wife's work in the home is just as valuable as a husband's work at his job. Therefore, in community-property states, a wife owns one-half of all the property and income her husband earns during their marriage, and he cannot take it away from her.

In Illinois, as a result of agitation by "equal rights" fanatics, the real-estate dower laws were repealed as of January 1, 1972. This means that in Illinois a husband can now sell the family home, spend the money on his girlfriend or gamble it away, and his faithful wife of 30 years can no longer stop him. "Equal rights" fanatics have also deprived women in Illinois and in some other states of most of their basic common-law rights to recover damages for breach of promise to marry, seduction, criminal conversation, and alienation of affections.

THE REAL LIBERATION OF WOMEN

3. The third reason why American women are so well off is that the great American free enterprise system has produced remarkable inventors who have lifted the backbreaking "women's work" from our shoulders.

In other countries and in other eras, it was truly said that "Man may work from sun to sun, but woman's work is never done." Other women have labored every waking hour—preparing food on wood-burning stoves, making flour, baking bread in stone ovens, spinning yarn, making clothes, making soap, doing the laundry by hand, heating irons, making candles for light and fires for warmth, and trying to nurse their babies through illnesses without medical care.

The real liberation of women from the backbreaking drudgery of centuries is the American free enterprise system which stimulated inventive geniuses to pursue their talents—and we all reap the profits. The great heroes of women's liberation are not the straggly-haired women on television talk shows and picket lines, but Thomas Edison who brought the miracle of electricity to our homes to give light and to run all those labor-saving devices – the equivalent, perhaps, of a half-dozen household servants for every middle-class American woman. Or Elias Howe who gave us the sewing machine which resulted in such an abundance of readymade clothing. Or Clarence Birdseye who invented the process for freezing foods. Or Henry Ford, who mass-produced the automobile so that it is within the price-range of every American, man or woman.

A major occupation of women in other countries is doing their daily shopping for food, which requires carrying their own containers and standing in line at dozens of small shops. They buy only small portions because they can't carry very much and have no refrigerator or freezer to keep a surplus anyway. Our American free enterprise system has given us the gigantic food and packaging industry and beautiful supermarkets, which provide an endless variety of foods, prepackaged for easy carrying and a minimum of waiting. In America, women have the freedom from the slavery of standing in line for daily food.

Thus, household duties have been reduced to only a few hours a day, leaving the American woman with plenty of time to moonlight. She can take a full or part-time paying job, or she can indulge to her heart's content in a tremendous selection of interesting educational or cultural or homemaking activities.

THE FRAUD OF THE EQUAL RIGHTS AMENDMENT

In the last couple of years, a noisy movement has sprung up agitating for "women's rights." Suddenly, everywhere we are afflicted with aggressive females on television talk shows yapping about how mistreated American women are, suggesting that marriage has put us in some kind of "slavery," that housework is menial and degrading, and—perish the thought—that women are discriminated against. New "women's liberation" organizations are popping up, agitating and demonstrating, serving demands on public officials, getting wide press coverage always, and purporting to speak for some 100,000,000 American women.

It's time to set the record straight. The claim that American women are downtrodden and unfairly treated is the fraud of the century. The truth is that American women never had it so good. Why should we lower ourselves to "equal rights" when we already have the status of special privilege?

The proposed Equal Rights Amendment states: "Equality of rights under the law shall not be denied or abridged by the United States or by any state on account of sex." So what's wrong with that? Well, here are a few examples of what's wrong with it.

This Amendment will absolutely and positively make women subject to the draft. Why any woman would support such a ridiculous and un-American proposal as this is beyond comprehension. Why any Congressman who had any regard for his wife, sister or daughter would support such a proposition is just as hard to understand. Foxholes are bad enough for men, but they certainly are not the place for women—and we should reject any proposal which would put them there in the name of "equal rights."

It is amusing to watch the semantic chicanery of the advocates of the Equal Rights Amendment when confronted with this issue of the draft. They evade, they sidestep, they try to muddy up the issue, but they cannot deny that the Equal Rights Amendment will positively make women subject to the draft. Congresswoman Margaret Heckler's answer to this question was, Don't worry, it will take two years for the Equal Rights Amendment to go into effect, and we can rely on President Nixon to end the Vietnam War before then!

Literature distributed by Equal Rights Amendment supporters confirms that "under the Amendment a draft law which applied to men would apply also to women." The Equal Rights literature argues that this would be good for women so they can achieve their "equal rights" in securing veterans' benefits.

Another bad effect of the Equal Rights Amendment is that it will abolish a woman's right to child support and alimony, and substitute what the women's libbers think is a more "equal" policy, that "such decisions should be within the discretion of the Court and should be made on the economic situation and need of the parties in the case."

Under present American laws, the man is *always* required to support his wife and each child he caused to be brought into the world. Why should women abandon these good laws—by trading them for something so nebulous and uncertain as the "discretion of the Court"?

The law now requires a husband to support his wife as best as his financial situation permits, but a wife is not required to support her husband (unless he is about to become a public charge). A husband cannot demand that his wife go to work to help pay for family expenses. He has the duty of financial support under our laws and customs. Why should we abandon these mandatory wife-support and child-support laws so that a wife would have an "equal" obligation to take a job?

By law and custom in America, in case of divorce, the mother always is given custody of her children unless there is overwhelming evidence of mistreatment, neglect or bad character. This is our special privilege because of the high rank that is placed on motherhood in our society. Do women really want to give up this special privilege and lower themselves to "equal rights", so that the mother gets one child and the father gets the other? I think not.

THE RIGHT NOT TO TAKE A JOB

Passage of the Equal Rights Amendment would open up a Pandora's box of trouble for women. It would deprive the American woman of many of the fundamental special privileges we now enjoy, and especially the greatest rights of all: (1) NOT to take a job, (2) to keep her baby, and (3) to be supported by her husband.

How have the proponents of the Equal Rights Amendment been so successful that it passed the House of Representatives in 1971 by a large margin? There are three reasons. First, most people mistakenly believe that "equal rights" means simply "equal pay for equal work," and we are all in favor of this. But this goal has already been practically achieved by legislation, and the remaining violations can also be wiped out by legislation. Only 12 states still have obsolete discriminatory laws.

Second, Equal Rights Amendment literature lists many women's organizations as supporters. Most of these organizations probably gave their endorsement after being told that this Amendment will bring better jobs and more pay for women, but were never told what basic rights women would give up. That is the way, for example, that it happened at the October 1971 Convention of the National Federation of Republican Women, where the tight little clique running things from the top presented speaker after speaker to promote the Equal Rights Amendment, but gave no "equal rights" to delegates who wanted to speak against it. The 1971 officers of the NFRW even published intemperate attacks on the Republican Congressmen who voted for an amendment to the Equal Rights Amendment which would exempt women from the draft and permit states to enact "reasonable" laws based on sex differences.

Thirdly, the women's lib agitators caught the Congressmen badly off guard and they felt they could not risk being labeled "anti-women". The Congressmen simply didn't hear from the millions of happily married women who believe in the laws which protect the family and require the husband to support his wife and children. They only heard from the few but noisy unhappy women.

EQUAL RIGHTS IN RUSSIA

At women's lib rallies, some of the fiery speakers cite Russia as an example of a country where women have equal rights. The Soviet Constitution guarantees: "Woman in the U.S.S.R. is accorded equal rights with men in all spheres of economic, stale, cultural, public and political life."

"Equal rights" in the Soviet Union means that the Russian woman is *obliged* to put her baby in a state-operated nursery or kindergarten so she can join the labor force. Under Soviet law, a woman (as well as a man) can be jailed for refusing to engage in "socially useful labor" or for leading a "parasitic way of life."

"Equal rights" in Russia means that the women do the heavy, dirty work American women do not do—but men are still the bosses. Russian women have "equal rights" to mine coal, load cargo ships, work in heavy construction, and labor in the fields. A typical garbage pickup learn consists of two women hauling the garbage and a man driving the truck. A typical road construction "brigade" consists of a dozen women digging ditches while a male "brigadier" supervises. Of course, the women still do all the housework (without electrical appliances) and all the standing in line to buy food for their families.

A Russian woman journalist recently wrote this in a report called "Unbearable Burden," about women's employment in heavy construction work: "The years given over to a 'male' occupation can rob her of the main thing: her happiness as a woman, the joy of motherhood." Abortions are available for the asking and the average Russian woman has had several, while limiting herself to one or two children.

Under Soviet-style "equal rights," the men still hold all the top jobs. Nine out of every ren plant managers are men. Three out of four school principals are men. There is no woman member in the all-powerful Politburo or Party Secretarial.

WHAT "WOMEN'S LIB" REALLY MEANS

Many women are under the mistaken impression that "women's lib" means more job employment opportunities for women, equal pay for equal work, appointments of women to high positions, admitting more women to medical schools, and other desirable objectives which all women favor. We all support these purposes, as well as any necessary legislation which would bring them about.

But all this is only a sweet syrup which covers the deadly poison masquerading as "women's lib." The women's libbers are radicals who are waging a total assault on the family, on marriage, and on children. Don't take my word for it—read their own literature and prove to yourself what these characters are trying to do.

The most pretentious of the women's liberation magazines is called *Ms.*, and subtitled "The New Magazine For Women," with Gloria Steinem listed as president and secretary.

Reading the Spring 1972 issue of *Ms.* gives a good understanding of women's lib, and the people who promote it. It is anti-family, anti-children, and pro-abortion. It is a series of sharp-tongued, high-pitched whining complaints by unmarried women. They view the home as a prison, and the wife and mother as a slave. To these women's libbers, marriage means dirty dishes and dirty laundry. One article lauds a woman's refusal to carry up the family laundry as "an act of extreme courage." Another tells how satisfying it is to be a lesbian. (page 117)

The women's libbers don't understand that most women want to be wife, mother and homemaker—and are happy in that role. The women's libbers actively resent the mother who stays at home with her children and likes it that way. The principal purpose of *Ms.*'s shrill tirade is to sow seeds of discontent among happy, married women so that all women can be unhappy in some new sisterhood of frustrated togetherness.

Obviously intrigued by the 170 clauses of exemptions from marital duties given to Jackie Kennedy, and the special burdens imposed on Aristotle Onassis, in the pre-marriage contract they signed, *Ms.* recommends two women's lib marriage contracts. The "utopian marriage contract" has a clause on "sexual rights and freedoms" which approves "arrangements such as having Tuesdays off from one another," and the husband giving "his consent to abortion in advance."

The "Shulmans' marriage agreement" includes such petty provisions as "wife strips beds, husband remakes them," and "Husband does dishes on Tuesday, Thursday and Sunday. Wife does Monday, Wednesday and Saturday, Friday is split . . ." If the baby cries in the night, the chore of "handling" the baby is assigned as follows: "Husband does Tuesday, Thursday and Sunday. Wife does Monday, Wednesday and Saturday, Friday is split . . ." Presumably, if the baby cries for his mother on Tuesday night, he would be informed that the marriage contract prohibits her from answering.

Of course, it is possible, in such a loveless home, that the baby would never call for his mother at all.

Who put up the money to launch this 130-page slick-paper assault on the family and motherhood? A count of the advertisements in *Ms.* shows that the principal financial backer is the liquor industry. There are 26 liquor ads in this one initial issue. Of these, 13 are expensive full-page color ads, as opposed to only 18 full-page ads from all other sources combined, most of which are in the cheaper black-and-white.

Another women's lib magazine, called *Women*, tells the American woman that she is a prisoner in the "solitary confinement" and "isolation" of marriage. The magazine promises that it will provide women with "escape from isolation . . . release from boredom," and that it will "break the barriers . . . that separate wife, mistress and secretary . . . heterosexual women and homosexual women."

These women's libbers do, indeed, intend to "break the barriers" of the Ten Commandments and the sanctity of the family. It hasn't occurred to them that a woman's best "escape from isolation and boredom" is—not a magazine subscription to boost her "stifled ego"—but a husband and children who love her.

The first issue of *Women* contains 68 pages of such proposals as "The BITCH Manifesto," which promotes the line that "Bitch is Beautiful and that we have nothing to lose. Nothing whatsoever." Another article promotes an organization called W.I.T.C.H. (Women's International Terrorist Conspiracy from Hell), "an action arm of Women's Liberation."

In intellectual circles, a New York University professor named Warren T. Farrell has provided the rationale for why men should support women's lib. When his speech to the American Political Science Association Convention is stripped of its egghead verbiage, his argument is that men should eagerly look forward to the day when they can enjoy free sex and not have to pay for it. The husband will no longer be "saddled with the tremendous guilt feelings" when he leaves his wife with nothing after she has given him her best years. If a husband loses his job, he will no longer feel compelled to take any job to support his family. A husband can go "out with the boys" to have a drink without feeling guilty. Alimony will be eliminated.

WOMEN'S LIBBERS DO NOT SPEAK FOR US

The "women's lib" movement is *not* an honest effort to secure better jobs for women who want or need to work outside the home. This is just the superficial sweet-talk to win broad support for a radical "movement." Women's lib is a total assault on the role of the American woman as wife and mother, and on the family as the basic unit of society.

Women's libbers are trying to make wives and mothers unhappy with their career, make them feel that they are "second-class citizens" and "abject slaves." Women's libbers are promoting free sex instead of the "slavery" of marriage. They are promoting Federal "day-care centers" for babies instead of homes. They are promoting abortions instead of families.

Why should we trade in our special privileges and honored status for the alleged advantage of working in an office or assembly line? Most women would rather cuddle a baby than a typewriter or factory machine. Most women find that it is easier to get along with a husband than a foreman or office manager. Offices and factories require many more menial and repetitious chores than washing dishes and ironing shirts.

Women's libbers *do not* speak for the majority of American women. American women do *not* want to be liberated from husbands and children. We do *not* want to trade our birthright of the special privileges of

American women—for the mess of pottage called the Equal Rights Amendment.

Modern technology and opportunity have not discovered any nobler or more satisfying or more creative career for a woman than marriage and motherhood. The wonderful advantage that American women have is that we can have all the rewards of that number-one career, and still moonlight with a second one to suit our intellectual, cultural or financial tastes or needs.

And why should the men acquiesce in a system which gives preferential rights and lighter duties to women? In return, the men get the pearl of great price: a happy home, a faithful wife, and children they adore.

If the women's libbers want to reject marriage and motherhood, it's a free country and that is their choice. But let's not permit these women's libbers to get away with pretending to speak for the rest of us. Let's not permit this tiny minority to degrade the role that most women prefer. Let's not let these women's libbers deprive wives and mothers of the rights we now possess.

Tell your Senators NOW that you want them to vote NO on the Equal Rights Amendment. Tell your television and radio stations that you want equal time to present the case FOR marriage and motherhood.

QUESTIONS TO CONSIDER

1. What does Schlafly fear will be the negative consequences of the ERA? How does the ERA conflict with her world view?
2. How would you describe Schlafly's philosophy of the American family? What does she value in relationships between men and women?

28.3 JERRY FALWELL, "THE FIVE MAJOR PROBLEMS MORAL AMERICANS NEED TO BE READY TO FACE" (1980)*

Jerry Falwell (1933–2007) was a Baptist pastor best known for founding Moral Majority, a political organization that encouraged a variety of socially conservative policies and the election of Republicans to office, in 1979. Falwell encouraged conservative evangelicals to register to vote and to be sure they voted regularly for candidates who held conservative views on a variety of social issues including opposition to pornography, abortion, prostitution, equal rights for gays and lesbians, and drug use. Falwell and Moral Majority were crucial to establishing an alliance between the Republican Party and conservative evangelical Christians. With the influence of Falwell and other socially conservative leaders, the Republicans embraced social conservatism as a core litmus test for the party.

In light of our present moral condition, we as a nation are quickly approaching the point of no return. There can be no doubt that the sin of America is severe. We are literally approaching the brink of national disaster. Many have exclaimed, "If God does not judge America soon, He will have to apologize to Sodom and Gomorrah." In almost every aspect of our society, we have flaunted our sinful behavior in the very face of God Himself. Our movies, television programs, magazines, and entertainment in general are morally bankrupt and spiritually corrupt.

We have become one of the most blatantly sinful nations of all time. We dare not continue to excuse ourselves on the basis of God's past blessing in our national heritage. The time for a national repentance of God's people has now come to America. . . .

Is there no hope? Is our doom inevitable? Can the hand of God's judgment not be stayed? Many of us are convinced that it can. We believe that there is yet an opportunity for a reprieve in God's judgment of this great nation. But that hope rests in the sincerity of national repentance led by the people of God. . . .

While sins of America are certainly many, let us summarize the five major problems that have political consequences, political implications, that moral Americans need to be ready to face.

1. ABORTION—Nine men, by majority vote, said it was okay to kill unborn children. In 1973, two hundred million Americans and four hundred thousand pastors stood by and did little to stop it. Every year millions of babies are murdered in America, and most of us want to forget that it is happening. The Nazis murdered six million Jews, and certainly the Nazis fell under the hand of the judgment of God for these atrocities. So-called Christian America has murdered more unborn innocents than that. How do we think that we shall escape the judgment of God?

2. HOMOSEXUALITY—In spite of the fact that the Bible clearly designates this sin as an act of a "reprobate mind" for which God "gave them up" (Rm. 1:26–28), our government seems determined to legalize homosexuals as a legitimate "minority." Even the ancient Greeks, among whom homosexuality was fairly prevalent, never legally condoned its practice. Plato himself called it "abnormal." If

our nation legally recognizes homosexuality, we will put ourselves under the same hand of judgment as Sodom and Gomorrah.

3. PORNOGRAPHY—The four-billion-dollar-per-year pornographic industry is probably the most devastating moral influence of all upon our young people. Sex magazines deliberately increase the problem of immoral lust and thus provoke increased adultery, prostitution, and sexual child abuse. . . .

4. HUMANISM—The contemporary philosophy that glorifies man as man, apart from God, is the ultimate outgrowth of evolutionary science and secular education. In his new book *The Battle for the Mind*, Dr. Tim LaHaye argues that the full admission of humanism as the religion of secular education came after prayer and Bible reading were excluded from our public schools. Ultimately, humanism rests upon the philosophy of existentialism, which emphasizes that one's present existence is the true meaning and purpose of life. Existentialism has become the religion of the public schools. Applied to psychology, it postulates a kind of moral neutrality that is detrimental to Christian ethics. In popular terminology it explains, "Do your own thing," and "If it feels good, do it!" It is an approach to life that has no room for God and makes man the measure of all things.

5. THE FRACTURED FAMILY—With a skyrocketing divorce rate, the American family may well be on the verge of extinction in the next twenty years. Even the recent White House Conference on Families has called for an emphasis on diverse family forums (common-law, communal, homosexual, and transsexual "marriages"). The Bible pattern of the family has been virtually discarded by modern American society. Our movies and magazines have glorified the physical and emotional experience of sex without love to the point that most Americans do not even consider love to be important at all anymore. Bent on self-gratification, we have reinterpreted our moral values in light of our immoral life styles. Since the family is the basic unit of society, and since the family is desperately in trouble today, we can conclude that our society itself is in danger of total collapse. We are not moving toward

an alternate family life style, we are moving closer to the brink of destruction. . . .

Moral Americans can make the difference in America if we are willing to exert the effort to make our feelings known and if we are willing to make the necessary sacrifices to get the job done. . . .

To change America we must be involved, and this includes three areas of political action:

1. REGISTRATION

A recent national poll indicated that eight million American evangelicals are not registered to vote. I am convinced that this is one of the major sins of the church today. Until concerned Christian citizens become registered voters there is very little that we can do to change the tide of political influence on the social issues in our nation. Those who object to Christians being involved in the political process are ultimately objecting to Christians being involved in the social process. The political process is really nothing more than a realization of the social process. For us to divorce ourselves from society would be to run into the kind of isolationism and monasticism that characterized the medieval hermits. Many Christians are not even aware of the importance of registering to vote. It is perfectly legal, for example, for a deputy registrar to come right to your local church at a designated time and register the entire congregation. I am convinced that those of us who are pastors have an obligation to urge our people to register to vote. I am more concerned that people exercise their freedom to vote than I am concerned for whom they vote.

2. INFORMATION

Many moral Americans are unaware of the real issues affecting them today. Many people do not know the voting record of their congressman and have no idea how he is representing them on political issues that have moral implications. This is one of the major reasons why we have established the Moral Majority organization. We want to keep the public informed on the vital moral issues. The Moral Majority, Inc., is a nonprofit organization, with headquarters in Washington, D.C. Our goal is to exert a significant influence on the spiritual and moral direction of our nation by: (a) mobilizing the grassroots of moral Americans in one clear and effective voice; (b) informing the moral majority what is going on behind their backs in Washington and in state legislatures across the country; (c) lobbying intensely in Congress to defeat left-wing, social welfare bills that will further erode our precious freedom; (d) pushing for positive legislation such as that to establish the Family Protection Agency, which will ensure a strong, enduring America; and (e) helping the moral majority in local communities to fight pornography, homosexuality, the advocacy of immorality in school textbooks, and other issues facing each and every one of us.

Christians must keep America great by being willing to go into the halls of Congress, by getting laws passed that will protect the freedom and liberty of her citizens. The Moral Majority, Inc., was formed to acquaint Americans everywhere with the tragic decline in our nation's morals and to provide leadership in establishing an effective coalition of morally active citizens who are (a) prolife, (b) profamily, (c) promoral, and (d) proAmerican. If the vast majority of Americans (84 per cent, according to George Gallup) still believe the Ten Commandments are valid today, why are we permitting a few leading amoral humanists and naturalists to take over the most influential positions in this nation?

Tim LaHaye has formed a code of minimum moral standards dictated by the Bible; his code would be used to evaluate the stand of candidates on moral issues. These minimum standards are:

a. Do you agree that this country was founded on a belief in God and the moral principles of the Bible? Do you concur that this country has been departing from those principles and needs to return to them?

b. Would you favor stricter laws relating to the sale of pornography?

c. Do you favor stronger laws against the use and sale of hard drugs?

d. Are you in favor of legalizing marijuana?

e. Would you favor legalizing prostitution?

f. Do you approve of abortions on demand when the life of the mother is not in danger?

g. Do you favor laws that would increase homosexual rights?

h. Would you vote to prevent known homosexuals to teach in schools?

i. Do you favor capital punishment for capital offenses?

j. Do you favor the right of parents to send their children to private schools?

k. Do you favor voluntary prayer in the public schools?

l. Do you favor removal of the tax-exempt status of churches?

m. Do you favor removal of the tax-exempt status of church-related schools?

n. Do you believe that government should remove children from their parents' home except in cases of physical abuse?

o. Do you favor sex education, contraceptives, or abortions for minors without parental consent?

p. Except in wartime or dire emergency, would you vote for government spending that exceeds revenue?

q. Do you favor a reduction in taxes to allow families more spendable income?

r. Do you favor a reduction in government?

s. Do you favor passage of the Equal Rights Amendment?

t. Do you favor busing schoolchildren out of their neighborhood to achieve racial integration?

u. Do you favor more federal involvement in education?

The answers to these questions would be evaluated in the light of scriptural principles. . . .

3. MOBILIZATION

The history of the church includes the history of Christians' involvement in social issues . . .

America was born in her churches, and she must be reborn there as well. The time has come for pastors and church leaders to clearly and boldly proclaim the Gospel of regeneration in Christ Jesus. We need a return to God and to the Bible as never before in the history of America. Undoubtedly we are at the edge of eternity. Some are already referring to us as "post-Christian America." We have stretched the rubber band of morality too far already. A few more stretches and it will undoubtedly snap forever. When that happens we will become like all the other nations preceding us who've fallen under the judgment of God. I love America not because of her pride, her wealth, or her prestige; I love America because she, above all the nations of the world, has honored the principles of the Bible. America has been great because she has been good . . .

I am convinced that we need a spiritual and moral revival in America if America is to survive the twentieth century. The time for action is now; we dare not wait for someone else to take up the banner of righteousness in our generation. We have already waited too long . . .

Right living must be re-established as an American way of life. We as American citizens must recommit ourselves to the faith of our fathers and to the premises and moral foundations upon which this country was established. Now is the time to begin calling America back to God, back to the Bible, back to morality! We must be willing to live by the moral convictions that we claim to believe. There is no way that we will ever be willing to die for something for which we are not willing to live. The authority of Bible morality must once again be recognized as the legitimate guiding principle of our nation. Our love for our fellow man must ever be grounded in the truth and never be allowed to blind us from the truth that is the basis of our love for our fellow man.

As a pastor and as a parent I am calling my fellow American citizens to unite in a moral crusade for righteousness in our generation. It is time to call America back to her moral roots. It is time to call America back to God. We need a revival of righteous living based on a proper confession of sin and repentance of heart if we are to remain the land of the free and the home of the brave! I am convinced that God is calling millions of Americans in the so-often silent majority to join in the moral-majority crusade to turn America around in our lifetime. Won't you begin now to pray with us for revival in America? Let us unite our hearts and lives together for the cause of a new America . . . a moral America in which righteousness will exalt this nation. Only as we do this can we exempt ourselves from one day having to look our children in the eyes and answer this searching question: "Mom and Dad, where were you the day freedom died in America?"

The choice is now ours.

QUESTIONS TO CONSIDER

1. What problems does Falwell identify in American society? What solutions does he propose?
2. What does Falwell understand the political role of Christians to be? In what ways does he think American laws and society ought to reflect his interpretation of Christian values?

28.4 NATIONAL SECURITY COUNCIL, DIRECTIVE NO. 75 ON US RELATIONS WITH THE USSR (1983)

This directive, authored two years into Ronald Reagan's (1911–2004) presidency, outlined the president's goals for how the United States should approach relations with the USSR. When he took office in 1981, Reagan sought to reverse the foreign policy of his predecessor, Jimmy Carter, who had encouraged détente or de-escalation with USSR leaders. Reagan authorized a renewed military buildup to confront the USSR, and approved money and arms for groups fighting the USSR in places such as Afghanistan. Reagan also supported ambitious but sometimes unfeasible defense programs such as the Strategic Defense Initiative (SDI), a plan to use space-based technology to prevent a ballistic missile attack on the United States. Reagan saw the USSR, and communism more generally, as an "evil empire" that required direct confrontation with military might.

U.S. policy toward the Soviet Union will consist of three elements: external resistance to Soviet imperialism; internal pressure on the USSR to weaken the sources of Soviet imperialism; and negotiations to eliminate, on the basis of strict reciprocity, outstanding disagreements. Specifically, U.S. tasks are:

1. To contain and over time reverse Soviet expansionism by competing effectively on a sustained basis with the Soviet Union in all international arenas—particularly in the overall military balance and in geographical regions of priority concern to the United States. This will remain the primary focus of U.S. policy toward the USSR.
2. To promote, within the narrow limits available to us, the process of change in the Soviet Union toward a more pluralistic political and economic system, in which the power of the privileged ruling elite is gradually reduced. The U.S. recognizes that Soviet aggressiveness has deep roots in the internal system and that relations with the USSR should therefore take into account whether or not they help to strengthen this system and its capacity to engage in aggression.
3. To engage the Soviet Union in negotiations to attempt to reach agreements which protect and enhance U.S. interests and which are consistent with the principle of strict reciprocity and mutual interest. This is important when the Soviet Union is in the midst of a process of political succession.

In order to implement this threefold strategy, the U.S. must convey clearly to Moscow that unacceptable behavior will incur costs that would outweigh any gains. At the same time, the U.S. must make clear to the Soviets that genuine restraint in their behavior would create the possibility of an East–West relationship that might bring important benefits for the Soviet Union. It is particularly important that this message be conveyed clearly during the succession period, since this may be a particularly opportune time for external forces to affect the policies of Brezhnev's successors.

SHAPING THE SOVIET ENVIRONMENT: ARENAS OF ENGAGEMENT

Implementation of U.S. policy must focus on shaping the environment in which Soviet decisions are made both in a wide variety of functional and geopolitical arenas and in the U.S.–Soviet bilateral relationship.

A. FUNCTIONAL

1. Military Strategy: The U.S. must modernize its military forces—both nuclear and conventional—so that Soviet leaders perceive that the U.S. is determined never to accept a second place or a deteriorating military posture. Soviet calculations of possible war outcomes under any contingency must always result in outcomes so unfavorable to the USSR that there would be no incentive for Soviet leaders to initiate an attack. The future strength of U.S. military capabilities must be assured. U.S. military technology advances must be exploited, while controls over transfer of military related/dual-use technology, products, and services must be tightened.

   In Europe, the Soviets must be faced with a reinvigorated NATO. In the Far East we must ensure that the Soviets cannot count on a secure flank in a global war. Worldwide, U.S. general purpose forces must be strong and flexible enough to affect Soviet calculations in a wide variety of contingencies. In the Third World, Moscow must know that areas of interest to the U.S. cannot be attacked or threatened without risk of serious U.S. military countermeasures.

2. Economic Policy: U.S. policy on economic relations with the USSR must serve strategic and foreign policy goals as well as economic interests. In this context, U.S. objectives are:

   - Above all, to ensure that East–West economic relations do not facilitate the Soviet military buildup. This requires prevention of the transfer of technology and equipment that would make a substantial contribution directly or indirectly to Soviet military power.
   - To avoid subsidizing the Soviet economy or unduly easing the burden of Soviet resource allocation decisions, so as not to dilute pressures for structural change in the Soviet system.
   - To seek to minimize the potential for Soviet exercise of reverse leverage on Western countries based on trade, energy supply, and financial relationships.
   - To permit mutual beneficial trade—without Western subsidization or the creation of Western dependence—with the USSR in non-strategic areas, such as grains.

   The U.S. must exercise strong leadership with its Allies and others to develop a common understanding of the strategic implications of East–West trade, building upon the agreement announced November 13, 1982 (see NSDD 66). This approach should involve efforts to reach agreements with the Allies on specific measures, such as: (a) no incremental deliveries of Soviet gas beyond the amounts contracted for from the first strand of the Siberian pipeline; (b) the addition of critical technologies and equipment to the COCOM list, the harmonization of national licensing procedures for COCOM, and the substantial improvement of the coordination and effectiveness of international enforcement efforts; (c) controls on advanced technology and equipment beyond the expanded COCOM list, including equipment in the oil and gas sector; (d) further restraints on officially-backed credits such as higher down payments, shortened maturities and an established framework to monitor this process; and (e) the strengthening of the role of the OECD and NATO in East–West trade analysis and policy.

   In the longer term, if Soviet behavior should worsen, e.g., an invasion of Poland, we would need to consider extreme measures. Should Soviet behavior improve, carefully calibrated positive economic signals, including a broadening of government-to-government economic contacts, could be considered as a means of demonstrating to the Soviets the benefits that real restraint in their conduct might bring. Such steps could not, however, alter the basic direction of U.S. policy.

3. Political Action: U.S. policy must have an ideological thrust which clearly affirms the superiority of U.S. and Western values of individual dignity and freedom, a free press, free trade unions, free

enterprise, and political democracy over the repressive features of Soviet Communism. We need to review and significantly strengthen U.S. instruments of political action including: (a) The President's London initiative to support democratic forces; (b) USG efforts to highlight Soviet human rights violations; and (c) U.S. radio broadcasting policy. The U.S. should:

– Expose at all available fora the double standards employed by the Soviet Union in dealing with difficulties within its own domain and the outside ("capitalist") world (e.g., treatment of labor, policies toward ethnic minorities, use of chemical weapons, etc.).

– Prevent the Soviet propaganda machine from seizing the semantic high-ground in the battle of ideas through the appropriation of such terms as "peace."

B. GEOPOLITICAL

1. The Industrial Democracies: An effective response to the Soviet challenge requires close partnership among the industrial democracies, including stronger and more effective collective defense arrangements. The U.S. must provide strong leadership and conduct effective consultations to build consensus and cushion the impact of intra-alliance disagreements. While Allied support of U.S. overall strategy is essential, the U.S. may on occasion be forced to act to protect vital interests without Allied support and even in the face of Allied opposition; even in this event, however, U.S. should consult to the maximum extent possible with its Allies.

2. The Third World: The U.S. must rebuild the credibility of its commitment to resist Soviet encroachment on U.S. interests and those of its Allies and friends, and to support effectively those Third World states that are willing to resist Soviet pressures or oppose Soviet initiatives hostile to the United States, or are special targets of Soviet policy. The U.S. effort in the Third World must involve an important role for security assistance and foreign military sales, as well as readiness to use U.S. military forces where necessary to protect vital interests

and support endangered Allies and friends. U.S. policy must also involve diplomatic initiatives to promote resolution of regional crises vulnerable to Soviet exploitation, and an appropriate mixture of economic assistance programs and private sector initiatives for Third World countries.

3. The Soviet Empire: There are a number of important weaknesses and vulnerabilities within the Soviet empire which the U.S. should exploit. U.S. policies should seek wherever possible to encourage Soviet allies to distance themselves from Moscow in foreign policy and to move toward democratization domestically.

   (a) Eastern Europe: The primary U.S. objective in Eastern Europe is to loosen Moscow's hold on the region while promoting the cause of human rights in individual East European countries. The U.S. can advance this objective by carefully discriminating in favor of countries that show relative independence from the USSR in their foreign policy, or show a greater degree of internal liberalization. U.S. policies must also make clear that East European countries which reverse movements of liberalization, or drift away from an independent stance in foreign policy, will incur significant costs in their relations with the U.S.

   (b) Afghanistan: The U.S. objective is to keep maximum pressure on Moscow for withdrawal and to ensure that the Soviets' political, military, and other costs remain high while the occupation continues.

   (c) Cuba: The U.S. must take strong countermeasures to affect the political/military impact of Soviet arms deliveries to Cuba. The U.S. must also provide economic and military assistance to states in Central America and the Caribbean Basin threatened by Cuban destabilizing activities. Finally, the U.S. will seek to reduce the Cuban presence and influence in southern Africa by energetic leadership of the diplomatic effort to achieve a Cuban withdrawal from Angola, or failing that, by increasing the costs of Cuba's role in southern Africa.

   (d) Soviet Third World Alliances: U.S. policy will seek to limit the destabilizing activities of

Soviet Third World allies and clients. It is a further objective to weaken and, where possible, undermine the existing links between them and the Soviet Union. U.S. policy will include active efforts to encourage democratic movements and forces to bring about political change inside these countries.

4. China: China continues to support U.S. efforts to strengthen the world's defenses against Soviet expansionism. The U.S. should over time seek to achieve enhanced strategic cooperation and policy coordination with China, and to reduce the possibility of a Sino-Soviet rapprochement. The U.S. will continue to pursue a policy of substantially liberalized technology transfer and sale of military equipment to China on a case-by-case basis within the parameters of the policy approved by the President in 1981, and defined further in 1982.

5. Yugoslavia: It is U.S. policy to support the independence, territorial integrity and national unity of Yugoslavia. Yugoslavia's current difficulties in paying its foreign debts have increased its vulnerability to Soviet pressures. The Yugoslav government, well aware of this vulnerability, would like to reduce its trade dependence on the Soviet Union. It is in our interest to prevent any deterioration in Yugoslavia's economic situation that might weaken its resolve to withstand Soviet pressure.

C. BILATERAL RELATIONSHIPS

1. Arms Control: The U.S. will enter into arms control negotiations when they serve U.S. national security objectives. At the same time, U.S. policy recognizes that arms control agreements are not an end in themselves but are, in combination with U.S. and Allied efforts to maintain the military balance, an important means for enhancing national security and global stability. The U.S. should make clear to the Allies as well as to the USSR that U.S. ability to reach satisfactory results in arms control negotiations will inevitably be influenced by the international situation, the overall state of U.S.–Soviet relations, and the difficulties in defining areas of mutual agreement with an adversary which often seeks unilateral gains. U.S. arms control proposals will be consistent with necessary force modernization plans and will seek to achieve balanced, significant, and verifiable reductions to equal levels of comparable armaments.

2. Official Dialogue: The U.S. should insist that Moscow address the full range of U.S. concerns about Soviet internal behavior and human rights violations, and should continue to resist Soviet efforts to return to a U.S.–Soviet agenda focused primarily on arms control. U.S.–Soviet diplomatic contacts on regional issues can serve U.S. interests if they are used to keep pressure on Moscow for responsible behavior. Such contacts can also be useful in driving home to Moscow that the costs of irresponsibility are high, and that the U.S. is prepared to work for pragmatic solutions of regional problems if Moscow is willing seriously to address U.S. concerns. At the same time, such contacts must be handled with care to avoid offering the Soviet Union a role in regional questions it would not otherwise secure.

A continuing dialogue with the Soviets at Foreign Minister level facilitates necessary diplomatic communication with the Soviet leadership and helps to maintain Allied understanding and support for U.S. approach to East–West relations. A summit between President Reagan and his Soviet counterpart might promise similarly beneficial results. At the same time, unless it were carefully handled a summit could be seen as registering an improvement in U.S.–Soviet relations without the changes in Soviet behavior which we have insisted upon. It could therefore generate unrealizable expectations and further stimulate unilateral Allied initiatives toward Moscow.

A summit would not necessarily involve signature of major new U.S.–Soviet agreements. Any summit meeting should achieve the maximum possible positive impact with U.S. Allies and the American public, while making clear to both audiences that improvement in Soviet–American relations depends on changes in Soviet conduct. A summit without such changes must not be understood to signal such improvement.

3. U.S.–Soviet Cooperative Exchanges: The role of U.S.–Soviet cultural, educational, scientific and other cooperative exchanges should be seen in light of the U.S. intention to maintain a strong

ideological component in relations with Moscow. The U.S. should not further dismantle the framework of exchanges; indeed those exchanges which could advance the U.S. objective of promoting positive evolutionary change within the Soviet system should be expanded. At the same time, the U.S. will insist on <u>full</u> reciprocity and encourage its Allies to do so as well. This recognizes that unless the U.S. has an effective official framework for handling exchanges, the Soviets will make separate arrangements with private U.S. sponsors, while denying reciprocal access to the Soviet Union. U.S. policy on exchanges must also take into account the necessity to prevent transfer of sensitive U.S. technology to the Soviet Union.

PRIORITIES IN THE U.S. APPROACH: MAXIMIZING RESTRAINING LEVERAGE OVER SOVIET BEHAVIOR

The interrelated tasks of containing and reversing Soviet expansion and promoting evolutionary change within the Soviet Union itself cannot be accomplished quickly. The coming 5–10 years will be a period of considerable uncertainty in which the Soviets may test U.S. resolve by continuing the kind of aggressive international behavior which the U.S. finds unacceptable.

The uncertainties will be exacerbated by the fact that the Soviet Union will be engaged in the unpredictable process of political succession to Brezhnev. The U.S. will not seek to adjust its policies to the Soviet internal conflict, but rather try to create incentives (positive and negative) for the new leadership to adopt policies less detrimental to U.S. interests. The U.S. will remain ready for improved U.S.–Soviet relations if the Soviet Union makes significant changes in policies of concern to it; the burden for any further deterioration in relations must fall squarely on Moscow. The U.S. must not yield to pressures to "take the first step."

The existing and projected gap between finite U.S. resources and the level of capabilities needed to implement U.S. strategy makes it essential that the U.S.: (1) establish firm priorities for the use of limited U.S. resources where they will have the greatest restraining impact on the Soviet Union; and (2) mobilize the resources of Allies and friends which are willing to join the U.S. in containing the expansion of Soviet power.

Underlying the full range of U.S. and Western policies must be a strong military capable of action across the entire spectrum of potential conflicts and guided by a well conceived political and military strategy. The heart of U.S. military strategy is to deter attack by the USSR and its allies against the U.S., its Allies, or other important countries, and to defeat such an attack should deterrence fail. Although unilateral U.S. efforts must lead the way in rebuilding Western military strength to counter the Soviet threat, the protection of Western interests will require increased U.S. cooperation with Allied and other states and greater utilization of their resources. This military strategy will be combined with a political strategy attaching high priority to the following objectives:

– <u>Sustaining steady, long-term growth in U.S. defense spending and capabilities—both nuclear and conventional</u>. This is the most important way of conveying to the Soviets U.S. resolve and political staying-power.

– <u>Creating a long-term Western consensus for dealing with the Soviet Union</u>. This will require that the U.S. exercise strong leadership in developing policies to deal with the multifaceted Soviet threat to Western interests. It will require that the U.S. take Allied concerns into account, and also that U.S. Allies take into equal account U.S. concerns. In this connection, and in addition to pushing Allies to spend more on defense, the U.S. must make a serious effort to negotiate arms control agreements consistent with U.S. military strategy and necessary force modernization plans, and should seek to achieve balanced, significant and verifiable reductions to equal levels of comparable armaments. The U.S. must also develop, together with the Allies, a unified Western approach to East–West economic relations, implementing the agreement announced on November 13, 1982.

– <u>Maintenance of a strategic relationship with China, and efforts to minimize opportunities for a Sino-Soviet rapprochement</u>.

– <u>Building and sustaining a major ideological/political offensive which, together with other efforts, will be designed to bring about evolutionary change of the Soviet system</u>. This must be a long-term and sophisticated program, given the nature of the Soviet system.

– Effective opposition to Moscow's efforts to consolidate its position in Afghanistan. This will require that the U.S. continue efforts to promote Soviet withdrawal in the context of a negotiated settlement of the conflict. At the same time, the U.S. must keep pressure on Moscow for withdrawal and ensure that Soviet costs on the ground are high.

– Blocking the expansion of Soviet influence in the critical Middle East and Southwest Asia regions. This will require both continued efforts to seek a political solution to the Arab–Israeli conflict and to bolster U.S. relations with moderate states in the region, and a sustained U.S. defense commitment to deter Soviet military encroachments.

– Maintenance of international pressure on Moscow to permit a relaxation of the current repression in Poland and a longer-term increase in diversity and independence throughout Eastern Europe. This will require that the U.S. continue to impose costs on the Soviet Union for its behavior in Poland. It will also require that the U.S. maintain a U.S. policy of differentiation among East European countries.

– Neutralization and reduction of the threat to U.S. national security interests posed by the Soviet–Cuban relationship. This will require that the U.S. use a variety of instruments, including diplomatic efforts and U.S. security and economic assistance. The U.S. must also retain the option of using of its military forces to protect vital U.S. security interests against threats which may arise from the Soviet–Cuban connection.

ARTICULATING THE U.S. APPROACH: SUSTAINING PUBLIC AND CONGRESSIONAL SUPPORT

The policy outlined above is one for the long haul. It is unlikely to yield a rapid breakthrough in bilateral relations with the Soviet Union. In the absence of dramatic near-term victories in the U.S. effort to moderate Soviet behavior, pressure is likely to mount for change in U.S. policy. There will be appeals from important segments of domestic opinion for a more "normal" U.S.–Soviet relationship, particularly in a period of political transition in Moscow.

It is therefore essential that the American people understand and support U.S. policy. This will require that official U.S. statements and actions avoid generating unrealizable expectations for near-term progress in U.S.–Soviet relations. At the same time, the U.S. must demonstrate credibly that its policy is not a blueprint for an open-ended, sterile confrontation with Moscow, but a serious search for a stable and constructive long-term basis for U.S.–Soviet relations.

Ronald Reagan

QUESTIONS TO CONSIDER

1. What are Reagan's priorities concerning the U.S. relationship with the U.S.S.R.? What does he hope to accomplish and how?
2. What is Reagan willing to offer the Soviets to secure the goals he has outlined?

28.5 VISUAL SOURCE: HERBLOCK, *SPEAK SOFTLY AND CARRY A BIG STICK* (1986)*

This cartoon by *Washington Post* cartoonist Herbert Block (1909–2001), also known as Herblock, satirizes President Reagan's explanation of what became known as the Iran–Contra Affair by comparing his explanation that "mistakes were made" with no-nonsense quotations attributed to past

* A 1986 Herblock Cartoon, © The Herb Block Foundation

presidents. In a convoluted plan, members of Reagan's administration had attempted to finance right-wing rebels in socialist Nicaragua using the proceeds of weapons they sold to Iran. At the time Iran was at war with Iraq, for whom the United States had also provided funding and support, and Congress had specifically denied any further funding for the Nicaraguan contras. Administration authorities had also hoped to secure the release of Americans held hostage by Lebanese militants with ties to Iran. When these negotiations came to light, public opinion of Reagan declined precipitously and numerous members of his administration were indicted.

QUESTIONS TO CONSIDER

1. What is Block saying about Reagan's approach to the presidency?
2. What is the point of the comparison to past presidents? What does Block think this contrast reveals about Reagan?

CHAPTER 29

NEW WORLD DISORDER, 1989–2004

29.1 GEORGE H. W. BUSH, "NEW WORLD ORDER" ADDRESS BEFORE CONGRESS (1990)*

President George H. W. Bush (1924–2018) addressed Congress in the midst of the Gulf War, in which a coalition of nations led by the United States sought to drive an occupying Iraqi army out of their neighboring country of Kuwait. Following the Iraqi invasion of Kuwait in August 1990, the UN Security Council passed a series of resolutions demanding an end to their invasion, eventually leading to an armed intervention by a US-led coalition. In this speech, President Bush characterized Saddam Hussein, Iraq's president and functional dictator at the time, as the leader of a rogue state, unconstrained by international norms and a threat to his neighbors. Bush portrayed the US response as an effort to help achieve a "new world order" that would replace the Cold War that had defined international relations for the past four decades. Bush's advocacy of a "new world order" based on shared responsibility among nations to prevent aggression and ensure justice was a rhetorical shift away from the military buildup and anti-Soviet hostility that had characterized the preceding Reagan administration.

Mr. President and Mr. Speaker and Members of the United States Congress, distinguished guests, fellow Americans, thank you very much for that warm welcome. We gather tonight, witness to events in the Persian Gulf as significant as they are tragic. In the early morning hours of August 2d, following negotiations and promises by Iraq's dictator Saddam Hussein not to use force, a powerful Iraqi army invaded its trusting and much weaker neighbor, Kuwait. Within 3 days, 120,000 Iraqi troops with 850 tanks had poured into Kuwait and moved south to threaten Saudi Arabia. It was then that I decided to act to check that aggression.

At this moment, our brave servicemen and women stand watch in that distant desert and on distant seas, side by side with the forces of more than 20 other nations. They are some of the finest men and women of the United States of America. And they're doing one terrific job. These valiant Americans were ready at a

* George H. W. Bush, "New World Order," Address Before a Joint Session of Congress, September 11, 1990. National Archives.

moment's notice to leave their spouses and their children, to serve on the front line halfway around the world. They remind us who keeps America strong: they do. In the trying circumstances of the Gulf, the morale of our service men and women is excellent. In the face of danger, they're brave, they're well-trained, and dedicated.

A soldier, Private First Class Wade Merritt of Knoxville, Tennessee, now stationed in Saudi Arabia, wrote his parents of his worries, his love of family, and his hope for peace. But Wade also wrote, "I am proud of my country and its firm stance against inhumane aggression. I am proud of my army and its men. I am proud to serve my country." Well, let me just say, Wade, America is proud of you and is grateful to every soldier, sailor, marine, and airman serving the cause of peace in the Persian Gulf. I also want to thank the Chairman of the Joint Chiefs of Staff, General Powell; the Chiefs here tonight; our commander in the Persian Gulf, General Schwartzkopf; and the men and women of the Department of Defense. What a magnificent job you all are doing. And thank you very, very much from a grateful people. I wish I could say that their work is done. But we all know it's not.

So, if there ever was a time to put country before self and patriotism before party, the time is now. And let me thank all Americans, especially those here in this Chamber tonight, for your support for our armed forces and for their mission. That support will be even more important in the days to come. So, tonight I want to talk to you about what's at stake—what we must do together to defend civilized values around the world and maintain our economic strength at home.

Our objectives in the Persian Gulf are clear, our goals defined and familiar: Iraq must withdraw from Kuwait completely, immediately, and without condition. Kuwait's legitimate government must be restored. The security and stability of the Persian Gulf must be assured. And American citizens abroad must be protected. These goals are not ours alone. They've been endorsed by the United Nations Security Council five times in as many weeks. Most countries share our concern for principle. And many have a stake in the stability of the Persian Gulf. This is not, as Saddam Hussein would have it, the United States against Iraq. It is Iraq against the world.

As you know, I've just returned from a very productive meeting with Soviet President Gorbachev. And I am pleased that we are working together to build a new relationship. In Helsinki, our joint statement affirmed to the world our shared resolve to counter Iraq's threat to peace. Let me quote: "We are united in the belief that Iraq's aggression must not be tolerated. No peaceful international order is possible if larger states can devour their smaller neighbors." Clearly, no longer can a dictator count on East–West confrontation to stymie concerted United Nations action against aggression. A new partnership of nations has begun.

We stand today at a unique and extraordinary moment. The crisis in the Persian Gulf, as grave as it is, also offers a rare opportunity to move toward an historic period of cooperation. Out of these troubled times, our fifth objective—a new world order—can emerge: a new era—freer from the threat of terror, stronger in the pursuit of justice, and more secure in the quest for peace. An era in which the nations of the world, East and West, North and South, can prosper and live in harmony. A hundred generations have searched for this elusive path to peace, while a thousand wars raged across the span of human endeavor. Today that new world is struggling to be born, a world quite different from the one we've known. A world where the rule of law supplants the rule of the jungle. A world in which nations recognize the shared responsibility for freedom and justice. A world where the strong respect the rights of the weak. This is the vision that I shared with President Gorbachev in Helsinki. He and other leaders from Europe, the Gulf, and around the world understand that how we manage this crisis today could shape the future for generations to come.

The test we face is great, and so are the stakes. This is the first assault on the new world that we seek, the first test of our mettle. Had we not responded to this first provocation with clarity of purpose, if we do not continue to demonstrate our determination, it would be a signal to actual and potential despots around the world. America and the world must defend common vital interests—and we will. America and the world must support the rule of law—and we will. America and the world must stand up to aggression—and we will. And one thing more: In the pursuit of these goals America will not be intimidated.

Vital issues of principle are at stake. Saddam Hussein is literally trying to wipe a country off the face of the Earth. We do not exaggerate. Nor do we exaggerate when we say Saddam Hussein will fail. Vital economic interests are at risk as well. Iraq itself controls some 10 percent of the world's proven oil reserves. Iraq plus Kuwait controls twice that. An Iraq permitted to swallow Kuwait would have the economic and military power, as well as the arrogance, to intimidate and coerce its neighbors—neighbors who control the lion's share of the world's remaining oil reserves. We cannot permit a resource so vital to be dominated by one so ruthless. And we won't.

Recent events have surely proven that there is no substitute for American leadership. In the face of tyranny, let no one doubt American credibility and reliability. Let no one doubt our staying power. We will stand by our friends. One way or another, the leader of Iraq must learn this fundamental truth. From the outset, acting hand in hand with others, we've sought to fashion the broadest possible international response to Iraq's aggression. The level of world cooperation and condemnation of Iraq is unprecedented. Armed forces from countries spanning four continents are there at the request of King Fahd of Saudi Arabia to deter and, if need be, to defend against attack. Moslems and non-Moslems, Arabs and non-Arabs, soldiers from many nations stand shoulder to shoulder, resolute against Saddam Hussein's ambitions.

We can now point to five United Nations Security Council resolutions that condemn Iraq's aggression. They call for Iraq's immediate and unconditional withdrawal, the restoration of Kuwait's legitimate government, and categorically reject Iraq's cynical and self-serving attempt to annex Kuwait. Finally, the United Nations has demanded the release of all foreign nationals held hostage against their will and in contravention of international law. It is a mockery of human decency to call these people "guests." They are hostages, and the whole world knows it.

Prime Minister Margaret Thatcher, a dependable ally, said it all: "We do not bargain over hostages. We will not stoop to the level of using human beings as bargaining chips ever." Of course, of course, our hearts go out to the hostages and to their families. But our policy cannot change, and it will not change. America and the world will not be blackmailed by this ruthless policy.

We're now in sight of a United Nations that performs as envisioned by its founders. We owe much to the outstanding leadership of Secretary-General Javier Perez de Cuellar. The United Nations is backing up its words with action. The Security Council has imposed mandatory economic sanctions on Iraq, designed to force Iraq to relinquish the spoils of its illegal conquest. The Security Council has also taken the decisive step of authorizing the use of all means necessary to ensure compliance with these sanctions. Together with our friends and allies, ships of the United States Navy are today patrolling Mideast waters. They've already intercepted more than 700 ships to enforce the sanctions. Three regional leaders I spoke with just yesterday told me that these sanctions are working. Iraq is feeling the heat. We continue to hope that Iraq's leaders will recalculate just what their aggression has cost them. They are cut off from world trade, unable to sell their oil. And only a tiny fraction of goods gets through.

The communique with President Gorbachev made mention of what happens when the embargo is so effective that children of Iraq literally need milk or the sick truly need medicine. Then, under strict international supervision that guarantees the proper destination, then food will be permitted.

At home, the material cost of our leadership can be steep. That's why Secretary of State Baker and Treasury Secretary Brady have met with many world leaders to underscore that the burden of this collective effort must be shared. We are prepared to do our share and more to help carry that load; we insist that others do their share as well.

The response of most of our friends and allies has been good. To help defray costs, the leaders of Saudi Arabia, Kuwait, and the UAE—the United Arab Emirates—have pledged to provide our deployed troops with all the food and fuel they need. Generous assistance will also be provided to stalwart front-line nations, such as Turkey and Egypt. I am also heartened to report that this international response extends to the neediest victims of this conflict—those refugees. For our part, we've contributed $28 million for relief efforts. This is but a portion of what is needed. I commend, in particular, Saudi Arabia, Japan, and several

European nations who have joined us in this purely humanitarian effort.

There's an energy-related cost to be borne as well. Oil-producing nations are already replacing lost Iraqi and Kuwaiti output. More than half of what was lost has been made up. And we're getting superb cooperation. If producers, including the United States, continue steps to expand oil and gas production, we can stabilize prices and guarantee against hardship. Additionally, we and several of our allies always have the option to extract oil from our strategic petroleum reserves if conditions warrant. As I've pointed out before, conservation efforts are essential to keep our energy needs as low as possible. And we must then take advantage of our energy sources across the board: coal, natural gas, hydro, and nuclear. Our failure to do these things has made us more dependent on foreign oil than ever before. Finally, let no one even contemplate profiteering from this crisis. We will not have it.

I cannot predict just how long it will take to convince Iraq to withdraw from Kuwait. Sanctions will take time to have their full intended effect. We will continue to review all options with our allies, but let it be clear: we will not let this aggression stand.

Our interest, our involvement in the Gulf is not transitory. It predated Saddam Hussein's aggression and will survive it. Long after all our troops come home—and we all hope it's soon, very soon—there will be a lasting role for the United States in assisting the nations of the Persian Gulf. Our role then: to deter future aggression. Our role is to help our friends in their own self-defense. And something else: to curb the proliferation of chemical, biological, ballistic missile and, above all, nuclear technologies.

Let me also make clear that the United States has no quarrel with the Iraqi people. Our quarrel is with Iraq's dictator and with his aggression. Iraq will not be permitted to annex Kuwait. That's not a threat, that's not a boast, that's just the way it's going to be.

Our ability to function effectively as a great power abroad depends on how we conduct ourselves at home. Our economy, our Armed Forces, our energy dependence, and our cohesion all determine whether we can help our friends and stand up to our foes. For America to lead, America must remain strong and vital. Our world leadership and domestic strength are mutual and reinforcing; a woven piece, strongly bound as Old Glory. To revitalize our leadership, our leadership capacity, we must address our budget deficit—not after election day, or next year, but now.

Higher oil prices slow our growth, and higher defense costs would only make our fiscal deficit problem worse. That deficit was already greater than it should have been—a projected $232 billion for the coming year. It must—it will—be reduced.

To my friends in Congress, together we must act this very month—before the next fiscal year begins on October 1st—to get America's economic house in order. The Gulf situation helps us realize we are more economically vulnerable than we ever should be. Americans must never again enter any crisis, economic or military, with an excessive dependence on foreign oil and an excessive burden of Federal debt.

Most Americans are sick and tired of endless battles in the Congress and between the branches over budget matters. It is high time we pulled together and get the job done right. It's up to us to straighten this out. This job has four basic parts. First, the Congress should, this month, within a budget agreement, enact growth-oriented tax measures—to help avoid recession in the short term and to increase savings, investment, productivity, and competitiveness for the longer term. These measures include extending incentives for research and experimentation; expanding the use of IRA's for new homeowners; establishing tax-deferred family savings accounts; creating incentives for the creation of enterprise zones and initiatives to encourage more domestic drilling; and, yes, reducing the tax rate on capital gains.

And second, the Congress should, this month, enact a prudent multiyear defense program, one that reflects not only the improvement in East–West relations but our broader responsibilities to deal with the continuing risks of outlaw action and regional conflict. Even with our obligations in the Gulf, a sound defense budget can have some reduction in real terms; and we're prepared to accept that. But to go beyond such levels, where cutting defense would threaten our vital margin of safety, is something I will never accept. The world is still dangerous. And surely, that is now clear. Stability's not secure. American interests are far reaching. Interdependence has increased. The consequences of regional instability can be global. This is no time to risk America's capacity to protect her vital interests.

And third, the Congress should, this month, enact measures to increase domestic energy production and energy conservation in order to reduce dependence on foreign oil. These measures should include my proposals to increase incentives for domestic oil and gas exploration, fuel-switching, and to accelerate the development of the Alaskan energy resources without damage to wildlife. As you know, when the oil embargo was imposed in the early 1970's, the United States imported almost 6 million barrels of oil a day. This year, before the Iraqi invasion, U.S. imports had risen to nearly 8 million barrels per day. And we'd moved in the wrong direction. And now we must act to correct that trend.

And fourth, the Congress should, this month, enact a 5-year program to reduce the projected debt and deficits by $500 billion—that's by half a trillion dollars. And if, with the Congress, we can develop a satisfactory program by the end of the month, we can avoid the ax of sequester—deep across-the-board cuts that would threaten our military capacity and risk substantial domestic disruption. I want to be able to tell the American people that we have truly solved the deficit problem. And for me to do that, a budget agreement must meet these tests: It must include the measures I've recommended to increase economic growth and reduce dependence on foreign oil. It must be fair. All should contribute, but the burden should not be excessive for any one group of programs or people. It must address the growth of government's hidden liabilities. It must reform the budget process and, further, it must be real.

I urge Congress to provide a comprehensive 5-year deficit reduction program to me as a complete legislative package, with measures to assure that it can be fully enforced. America is tired of phony deficit reduction or promise-now, save-later plans. It is time for a program that is credible and real. And finally, to the extent that the deficit reduction program includes new revenue measures, it must avoid any measure that would threaten economic growth or turn us back toward the days of punishing income tax rates. That is one path we should not head down again.

I have been pleased with recent progress, although it has not always seemed so smooth. But now it's time to produce. I hope we can work out a responsible plan. But with or without agreement from the budget summit, I ask both Houses of the Congress to allow a straight up-or-down vote on a complete $500-billion deficit reduction package not later than September 28. If the Congress cannot get me a budget, then Americans will have to face a tough, mandated sequester. I'm hopeful, in fact, I'm confident that the Congress will do what it should. And I can assure you that we in the executive branch will do our part.

In the final analysis, our ability to meet our responsibilities abroad depends upon political will and consensus at home. This is never easy in democracies, for we govern only with the consent of the governed. And although free people in a free society are bound to have their differences, Americans traditionally come together in times of adversity and challenge.

Once again, Americans have stepped forward to share a tearful goodbye with their families before leaving for a strange and distant shore. At this very moment, they serve together with Arabs, Europeans, Asians, and Africans in defense of principle and the dream of a new world order. That's why they sweat and toil in the sand and the heat and the sun. If they can come together under such adversity, if old adversaries like the Soviet Union and the United States can work in common cause, then surely we who are so fortunate to be in this great Chamber—Democrats, Republicans, liberals, conservatives—can come together to fulfill our responsibilities here.

Thank you. Good night. And God bless the United States of America.

QUESTIONS TO CONSIDER

1. According to President Bush, what stake does the United States have in the fate of Iraq and Kuwait? Why does he believe the US must intervene?
2. Why are international cooperation and the United Nations important to President Bush? What is the significance of the United Nations to the New World Order he imagines?

29.2 GEORGE W. BUSH, "WAR ON TERROR" ADDRESS BEFORE CONGRESS (2001)*

Nine days after the September 11 attacks, President George W. Bush (b. 1946) addressed both houses of Congress to discuss the attacks and his administration's response. Calling the aggression an "act of war," against the United States and drawing parallels to Pearl Harbor, Bush declared his determination to hunt down al Qaeda, the terrorist group that perpetrated the airplane hijackings. After thanking international allies for their support during the crisis, Bush also delivered a warning to the rest of the world: "Either you are with us, or you are with the terrorists."

The Bush administration's response to 9/11 began the decades-long "war on terror," as Bush declared his ambition to eliminate not just al Qaeda but "every terrorist group of global reach." As part of the war on terror, the Bush administration passed new laws like the USA PATRIOT Act, which expanded the federal government's ability to surveil Americans. His administration also launched invasions of Iraq and Afghanistan, beginning decades-long conflicts to eliminate terrorist groups and rebuild those countries. The goals laid out in President Bush's speech would define American foreign policy for years to come.

Mr. Speaker, Mr. President Pro Tempore, members of Congress, and fellow Americans:

In the normal course of events, Presidents come to this chamber to report on the state of the Union. Tonight, no such report is needed. It has already been delivered by the American people.

We have seen it in the courage of passengers, who rushed terrorists to save others on the ground—passengers like an exceptional man named Todd Beamer. And would you please help me to welcome his wife, Lisa Beamer, here tonight. (Applause.)

We have seen the state of our Union in the endurance of rescuers, working past exhaustion. We have seen the unfurling of flags, the lighting of candles, the giving of blood, the saying of prayers—in English, Hebrew, and Arabic. We have seen the decency of a loving and giving people who have made the grief of strangers their own.

My fellow citizens, for the last nine days, the entire world has seen for itself the state of our Union—and it is strong. (Applause.)

Tonight we are a country awakened to danger and called to defend freedom. Our grief has turned to anger, and anger to resolution. Whether we bring our enemies to justice, or bring justice to our enemies, justice will be done. (Applause.)

I thank the Congress for its leadership at such an important time. All of America was touched on the evening of the tragedy to see Republicans and Democrats joined together on the steps of this Capitol, singing "God Bless America." And you did more than sing; you acted, by delivering $40 billion to rebuild our communities and meet the needs of our military.

Speaker Hastert, Minority Leader Gephardt, Majority Leader Daschle and Senator Lott, I thank you for your friendship, for your leadership and for your service to our country. (Applause.)

And on behalf of the American people, I thank the world for its outpouring of support. America will never forget the sounds of our National Anthem playing at Buckingham Palace, on the streets of Paris, and at Berlin's Brandenburg Gate.

---

* The White House, "Address to a Joint Session of Congress and the American People," September 20, 2001, https://georgewbush-whitehouse.archives.gov/news/releases/2001/09/20010920-8.html.

We will not forget South Korean children gathering to pray outside our embassy in Seoul, or the prayers of sympathy offered at a mosque in Cairo. We will not forget moments of silence and days of mourning in Australia and Africa and Latin America.

Nor will we forget the citizens of 80 other nations who died with our own: dozens of Pakistanis; more than 130 Israelis; more than 250 citizens of India; men and women from El Salvador, Iran, Mexico and Japan; and hundreds of British citizens. America has no truer friend than Great Britain. (Applause.) Once again, we are joined together in a great cause—so honored the British Prime Minister has crossed an ocean to show his unity of purpose with America. Thank you for coming, friend. (Applause.)

On September the 11th, enemies of freedom committed an act of war against our country. Americans have known wars—but for the past 136 years, they have been wars on foreign soil, except for one Sunday in 1941. Americans have known the casualties of war—but not at the center of a great city on a peaceful morning. Americans have known surprise attacks—but never before on thousands of civilians. All of this was brought upon us in a single day—and night fell on a different world, a world where freedom itself is under attack.

Americans have many questions tonight. Americans are asking: Who attacked our country? The evidence we have gathered all points to a collection of loosely affiliated terrorist organizations known as al Qaeda. They are the same murderers indicted for bombing American embassies in Tanzania and Kenya, and responsible for bombing the USS *Cole*.

Al Qaeda is to terror what the mafia is to crime. But its goal is not making money; its goal is remaking the world—and imposing its radical beliefs on people everywhere.

The terrorists practice a fringe form of Islamic extremism that has been rejected by Muslim scholars and the vast majority of Muslim clerics—a fringe movement that perverts the peaceful teachings of Islam. The terrorists' directive commands them to kill Christians and Jews, to kill all Americans, and make no distinction among military and civilians, including women and children.

This group and its leader—a person named Osama bin Laden—are linked to many other organizations in different countries, including the Egyptian Islamic Jihad and the Islamic Movement of Uzbekistan. There are thousands of these terrorists in more than 60 countries. They are recruited from their own nations and neighborhoods and brought to camps in places like Afghanistan, where they are trained in the tactics of terror. They are sent back to their homes or sent to hide in countries around the world to plot evil and destruction.

The leadership of al Qaeda has great influence in Afghanistan and supports the Taliban regime in controlling most of that country. In Afghanistan, we see al Qaeda's vision for the world.

Afghanistan's people have been brutalized—many are starving and many have fled. Women are not allowed to attend school. You can be jailed for owning a television. Religion can be practiced only as their leaders dictate. A man can be jailed in Afghanistan if his beard is not long enough.

The United States respects the people of Afghanistan—after all, we are currently its largest source of humanitarian aid—but we condemn the Taliban regime. (Applause.) It is not only repressing its own people, it is threatening people everywhere by sponsoring and sheltering and supplying terrorists. By aiding and abetting murder, the Taliban regime is committing murder.

And tonight, the United States of America makes the following demands on the Taliban: Deliver to United States authorities all the leaders of al Qaeda who hide in your land. (Applause.) Release all foreign nationals, including American citizens, you have unjustly imprisoned. Protect foreign journalists, diplomats and aid workers in your country. Close immediately and permanently every terrorist training camp in Afghanistan, and hand over every terrorist, and every person in their support structure, to appropriate authorities. (Applause.) Give the United States full access to terrorist training camps, so we can make sure they are no longer operating.

These demands are not open to negotiation or discussion. (Applause.) The Taliban must act, and act immediately. They will hand over the terrorists, or they will share in their fate.

I also want to speak tonight directly to Muslims throughout the world. We respect your faith. It's practiced freely by many millions of Americans, and by millions more in countries that America counts as friends. Its teachings are good and peaceful, and those who commit evil in the name of Allah blaspheme the name of Allah. (Applause.) The terrorists are traitors to their own faith, trying, in effect, to hijack Islam itself. The enemy of America is not our many Muslim friends; it is not our many Arab friends. Our enemy is a radical network of terrorists, and every government that supports them. (Applause.)

Our war on terror begins with al Qaeda, but it does not end there. It will not end until every terrorist group of global reach has been found, stopped and defeated. (Applause.)

Americans are asking, why do they hate us? They hate what we see right here in this chamber—a democratically elected government. Their leaders are self-appointed. They hate our freedoms—our freedom of religion, our freedom of speech, our freedom to vote and assemble and disagree with each other.

They want to overthrow existing governments in many Muslim countries, such as Egypt, Saudi Arabia, and Jordan. They want to drive Israel out of the Middle East. They want to drive Christians and Jews out of vast regions of Asia and Africa.

These terrorists kill not merely to end lives, but to disrupt and end a way of life. With every atrocity, they hope that America grows fearful, retreating from the world and forsaking our friends. They stand against us, because we stand in their way.

We are not deceived by their pretenses to piety. We have seen their kind before. They are the heirs of all the murderous ideologies of the 20th century. By sacrificing human life to serve their radical visions—by abandoning every value except the will to power—they follow in the path of fascism, and Nazism, and totalitarianism. And they will follow that path all the way, to where it ends: in history's unmarked grave of discarded lies. (Applause.)

Americans are asking: How will we fight and win this war? We will direct every resource at our command—every means of diplomacy, every tool of intelligence, every instrument of law enforcement, every financial influence, and every necessary weapon of war—to the disruption and to the defeat of the global terror network.

This war will not be like the war against Iraq a decade ago, with a decisive liberation of territory and

a swift conclusion. It will not look like the air war above Kosovo two years ago, where no ground troops were used and not a single American was lost in combat.

Our response involves far more than instant retaliation and isolated strikes. Americans should not expect one battle, but a lengthy campaign, unlike any other we have ever seen. It may include dramatic strikes, visible on TV, and covert operations, secret even in success. We will starve terrorists of funding, turn them one against another, drive them from place to place, until there is no refuge or no rest. And we will pursue nations that provide aid or safe haven to terrorism. Every nation, in every region, now has a decision to make. Either you are with us, or you are with the terrorists. (Applause.) From this day forward, any nation that continues to harbor or support terrorism will be regarded by the United States as a hostile regime.

Our nation has been put on notice: We are not immune from attack. We will take defensive measures against terrorism to protect Americans. Today, dozens of federal departments and agencies, as well as state and local governments, have responsibilities affecting homeland security. These efforts must be coordinated at the highest level. So tonight I announce the creation of a Cabinet-level position reporting directly to me—the Office of Homeland Security.

And tonight I also announce a distinguished American to lead this effort, to strengthen American security: a military veteran, an effective governor, a true patriot, a trusted friend—Pennsylvania's Tom Ridge. (Applause.) He will lead, oversee and coordinate a comprehensive national strategy to safeguard our country against terrorism, and respond to any attacks that may come.

These measures are essential. But the only way to defeat terrorism as a threat to our way of life is to stop it, eliminate it, and destroy it where it grows. (Applause.)

Many will be involved in this effort, from FBI agents to intelligence operatives to the reservists we have called to active duty. All deserve our thanks, and all have our prayers. And tonight, a few miles from the damaged Pentagon, I have a message for our military: Be ready. I've called the Armed Forces to alert, and there is a reason. The hour is coming when America will act, and you will make us proud. (Applause.)

This is not, however, just America's fight. And what is at stake is not just America's freedom. This is the world's fight. This is civilization's fight. This is the fight of all who believe in progress and pluralism, tolerance and freedom.

We ask every nation to join us. We will ask, and we will need, the help of police forces, intelligence services, and banking systems around the world. The United States is grateful that many nations and many international organizations have already responded—with sympathy and with support. Nations from Latin America, to Asia, to Africa, to Europe, to the Islamic world. Perhaps the NATO Charter reflects best the attitude of the world: An attack on one is an attack on all.

The civilized world is rallying to America's side. They understand that if this terror goes unpunished, their own cities, their own citizens may be next. Terror, unanswered, can not only bring down buildings, it can threaten the stability of legitimate governments. And you know what—we're not going to allow it. (Applause.)

Americans are asking: What is expected of us? I ask you to live your lives, and hug your children. I know many citizens have fears tonight, and I ask you to be calm and resolute, even in the face of a continuing threat.

I ask you to uphold the values of America, and remember why so many have come here. We are in a fight for our principles, and our first responsibility is to live by them. No one should be singled out for unfair treatment or unkind words because of their ethnic background or religious faith. (Applause.)

I ask you to continue to support the victims of this tragedy with your contributions. Those who want to give can go to a central source of information, libertyunites.org, to find the names of groups providing direct help in New York, Pennsylvania, and Virginia.

The thousands of FBI agents who are now at work in this investigation may need your cooperation, and I ask you to give it.

I ask for your patience, with the delays and inconveniences that may accompany tighter security; and for your patience in what will be a long struggle.

I ask your continued participation and confidence in the American economy. Terrorists attacked a symbol of American prosperity. They did not touch its source.

America is successful because of the hard work, and creativity, and enterprise of our people. These were the true strengths of our economy before September 11th, and they are our strengths today. (Applause.)

And, finally, please continue praying for the victims of terror and their families, for those in uniform, and for our great country. Prayer has comforted us in sorrow, and will help strengthen us for the journey ahead.

Tonight I thank my fellow Americans for what you have already done and for what you will do. And ladies and gentlemen of the Congress, I thank you, their representatives, for what you have already done and for what we will do together.

Tonight, we face new and sudden national challenges. We will come together to improve air safety, to dramatically expand the number of air marshals on domestic flights, and take new measures to prevent hijacking. We will come together to promote stability and keep our airlines flying, with direct assistance during this emergency. (Applause.)

We will come together to give law enforcement the additional tools it needs to track down terror here at home. (Applause.) We will come together to strengthen our intelligence capabilities to know the plans of terrorists before they act, and find them before they strike. (Applause.) We will come together to take active steps that strengthen America's economy, and put our people back to work.

Tonight we welcome two leaders who embody the extraordinary spirit of all New Yorkers: Governor George Pataki, and Mayor Rudolph Giuliani. (Applause.) As a symbol of America's resolve, my administration will work with Congress, and these two leaders, to show the world that we will rebuild New York City. (Applause.)

After all that has just passed—all the lives taken, and all the possibilities and hopes that died with them—it is natural to wonder if America's future is one of fear. Some speak of an age of terror. I know there are struggles ahead, and dangers to face. But this country will define our times, not be defined by them. As long as the United States of America is determined and strong, this will not be an age of terror; this will be an age of liberty, here and across the world. (Applause.)

Great harm has been done to us. We have suffered great loss. And in our grief and anger we have found our mission and our moment. Freedom and fear are at war. The advance of human freedom—the great achievement of our time, and the great hope of every time—now depends on us. Our nation—this generation—will lift a dark threat of violence from our people and our future. We will rally the world to this cause by our efforts, by our courage. We will not tire, we will not falter, and we will not fail. (Applause.)

It is my hope that in the months and years ahead, life will return almost to normal. We'll go back to our lives and routines, and that is good. Even grief recedes with time and grace. But our resolve must not pass. Each of us will remember what happened that day, and to whom it happened. We'll remember the moment the news came—where we were and what we were doing. Some will remember an image of a fire, or a story of rescue. Some will carry memories of a face and a voice gone forever.

And I will carry this: It is the police shield of a man named George Howard, who died at the World Trade Center trying to save others. It was given to me by his mom, Arlene, as a proud memorial to her son. This is my reminder of lives that ended, and a task that does not end. (Applause.)

I will not forget this wound to our country or those who inflicted it. I will not yield; I will not rest; I will not relent in waging this struggle for freedom and security for the American people. The course of this conflict is not known, yet its outcome is certain. Freedom and fear, justice and cruelty, have always been at war, and we know that God is not neutral between them. (Applause.)

Fellow citizens, we'll meet violence with patient justice—assured of the rightness of our cause, and confident of the victories to come. In all that lies before us, may God grant us wisdom, and may He watch over the United States of America.

Thank you. (Applause.)

QUESTIONS TO CONSIDER

1. How does President Bush define America's enemies in this speech? According to him, why are terrorist groups enemies of America?
2. What does President Bush say about the Islamic faith? How does Bush distinguish everyday Muslims throughout the world from fringe groups like al Qaeda?

29.3 MOUSTAFA BAYOUMI, EXCERPTS FROM "HOW DOES IT FEEL TO BE A PROBLEM?" (2001)*

American writer Moustafa Bayoumi (b. 1966) wrote this essay in the wake of the September 11 attacks, when he and many other Muslims and people of Arab descent experienced increasing hostility in the United States. Because the September 11 attacks were carried out by members of an Islamic extremist group, many Americans expressed worry about Muslims in America, associating American Muslims, many of whom were US citizens, with extremists on the other side of the world. Although counts vary, hate crimes and attacks on people of Arab and South Asian descent increased dramatically in

* Moustafa Bayoumi, "How Does It Feel to Be a Problem?" *Amerasia Journal* 27, no. 3/28, no. 1 (2001/2002): 69–77, copyright © The Regents of the University of California, reprinted by permission of Taylor & Francis Ltd, http://www.tandfonline.com on behalf of The Regents of the University of California.

the year following the attacks. As Bayoumi observes, this hostility was aimed toward anyone who might be perceived as Arab or Muslim, regardless of their actual ethnicity or religious beliefs. The hostility that Arab Americans and Asian Americans experienced following September 11 made many, such as Bayoumi, feel misunderstood. They felt that many Americans did not understand the difference between a Sikh turban or a Muslim hijab, did not distinguish between an Egyptian and an Iranian, and did not understand that Islam as practiced by Americans had nothing to do with the extremism of al Qaeda.

Thankfully, I was spared any personal loss. Like so many others in the city which I love, I have spent much of the past two weeks reeling from the devastation. Mostly this has meant getting back in touch with friends, frantically calling them on the phone, rushing around the city to meet with them to give them a consoling hug, but knowing that really it was me looking for the hug. I dash off simple one-line emails, "let me know you're okay, okay?"

Old friends from around the world responded immediately. An email from Canada asks simply if I am all right. Another arrives from friends in Germany telling me how they remember, during their last visit to see me, the view from the top of the towers. A cousin in Egypt states in awkward English, "I hope this attack will not affect you. We hear that some of the Americans attack Arabs and Muslims. I will feel happy if you be in contact with me."

I am all right, of course, but I am devastated. In the first days, I scoured the lists of the dead and missing hoping not to find any recognizable names, but I come across the name of a three-year-old child, and my heart collapses. I hear my neighbor, who works downtown, arrive home, and I knock on her door. She tells me how she was chased by a cloud of debris into a building, locked in there for over an hour, and then, like thousands of others, walked home. I can picture her with the masses in the streets, trudging bewildered like refugees, covered in concrete and human dust. Later, I ride the subway and see a full-page picture of the towers on fire with tiny figures in the frame silently diving to their deaths, and I start to cry.

In the following days, I cried a lot. Then, with friends, I attended a somber peace march in Brooklyn, sponsored by the Arab community. Thousands, overwhelmingly non-Arab and non-Muslim, show up, and

I feel buoyed by the support. A reporter from Chile notices my Arab appearance and asks if she can interview me. I talk to her but am inwardly frightened by her locating me so easily among the thousands. Many people are wearing stickers reading: "We Support Our Arab neighbors," which leaves me both happy and, strangely, crushed. Has it really come to this? Now it has become not just a question of whether we—New Yorkers—are so vulnerable as a city but whether we—in the Arab and Muslim communities—are so vulnerable by our appearances. Is our existence so precarious here? I want to show solidarity with the people wearing the stickers, so how can I possibly explain to them how those stickers scare me?

. . . For the first four weeks after the attacks, I felt a bubble of hope in the dank air of New York. The blunt smell of smoke and death that hung in the atmosphere slowed the city down like I had never experienced it before. New York was solemn, lugubrious, and, for once, without a quick comeback. For a moment, it felt that the trauma of suffering—not the exercise of reason, not the belief in any God, not the universal consumption of a fizzy drink, but the simple and tragic reality that it hurts when we feel pain—was understood as the thread that connects all of humanity. From this point, I had hope that a lesson was being learned, that inflicting more misery cannot alleviate the ache of collective pain.

When the bombing began, the bubble burst. Where there was apprehension, now there was relief in the air. It felt like the city was taking a collective sigh, saying to itself that finally, with the bombing, we can get back to our own lives again. With a perverted logic, dropping munitions meant all's right with the world again.

. . . For years, the organized Arab American community has been lobbying to be recognized with minority status. The check boxes on application forms have always stared defiantly out at me. Go ahead, try to find yourself, they seem to be taunting me. I search and find that, in the eyes of the government, I am a white man.

It is a strange thing, to be brown in reality and white in bureaucracy. Now, however, it is stranger than ever. Since 1909, when the government began questioning whether Syrian immigrants were of "white" stock (desirable) or Asian stock (excludable), Arab immigrants in this country have had to contend with fitting their mixed hues into the primary colors of the state. As subjects of the Ottoman empire, and thus somehow comingled with Turkish stock (who themselves claim descent from the Caucasus, birthplace of the original white people in nineteenth century thinking, even though the location is Asia Minor), Arabs, Armenians, and other Western Asians caused a good deal of consternation among the legislators of race in this country. Syrians and Palestinians were in 1899 classified as white, but by 1910 they were reclassified as "Asiatics."

. . . In the twenty-first century, we are back to being white on paper and brown in reality. After the attacks of September 11, the flood to classify Arabs in this country was drowning our community like a break in a dam. This impact? Hundreds of hate crimes, many directed at South Asians and Iranians, whom the perpetrators mis-identified as Arab (or, more confusingly, as "Muslim": again as if that were a racial category). In the days following the attack (September 14/15), a Gallup Poll revealed that 49 percent of Americans supported "requiring Arabs, including those who are U.S. citizens, to carry a special ID." Fifty-eight percent also supported "requiring Arabs, including those who are U.S. citizens, to undergo special, more intensive security checks before boarding airplanes in the U.S."

Debate rages across the nation as to the legitimacy of using "racial profiling" in these times (overwhelmingly pro). The irony, delicious if it were not so tragic, is that they are racially profiling a people whom they don't even recognize as a race.

. . . These horrific, terrible, and inexcusable acts have no foundation in any ethics of any kind. Such crimes against humanity are to be rejected out of hand, denounced and done away with in any world which operates on principles of ethics, the sanctity of human life, belief in the ideas of human dignity and opportunity. How do we get there?

From the fall to the fallout, I have been living these days in some kind of limbo. The horrific attacks of September 11 have damaged everyone's sense of security, a principle enshrined in the Universal Declaration of Human Rights, and I wonder if for the first that I can remember in the United States, we can start to reflect on that notion more carefully. All the innocents who have perished in this horrendous crime deserve to be mourned, whether they be the rescue workers, the financiers, the tourists, or the service employees in the buildings. An imam in the city has told me how a local union requested his services for a September 11 memorial of their loss since a quarter of their membership was Muslim. Foreign nationals from over eighty countries lost their lives, and the spectacular nature of the attacks meant that the world could witness the United States' own sense of security crumble with the towers. The tragedy of September 11 is truly of heartbreaking proportions. The question remains whether the United States will understand its feelings of stolen security as an unique circumstance, woven into the familiar narrative of American exceptionalism, or whether the people of this country will begin to see how security of person must be guaranteed for all. Aren't we all in this together?

QUESTIONS TO CONSIDER

1.   What aspects of Bayoumi's identity inform his response to September 11? How does his experience as both a New Yorker and an Arab American influence his experiences in the weeks following the attacks?

2.   What frustrates Bayoumi about other Americans' response to the September 11 attacks?

29.4 NAACP ON VOTER IRREGULARITIES IN FLORIDA (2000)*

The 2000 presidential election was the closest in modern history and was beset by numerous voting issues in the state of Florida. Confusing "butterfly ballots" appeared to have led hundreds of voters who intended to vote for Democrat Al Gore to mistakenly vote for Reform Party candidate Pat Buchanan. Voters alleged that some polling locations had been inadequately staffed or subject to a heavy police presence, deterring some voters from casting a ballot. Some legal voters were turned away at the polls because their names were erroneously recorded on a list of felons who were ineligible to vote. The Democratic Party contested the election, which had produced a margin of victory for Republican George W. Bush of less than five hundred votes, but the resulting recount was overseen by Florida secretary of state Katherine Harris, who had been a senior member of the Bush campaign in Florida.

Some of these issues, specifically the understaffing of polling locations and erroneous rejections of legal voters, affected Black Floridians in particular, leading to the involvement of the NAACP. The NAACP eventually filed suit against Harris, and in the resulting settlement the company Florida had contracted to produce lists of ineligible voters agreed to reprocess the lists. The below letter was written by Kweisi Mfume (b. 1948), then president and chief executive of the NAACP, to activist Amy T. Billingsley after the election.

Dear Amy:

Thank you for your letter of support regarding our efforts with respect to violations of voter rights in the recent presidential election, and please forgive the delay of my response. I also thank you for your life membership payment and generous additional donation. It will go a long way to ensuring that we are able to continue our efforts.

Please know that your own dedication and countless hours of work to successfully mobilize volunteers are deeply appreciated. I realize that after working as hard as you did, it must have been disparaging to witness the minimization of the exigencies in Florida by the national media, and even more disheartening to find the Justice Department largely unresponsive to our requests for intervention.

As a non-partisan organization, we have an obligation to insist that all eligible voters be allowed to cast an unfettered ballot and be free from intimidation and harassment. By committing our own resources in order to investigate, publicize, and seek legal remedy for the multitude of non-uniform election practices that impeded or denied exercise of the franchise, we do hope to, as you suggest, turn the tide of public opinion and help the entire country live up to its ideals.

I know you will continue to work with the NAACP in the knowledge that we will prevail in our quest to ensure that all Americans are able to express their hard-won right to vote. I thank you again for your devotion to cause and extend to you my warmest personal regards.

Sincerely,
Kweisi Mfume
President and CEO

---

* NAACP Records, Manuscript Division, Library of Congress (153.00.00), Courtesy of the NAACP. [Digital ID # na0153p1].

QUESTIONS TO CONSIDER

1. Why would the NAACP be particularly interested in preventing voting irregularities in Southern states such as Florida?
2. What problems might arise if voters believe that they may not be allowed to cast a ballot when they arrive at a polling place, and that their ballot may not be counted fairly?

29.5 VISUAL SOURCE: ANN TELNAES, *THE BUSH DECISION* (2000)*

The 2000 presidential election had the closest result in modern history. Although Democrat Al Gore (b. 1948) led the popular vote, it seemed that by securing the heavily contested state of Florida, Republican George W. Bush (b. 1946) would win the election. However, because of numerous voting irregularities in Florida and Bush's small lead in the state, the Gore campaign pursued recounts throughout the state. After Gore's campaign secured an order from the Florida Supreme Court to recount over sixty thousand ballots, the Bush campaign appealed to the United States Supreme Court, who days later delivered a decision in the case, *Bush v. Gore*, in which it ordered the recount to cease, effectively making Bush the winner of the election.

The decision in *Bush v. Gore* was close, being decided by a vote of five to four, with all five votes of the majority coming from justices appointed by Republican presidents. Many Americans felt that the justices had betrayed their commitment to adjudicate as impartial judges and had instead handed an important victory to the candidate whose ideology matched their own. The Pulitzer Prize–winning editorial cartoonist Ann Telnaes (b. 1960) captured this sentiment in this pair of drawings commenting on the Supreme Court's handling of the case.

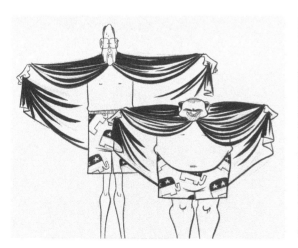 

QUESTIONS TO CONSIDER

1. Why are the justices shown exposing their underwear? What does this tell us about cartoonist Ann Telnaes's perspective on the Court?
2. What potential problems may arise from a court determining the outcome to an election?

CHAPTER 30

DESTINIES, 2005–THE PRESENT

30.1 TA-NEHISI COATES, EXCERPT FROM "FEAR OF A BLACK PRESIDENT" (2012)*

Ta-Nehisi Coates (b. 1975) is an American writer and journalist most notable for his numerous books and articles on the influence of race and white supremacy on American politics and culture. In this 2012 essay, published in *The Atlantic* two months before the 2012 presidential election in which President Barack Obama ran for re-election, Coates reflects on how race and Blackness have impacted Obama's presidency. Although Obama had won the election decisively in 2008, both his campaign and his first term in office were marred by persistent baseless myths about his religious faith and place of birth designed to cast him as un-American and as an illegitimate president.

Coates examines Obama's approach to race in his first term, noting that, despite being the first Black president in American history, Obama had largely avoided discussing race during his time in office. Coates attributes this to a persistent double standard of racial integration—namely, that for Black Americans to be accepted by white audiences, they must be "twice as good" and "half as Black." Coates notes that when Obama did address race, his political opponents responded with not just disagreement but anger.

The irony of President Barack Obama is best captured in his comments on the death of Trayvon Martin, and the ensuing fray. Obama has pitched his presidency as a monument to moderation. He peppers his speeches with nods to ideas originally held by conservatives. He routinely cites Ronald Reagan. He effusively praises the enduring wisdom of the American people, and believes that the height of insight lies in the town square. Despite his sloganeering for change and progress, Obama is a conservative revolutionary, and nowhere is his conservative character revealed more than in the very sphere where he holds singular gravity—race.

Part of that conservatism about race has been reflected in his reticence: for most of his term in office, Obama has declined to talk about the ways in which race complicates the American present and, in particular, his own presidency. But then, last February, George

* Courtesy of Atlantic Media

185

Zimmerman, a 28-year-old insurance underwriter, shot and killed a black teenager, Trayvon Martin, in Sanford, Florida. Zimmerman, armed with a 9 mm handgun, believed himself to be tracking the movements of a possible intruder. The possible intruder turned out to be a boy in a hoodie, bearing nothing but candy and iced tea. The local authorities at first declined to make an arrest, citing Zimmerman's claim of self-defense. Protests exploded nationally. Skittles and Arizona Iced Tea assumed totemic power. Celebrities—the actor Jamie Foxx, the former Michigan governor Jennifer Granholm, members of the Miami Heat—were photographed wearing hoodies. When Representative Bobby Rush of Chicago took to the House floor to denounce racial profiling, he was removed from the chamber after donning a hoodie mid-speech.

The reaction to the tragedy was, at first, trans-partisan. Conservatives either said nothing or offered tepid support for a full investigation—and in fact it was the Republican governor of Florida, Rick Scott, who appointed the special prosecutor who ultimately charged Zimmerman with second-degree murder. As civil-rights activists descended on Florida, *National Review*, a magazine that once opposed integration, ran a column proclaiming "Al Sharpton Is Right." The belief that a young man should be able to go to the store for Skittles and an iced tea and not be killed by a neighborhood-watch patroller seemed uncontroversial.

By the time reporters began asking the White House for comment, the president likely had already given the matter considerable thought. Obama is not simply America's first black president—he is the first president who could credibly teach a black-studies class. He is fully versed in the works of Richard Wright and James Baldwin, Frederick Douglass and Malcolm X. Obama's two autobiographies are deeply concerned with race, and in front of black audiences he is apt to cite important but obscure political figures such as George Henry White, who served from 1897 to 1901 and was the last African American congressman to be elected from the South until 1970. But with just a few notable exceptions, the president had, for the first three years of his presidency, strenuously avoided talk of race. And yet, when Trayvon Martin died, talk Obama did:

> When I think about this boy, I think about my own kids, and I think every parent in America should be

able to understand why it is absolutely imperative that we investigate every aspect of this, and that everybody pulls together—federal, state, and local—to figure out exactly how this tragedy happened. . . .

> But my main message is to the parents of Trayvon Martin. If I had a son, he'd look like Trayvon. I think they are right to expect that all of us as Americans are going to take this with the seriousness it deserves, and that we're going to get to the bottom of exactly what happened.

The moment Obama spoke, the case of Trayvon Martin passed out of its national-mourning phase and lapsed into something darker and more familiar—racialized political fodder. The illusion of consensus crumbled. Rush Limbaugh denounced Obama's claim of empathy. *The Daily Caller*, a conservative Web site, broadcast all of Martin's tweets, the most loutish of which revealed him to have committed the unpardonable sin of speaking like a 17-year-old boy. A white-supremacist site called Stormfront produced a photo of Martin with pants sagging, flipping the bird. *Business Insider* posted the photograph and took it down without apology when it was revealed to be a fake.

Newt Gingrich pounced on Obama's comments: "Is the president suggesting that if it had been a white who had been shot, that would be okay because it wouldn't look like him?" Reverting to form, *National Review* decided the real problem was that we were interested in the deaths of black youths only when nonblacks pulled the trigger. John Derbyshire, writing for *Taki's Magazine*, an iconoclastic libertarian publication, composed a racist advice column for his children inspired by the Martin affair. (Among Derbyshire's tips: never help black people in any kind of distress; avoid large gatherings of black people; cultivate black friends to shield yourself from charges of racism.)

The notion that Zimmerman might be the real victim began seeping out into the country, aided by PR efforts by his family and legal team, as well as by various acts of stupidity—Spike Lee tweeting Zimmerman's address (an act made all the more repugnant by the fact that he had the wrong Zimmerman), NBC misleadingly editing a tape of Zimmerman's phone conversation with a police dispatcher to make Zimmerman seem to be racially profiling Martin. In April, when Zimmerman set up a Web site to collect donations for his defense, he raised more than $200,000 in two weeks, before his lawyer asked that he close the site and launched a new, independently managed legal-defense fund. Although the trial date has yet to be set, as of July the fund was still raking in up to $1,000 in donations daily.

But it would be wrong to attribute the burgeoning support for Zimmerman to the blunders of Spike Lee or an NBC producer. Before President Obama spoke, the death of Trayvon Martin was generally regarded as a national tragedy. After Obama spoke, Martin became material for an Internet vendor flogging paper gun-range targets that mimicked his hoodie and his bag of Skittles. (The vendor sold out within a week.) Before the president spoke, George Zimmerman was arguably the most reviled man in America. After the president spoke, Zimmerman became the patron saint of those who believe that an apt history of racism begins with Tawana Brawley and ends with the Duke lacrosse team.

The irony of Barack Obama is this: he has become the most successful black politician in American history by avoiding the radioactive racial issues of yesteryear, by being "clean" (as Joe Biden once labeled him)—and yet his indelible blackness irradiates everything he touches. This irony is rooted in the greater ironies of the country he leads. For most of American history, our political system was premised on two conflicting facts—one, an oft-stated love of democracy; the other, an undemocratic white supremacy inscribed at every level of government. In warring against that paradox, African Americans have historically been restricted to the realm of protest and agitation. But when President Barack Obama pledged to "get to the bottom of exactly what happened," he was not protesting or agitating. He was not appealing to federal power—he was employing it. The power was black—and, in certain quarters, was received as such.

No amount of rhetorical moderation could change this. It did not matter that the president addressed himself to "every parent in America." His insistence that "everybody [pull] together" was irrelevant. It meant nothing that he declined to cast aspersions on the investigating authorities, or to speculate on events. Even the fact that Obama expressed his own connection to Martin in the quietest way imaginable—"If I had a son, he'd look like Trayvon"—would not mollify his opposition. It is, after all, one thing to hear "I am Trayvon Martin" from the usual placard-waving rabble-rousers. Hearing it from the commander of the greatest military machine in human history is another.

By virtue of his background—the son of a black man and a white woman, someone who grew up in multiethnic communities around the world—Obama has enjoyed a distinctive vantage point on race relations in America. Beyond that, he has displayed enviable dexterity at navigating between black and white America, and at finding a language that speaks to a critical mass in both communities. He emerged into national view at the Democratic National Convention in 2004, with a speech heralding a nation uncolored by old prejudices and shameful history. There was no talk of the effects of racism. Instead Obama stressed the power of parenting, and condemned those who would say that a black child carrying a book was "acting white." He cast himself as the child of a father from Kenya and a mother from Kansas and asserted, "In no other country on Earth is my story even possible." When, as a senator, he was asked if the response to Hurricane Katrina evidenced racism, Obama responded by calling the "ineptitude" of the response "color-blind."

Racism is not merely a simplistic hatred. It is, more often, broad sympathy toward some and broader skepticism toward others. Black America ever lives under that skeptical eye. Hence the old admonishments to be "twice as good." Hence the need for a special "talk" administered to black boys about how to be extra careful when relating to the police. And hence Barack Obama's insisting that there was no racial component to Katrina's effects; that name-calling among children somehow has the same import as one of the oldest guiding principles of American policy—white supremacy. The election of an African American to our highest political office was alleged to demonstrate a triumph of integration. But when President Obama addressed the tragedy of Trayvon Martin, he demonstrated integration's great limitation—that acceptance depends not just on being twice as good but on being half as black. And even then, full acceptance is still withheld. The larger effects of this withholding constrict Obama's presidential potential in areas affected tangentially—or seemingly not at all—by race. Meanwhile, across the country, the community in which Obama is rooted sees this fraudulent equality, and quietly seethes.

Obama's first term has coincided with a strategy of massive resistance on the part of his Republican opposition in the House, and a record number of filibuster threats in the Senate. It would be nice if this were merely a reaction to Obama's politics or his policies—if this resistance truly were, as it is generally described, merely one more sign of our growing "polarization" as a nation. But the greatest abiding challenge to Obama's national political standing has always rested on the existential fact that if he had a son, he'd look like Trayvon Martin. As a candidate, Barack Obama understood this.

"The thing is, a *black man* can't be president in America, given the racial aversion and history that's still out there," Cornell Belcher, a pollster for Obama, told the journalist Gwen Ifill after the 2008 election. "However, an extraordinary, gifted, and talented young man who happens to be black can be president."

Belcher's formulation grants the power of anti-black racism, and proposes to defeat it by not acknowledging it. His is the perfect statement of the Obama era, a time marked by a revolution that must never announce itself, by a democracy that must never acknowledge the weight of race, even while being shaped by it. Barack Obama governs a nation enlightened enough to send an African American to the White House, but not enlightened enough to accept a black man as its president.

Before Barack Obama, the "black president" lived in the African American imagination as a kind of cosmic joke, a phantom of all that could never be. White folks, whatever their talk of freedom and liberty, would not allow a black president. They could not tolerate Emmett's boyish gaze. Dr. King turned the other cheek, and they blew it off. White folks shot Lincoln over "nigger equality," ran Ida Wells out of Memphis, beat Freedom Riders over bus seats, slaughtered Medgar in his driveway like a dog. The comedian Dave Chappelle joked that the first black president would need a "Vice President Santiago"—because the only thing that would ensure his life in the White House was a Hispanic president-in-waiting. A black president signing a bill into law might as well sign his own death certificate.

The moment Obama spoke, the Trayvon case passed out of its mourning phase and into something dark and familiar—racialized political fodder.

And even if white folks could moderate their own penchant for violence, we could not moderate our own. A long-suffering life on the wrong side of the color line had denuded black people of the delicacy necessary to lead the free world. In a skit on his 1977 TV comedy show, Richard Pryor, as a black president, conceded that he was "courting an awful lot of white women" and held a press conference that erupted into a riot after a reporter requested that the president's momma clean his house. More recently, the comedian Cedric the Entertainer joked that a black president would never have made it through Monicagate without turning a press conference into a battle royal. When Chappelle tried to imagine how a black George W. Bush would have justified the war against Saddam Hussein, his character ("Black Bush") simply yelled, "The nigger tried to kill my father!"

Thus, in hard jest, the paradoxes and problems of a theoretical black presidency were given voice. Racism would not allow a black president. Nor would a blackness, forged by America's democratic double-talk, that was too ghetto and raw for the refinement of the Oval Office. Just beneath the humor lurked a resonant pain, the scars of history, an aching doubt rooted in the belief that "they" would never accept us. And so in our Harlems and Paradise Valleys, we invoked a black presidency the way a legion of 5-foot point guards might invoke the dunk—as evidence of some great cosmic injustice, weighty in its import, out of reach.

And yet Spud Webb lives.

When presidential candidate Barack Obama presented himself to the black community, he was not to be believed. It strained credulity to think that a man sporting the same rigorously managed haircut as Jay-Z, a man who was a hard-core pickup basketball player, and who was married to a dark-skinned black woman from the South Side, could coax large numbers of white voters into the booth. Obama's blackness quotient is often a subject of debate. (He himself once joked, while speaking to the National Association of Black Journalists in 2007, "I want to apologize for being a little bit late, but you guys keep on asking whether I'm black enough.") But despite Obama's post-election reluctance to talk about race, he has always displayed both an obvious affinity for black culture and a distinct ability to defy black America's worst self-conceptions.

The crude communal myth about black men is that we are in some manner unavailable to black women—either jailed, dead, gay, or married to white women. A corollary myth posits a direct and negative relationship between success and black culture. Before we actually had one, we could not imagine a black president who loved being black. In *The Audacity of Hope*, Obama describes his first kiss with the woman who would become his wife as tasting "of chocolate." The line sounds ripped from *Essence* magazine. That's the point.

These cultural cues became important during Obama's presidential run and beyond. Obama doesn't merely evince blackness; he uses his blackness to signal and court African Americans, semaphoring in a cultural dialect of our creation—crooning Al Green at the Apollo, name-checking Young Jeezy, regularly appearing on the cover of black magazines, weighing the merits of Jay-Z versus Kanye West, being photographed in the White House with a little black boy touching his hair. There is often something mawkish about this signaling—like a Virginia politico thickening his southern accent when talking to certain audiences. If you've often been the butt of political signaling (Sister Souljah, Willie Horton), and rarely the recipient, these displays of cultural affinity are powerful. And they are all the more powerful because Obama has been successful. Whole sections of America that we had assumed to be negrophobic turned out in support of him in 2008. Whatever Obama's other triumphs, arguably his greatest has been an expansion of the black imagination to encompass this: the idea that a man can be culturally black and many other things also—biracial, Ivy League, intellectual, cosmopolitan, temperamentally conservative, presidential.

It is often said that Obama's presidency has given black parents the right to tell their kids with a straight face that they can do anything. This is a function not only of Obama's election to the White House but of the way his presidency broadcasts an easy, almost mystic, blackness to the world. The Obama family represents our ideal imagining of ourselves—an ideal we so rarely see on any kind of national stage.

What black people are experiencing right now is a kind of privilege previously withheld—seeing our most sacred cultural practices and tropes validated in the world's highest office. Throughout the whole of American history, this kind of cultural power was wielded solely by whites, and with such ubiquity that it was not even commented upon. The expansion of this cultural power beyond the private province of whites has been a tremendous advance for black America. Conversely, for those who've long treasured white exclusivity, the existence of a President Barack Obama is discombobulating, even terrifying. For as surely as the iconic picture of the young black boy reaching out to touch the president's curly hair sends one message to black America, it sends another to those who have enjoyed the power of whiteness.

In America, the rights to own property, to serve on a jury, to vote, to hold public office, to rise to the presidency have historically been seen as belonging only to those people who showed particular integrity. Citizenship was a social contract in which persons of moral standing were transformed into stakeholders who swore to defend the state against threats external and internal. Until a century and a half ago, slave rebellion ranked high in the fevered American imagination of threats necessitating such an internal defense.

In the early years of our republic, when democracy was still an unproven experiment, the Founders were not even clear that all white people should be entrusted with this fragile venture, much less the bestial African. Thus Congress, in 1790, declared the following:

> All free white persons who have, or shall migrate into the United States, and shall give satisfactory proof, before a magistrate, by oath, that they intend to reside therein, and shall take an oath of allegiance, and shall have resided in the United States for one whole year, shall be entitled to all the rights of citizenship.

In such ways was the tie between citizenship and whiteness in America made plain from the very beginning. By the 19th century, there was, as Matthew Jacobson, a professor of history and American studies at Yale, has put it, "an unquestioned acceptance of whiteness as a prerequisite for naturalized citizenship." Debating Abraham Lincoln during the race for a

U.S. Senate seat in Illinois in 1858, Stephen Douglas asserted that "this government was made on the white basis" and that the Framers had made "no reference either to the Negro, the savage Indians, the Feejee, the Malay, or an other inferior and degraded race, when they spoke of the equality of men."

After the Civil War, Andrew Johnson, Lincoln's successor as president and a unionist, scoffed at awarding the Negro the franchise:

> The peculiar qualities which should characterize any people who are fit to decide upon the management of public affairs for a great state have seldom been combined. It is the glory of white men to know that they have had these qualities in sufficient measure to build upon this continent a great political fabric and to preserve its stability for more than ninety years, while in every other part of the world all similar experiments have failed. But if anything can be proved by known facts, if all reasoning upon evidence is not abandoned, it must be acknowledged that in the progress of nations Negroes have shown less capacity for government than any other race of people. No independent government of any form has ever been successful in their hands. On the contrary, wherever they have been left to their own devices they have shown a constant tendency to relapse into barbarism.

The notion of blacks as particularly unfit for political equality persisted well into the 20th century. As the nation began considering integrating its military, a young West Virginian wrote to a senator in 1944:

> I am a typical American, a southerner, and 27 years of age . . . I am loyal to my country and know but reverence to her flag, BUT I shall never submit to fight beneath that banner with a negro by my side. Rather I should die a thousand times, and see Old Glory trampled in the dirt never to rise again, than to see this beloved land of ours become degraded by race mongrels, a throw back to the blackest specimen from the wilds.

The writer—who never joined the military, but did join the Ku Klux Klan—was Robert Byrd, who died in 2010 as the longest-serving U.S. senator in history. Byrd's rejection of political equality was echoed in 1957 by William F. Buckley Jr., who addressed the moral disgrace of segregation by endorsing disenfranchisement strictly based on skin color:

> The central question that emerges—and it is not a parliamentary question or a question that is answered by merely consulting a catalog of the rights of American citizens, born Equal—is whether the White community in the South is entitled to take such measures as are necessary to prevail, politically and culturally, in areas in which it does not predominate numerically? The sobering answer is Yes—the White community is so entitled because, for the time being, it is the advanced race.

Buckley, the founder of *National Review*, went on to assert, "The great majority of the Negroes of the South who do not vote do not care to vote and would not know for what to vote if they could."

The myth of "twice as good" that makes Obama possible also smothers him. It holds that blacks feel no anger toward their tormentors.

The idea that blacks should hold no place of consequence in the American political future has affected every sector of American society, transforming whiteness itself into a monopoly on American possibilities. White people like Byrd and Buckley were raised in a time when, by law, they were assured of never having to compete with black people for the best of anything. Blacks used inferior public pools and inferior washrooms, attended inferior schools. The nicest restaurants turned them away. In large swaths of the country, blacks paid taxes but could neither attend the best universities nor exercise the right to vote. The best jobs, the richest neighborhoods, were giant set-asides for whites—universal affirmative action, with no pretense of restitution.

Slavery, Jim Crow, segregation: these bonded white people into a broad aristocracy united by the salient fact of unblackness. What Byrd saw in an integrated military was the crumbling of the ideal of whiteness, and thus the crumbling of an entire society built around it. Whatever the saintly nonviolent rhetoric used to herald it, racial integration was a brutal assault on whiteness. The American presidency, an unbroken streak of nonblack men, was, until 2008, the greatest symbol of that old order.

Watching Obama rack up victories in states like Virginia, New Mexico, Ohio, and North Carolina on Election Night in 2008, anyone could easily conclude that racism, as a national force, had been defeated.

The thought should not be easily dismissed: Obama's victory demonstrates the incredible distance this country has traveled. (Indeed, William F. Buckley Jr. later revised his early positions on race; Robert Byrd spent decades in Congress atoning for his.) That a country that once took whiteness as the foundation of citizenship would elect a black president is a victory. But to view this victory as racism's defeat is to forget the precise terms on which it was secured, and to ignore the quaking ground beneath Obama's feet.

During the 2008 primary, *The New Yorker*'s George Packer journeyed to Kentucky and was shocked by the brazen declarations of white identity. "I think he would put too many minorities in positions over the white race," one voter told Packer. "That's my opinion." That voter was hardly alone. In 2010, Michael Tesler, a political scientist at Brown University, and David Sears, a professor of psychology and political science at UCLA, were able to assess the impact of race in the 2008 primary by comparing data from two 2008 campaign and election studies with previous surveys of racial resentment and voter choice. As they wrote in *Obama's Race: The 2008 Election and the Dream of a Post-Racial America*:

> No other factor, in fact, came close to dividing the Democratic primary electorate as powerfully as their feelings about African Americans. The impact of racial attitudes on individual vote decisions . . . was so strong that it appears to have even outstripped the substantive impact of racial attitudes on Jesse Jackson's more racially charged campaign for the nomination in 1988.

Seth Stephens-Davidowitz, a doctoral candidate in economics at Harvard, is studying how racial animus may have cost Obama votes in 2008. First, Stephens-Davidowitz ranked areas of the country according to how often people there typed racist search terms into Google. (The areas with the highest rates of racially charged search terms were West Virginia, western Pennsylvania, eastern Ohio, upstate New York, and southern Mississippi.) Then he compared Obama's voting results in those areas with John Kerry's four years earlier. So, for instance, in 2004 Kerry received 50 percent of the vote in the media markets of both Denver and Wheeling (which straddles the Ohio–West

Virginia border). Based on the Democratic groundswell in 2008, Obama should have received about 57 percent of the popular vote in both regions. But that's not what happened. In the Denver area, which had one of the nation's lowest rates of racially charged Google searching, Obama received the predicted 57 percent. But in Wheeling, which had a high rate of racially charged Google searching, Obama's share of the popular vote was only 48 percent. Of course, Obama also picked up some votes because he is black. But, aggregating his findings nationally, Stephens-Davidowitz has concluded that Obama lost between 3 and 5 percentage points of the popular vote to racism.

After Obama won, the longed-for post-racial moment did not arrive; on the contrary, racism intensified. At rallies for the nascent Tea Party, people held signs saying things like Obama Plans White Slavery. Steve King, an Iowa congressman and Tea Party favorite, complained that Obama "favors the black person." In 2009, Rush Limbaugh, bard of white decline, called Obama's presidency a time when "the white kids now get beat up, with the black kids cheering 'Yeah, right on, right on, right on.' And of course everybody says the white kid deserved it—he was born a racist, he's white." On *Fox & Friends*, Glenn Beck asserted that Obama had exposed himself as a guy "who has a deep-seated hatred for white people or the white culture. . . . This guy is, I believe, a racist." Beck later said he was wrong to call Obama a racist. That same week he also called the president's health-care plan "reparations."

One possible retort to this pattern of racial paranoia is to cite the Clinton years, when an ideological fever drove the right wing to derangement, inspiring militia movements and accusations that the president had conspired to murder his own lawyer, Vince Foster. The upshot, by this logic, is that Obama is experiencing run-of-the-mill political opposition in which race is but a minor factor among much larger ones, such as party affiliation. But the argument assumes that party affiliation itself is unconnected to race. It pretends that only Toni Morrison took note of Clinton's particular appeal to black voters. It forgets that Clinton felt compelled to attack Sister Souljah. It forgets that whatever ignoble labels the right wing pinned on Clinton's health-care plan, "reparations" did not rank among them.

Michael Tesler, following up on his research with David Sears on the role of race in the 2008 campaign, recently published a study assessing the impact of race on opposition to and support for health-care reform. The findings are bracing. Obama's election effectively racialized white Americans' views, even of health-care policy. As Tesler writes in a paper published in July in *The American Journal of Political Science,* "Racial attitudes had a significantly greater impact on health care opinions when framed as part of President Obama's plan than they had when the exact same policies were attributed to President Clinton's 1993 health care initiative."

While Beck and Limbaugh have chosen direct racial assault, others choose simply to deny that a black president actually exists. One in four Americans (and more than half of all Republicans) believe Obama was not born in this country, and thus is an illegitimate president. More than a dozen state legislatures have introduced "birther bills" demanding proof of Obama's citizenship as a condition for putting him on the 2012 ballot. Eighteen percent of Republicans believe Obama to be a Muslim. The goal of all this is to delegitimize Obama's presidency. If Obama is not truly American, then America has still never had a black president.

White resentment has not cooled as the Obama presidency has proceeded. Indeed, the GOP presidential-primary race featured candidates asserting that the black family was better off under slavery (Michele Bachmann, Rick Santorum); claiming that Obama, as a black man, should oppose abortion (Santorum again); or denouncing Obama as a "food-stamp president" (Newt Gingrich).

The resentment is not confined to Republicans. Earlier this year, West Virginia gave 41 percent of the popular vote during the Democratic primary to Keith Judd, a white incarcerated felon (Judd actually defeated Obama in 10 counties). Joe Manchin, one of West Virginia's senators, and Earl Ray Tomblin, its governor, are declining to attend this year's Democratic convention, and will not commit to voting for Obama.

It is often claimed that Obama's unpopularity in coal-dependent West Virginia stems from his environmental policies. But recall that no state ranked higher on Seth Stephens-Davidowitz's racism scale than West

Virginia. Moreover, Obama was unpopular in West Virginia before he became president: even at the tail end of the Democratic primaries in 2008, Hillary Clinton walloped Obama by 41 points. A fifth of West Virginia Democrats openly professed that race played a role in their vote.

What we are now witnessing is not some new and complicated expression of white racism—rather, it's the dying embers of the same old racism that once rendered the best pickings of America the exclusive province of unblackness. Confronted by the thoroughly racialized backlash to Obama's presidency, a stranger to American politics might conclude that Obama provoked the response by relentlessly pushing an agenda of radical racial reform. Hardly. Daniel Gillion, a political scientist at the University of Pennsylvania who studies race and politics, examined the Public Papers of the Presidents, a compilation of nearly all public presidential utterances—proclamations, news-conference remarks, executive orders—and found that in his first two years as president, Obama talked less about race than any other Democratic president since 1961. Obama's racial strategy has been, if anything, the opposite of radical: he declines to use his bully pulpit to address racism, using it instead to engage in the time-honored tradition of black self-hectoring, railing against the perceived failings of black culture.

His approach is not new. It is the approach of Booker T. Washington, who, amid a sea of white terrorists during the era of Jim Crow, endorsed segregation and proclaimed the South to be a land of black opportunity. It is the approach of L. Douglas Wilder, who, in 1986, not long before he became Virginia's first black governor, kept his distance from Jesse Jackson and told an NAACP audience: "Yes, dear Brutus, the fault is not in our stars, but in ourselves. . . . Some blacks don't particularly care for me to say these things, to speak to values. . . . Somebody's got to. We've been too excusing." It was even, at times, the approach of Jesse Jackson himself, who railed against "the rising use of drugs, and babies making babies, and violence . . . cutting away our opportunity."

The strategy can work. Booker T.'s Tuskegee University still stands. Wilder became the first black governor in America since Reconstruction. Jackson's campaign moved the Democratic nominating process toward proportional allocation of delegates, a shift that Obama exploited in the 2008 Democratic primaries by staying competitive enough in big states to rack up delegates even where he was losing, and rolling up huge vote margins (and delegate-count victories) in smaller ones.

And yet what are we to make of an integration premised, first, on the entire black community's emulating the Huxtables? An equality that requires blacks to be twice as good is not equality—it's a double standard. That double standard haunts and constrains the Obama presidency, warning him away from candor about America's sordid birthmark.

Another political tradition in black America, running counter to the one publicly embraced by Obama and Booker T. Washington, casts its skepticism not simply upon black culture but upon the entire American project. This tradition stretches back to Frederick Douglass, who, in 1852, said of his native country, "There is not a nation on the earth guilty of practices more shocking and bloody than are the people of the United States at this very hour." It extends through Martin Delany, through Booker T.'s nemesis W. E. B. Du Bois, and through Malcolm X. It includes Martin Luther King Jr., who at the height of the Vietnam War called America "the greatest purveyor of violence in the world today." And it includes Obama's former pastor, he of the famous "God Damn America" sermon, Jeremiah Wright.

The Harvard Law professor Randall Kennedy, in his 2011 book, *The Persistence of the Color Line: Racial Politics and the Obama Presidency*, examines this tradition by looking at his own father and Reverend Wright in the context of black America's sense of patriotism. Like Wright, the elder Kennedy was a veteran of the U.S. military, a man seared and radicalized by American racism, forever remade as a vociferous critic of his native country: in virtually any American conflict, Kennedy's father rooted for the foreign country.

The deep skepticism about the American project that Kennedy's father and Reverend Wright evince is an old tradition in black America. Before Frederick Douglass worked, during the Civil War, for the preservation of the Union, he called for his country's destruction. "I have no love for America," he declaimed in a lecture to the American Anti-Slavery Society in 1847. "I have no

patriotism . . . I desire to see [the government] overthrown as speedily as possible and its Constitution shivered in a thousand fragments."

Kennedy notes that Douglass's denunciations were the words of a man who not only had endured slavery but was living in a country where whites often selected the Fourth of July as a special day to prosecute a campaign of racial terror:

> On July 4, 1805, whites in Philadelphia drove blacks out of the square facing Independence Hall. For years thereafter, blacks attended Fourth of July festivities in that city at their peril. On July 4, 1834, a white mob in New York City burned down the Broadway Tabernacle because of the antislavery and antiracist views of the church's leaders. Firefighters in sympathy with the arsonists refused to douse the conflagration. On July 4, 1835, a white mob in Canaan, New Hampshire, destroyed a school open to blacks that was run by an abolitionist. The antebellum years were liberally dotted with such episodes.

Jeremiah Wright was born into an America of segregation—overt in the South and covert in the North, but wounding wherever. He joined the Marines, vowing service to his country, at a time when he wouldn't have been allowed to vote in some states. He built his ministry in a community reeling from decades of job and housing discrimination, and heaving under the weight of drugs, gun violence, and broken families. Wright's world is emblematic of the African Americans he ministered to, people reared on the anti-black-citizenship tradition—poll taxes, states pushing stringent voter-ID laws—of Stephen Douglas and Andrew Johnson and William F. Buckley Jr. The message is "You are not American." The countermessage—God damn America—is an old one, and is surprising only to people unfamiliar with the politics of black life in this country. Unfortunately, that is an apt description of large swaths of America.

Whatever the context for Wright's speech, the surfacing of his remarks in 2008 was utterly inconvenient not just for the Obama campaign but for much of black America. One truism holds that black people are always anxious to talk about race, eager to lecture white people at every juncture about how wrong they are and about the price they must pay for past and ongoing sins. But one reason Obama rose so quickly was that African Americans are war-weary. It was not simply the country at large that was tired of the old Baby Boomer debates. Blacks, too, were sick of talking about affirmative action and school busing. There was a broad sense that integration had failed us, and a growing disenchantment with our appointed spokespeople. Obama's primary triumphs in predominantly white states gave rise to rumors of a new peace, one many blacks were anxious to achieve.

And even those black Americans who embrace the tradition of God Damn America do so not with glee but with deep pain and anguish. Both Kennedy's father and Wright were military men. My own father went to Vietnam dreaming of John Wayne, but came back quoting Malcolm X. The poet Lucille Clifton once put it succinctly:

They act like they don't love their country
No
what it is
is they found out
their country don't love them.

In 2008, as Obama's election became imaginable, it seemed possible that our country had indeed, at long last, come to love us. We did not need our Jeremiah Wrights, our Jesse Jacksons, our products of the polarized '60s getting in the way. Indeed, after distancing himself from Wright, Obama lost almost no black support.

Obama offered black America a convenient narrative that could be meshed with the larger American story. It was a narrative premised on Crispus Attucks, not the black slaves who escaped plantations and fought for the British; on the 54th Massachusetts, not Nat Turner; on stoic and saintly Rosa Parks, not young and pregnant Claudette Colvin; on a Christlike Martin Luther King Jr., not an avenging Malcolm X. Jeremiah Wright's presence threatened to rupture that comfortable narrative by symbolizing that which makes integration impossible—black rage.

From the "inadequate black male" diatribe of the Hillary Clinton supporter Harriet Christian in 2008, to Rick Santelli's 2009 rant on CNBC against subsidizing "losers' mortgages," to Representative Joe Wilson's "You lie!" outburst during Obama's September 2009 address to Congress, to John Boehner's screaming

"Hell no!" on the House floor about Obamacare in 2010, politicized rage has marked the opposition to Obama. But the rules of our racial politics require that Obama never respond in like fashion. So frightening is the prospect of black rage given voice and power that when Obama was a freshman senator, he was asked, on national television, to denounce the rage of Harry Belafonte. This fear continued with demands that he keep his distance from Louis Farrakhan and culminated with Reverend Wright and a presidency that must never betray any sign of rage toward its white opposition.

Thus the myth of "twice as good" that makes Barack Obama possible also smothers him. It holds that African Americans—enslaved, tortured, raped, discriminated against, and subjected to the most lethal homegrown terrorist movement in American history—feel no anger toward their tormentors. Of course, very little in our history argues that those who seek to tell bold truths about race will be rewarded. But it was Obama himself, as a presidential candidate in 2008, who called for such truths to be spoken. "Race is an issue that I believe this nation cannot afford to ignore right now," he said in his "More Perfect Union" speech, which he delivered after a furor erupted over Reverend Wright's "God Damn America" remarks. And yet, since taking office, Obama has virtually ignored race.

Whatever the political intelligence of this calculus, it has broad and deep consequences. The most obvious result is that it prevents Obama from directly addressing America's racial history, or saying anything meaningful about present issues tinged by race, such as mass incarceration or the drug war. There have been calls for Obama to take a softer line on state-level legalization of marijuana or even to stand for legalization himself. Indeed, there is no small amount of inconsistency in our black president's either ignoring or upholding harsh drug laws that every day injure the prospects of young black men—laws that could have ended his own, had he been of another social class and arrested for the marijuana use he openly discusses. But the intellectual argument doubles as the counterargument. If the fact of a black president is enough to racialize the wonkish world of health-care reform, what havoc would the Obama touch wreak upon the already racialized world of drug policy?

What we are witnessing is not some new racism—it's the dying embers of the same old racism that rendered the best pickings the province of unblackness.

The political consequences of race extend beyond the domestic. I am, like many liberals, horrified by Obama's embrace of a secretive drone policy, and particularly the killing of American citizens without any restraints. A president aware of black America's tenuous hold on citizenship, of how the government has at times secretly conspired against its advancement—a black president with a broad sense of the world—should know better. Except a black president with Obama's past is the perfect target for right-wing attacks depicting him as weak on terrorism. The president's inability to speak candidly on race cannot be bracketed off from his inability to speak candidly on everything. Race is not simply a portion of the Obama story. It is the lens through which many Americans view all his politics.

But whatever the politics, a total submission to them is a disservice to the country. No one knows this better than Obama himself, who once described patriotism as more than pageantry and the scarfing of hot dogs. "When our laws, our leaders, or our government are out of alignment with our ideals, then the dissent of ordinary Americans may prove to be one of the truest expressions of patriotism," Obama said in Independence, Missouri, in June 2008. Love of country, like all other forms of love, requires that you tell those you care about not simply what they want to hear but what they need to hear.

But in the age of the Obama presidency, expressing that kind of patriotism is presumably best done quietly, politely, and with great deference.

This spring I flew down to Albany, Georgia, and spent the day with Shirley Sherrod, a longtime civil-rights activist who embodies exactly the kind of patriotism that Obama esteems. Albany is in Dougherty County, where the poverty rate hangs around 30 percent—double that of the rest of the state. On the drive in from the airport, the selection of vendors—payday loans, title loans, and car dealers promising no credit check—evidenced the statistic.

When I met Sherrod at her office, she was working to get a birthday card out to Roger Spooner, whose farm she'd once fought to save. In July 2010, the conservative commentator Andrew Breitbart posted video

clips on his Web site of a speech Sherrod had delivered to the NAACP the previous March. The video was edited so that Sherrod, then an official at the U.S. Department of Agriculture, appeared to be bragging about discriminating against a white farmer and thus enacting a fantasy of racial revenge. The point was to tie Obama to the kind of black rage his fevered enemies often impute to him. Fearing exactly that, Sherrod's supervisors at the USDA called her in the middle of a long drive and had her submit her resignation via BlackBerry, telling her, "You're going to be on *Glenn Beck* tonight."

Glenn Beck did eventually do a segment on Sherrod—one in which he attacked the administration for forcing her out. As it turned out, the full context showed that Sherrod was actually documenting her own turn *away* from racial anger. The farmer who was the subject of the story came forward, along with his wife, and explained that Sherrod had worked tirelessly to help the family. The farmer was Roger Spooner.

Sherrod's career as an activist, first in civil rights and then later in the world of small farmers like Roger Spooner, was not chosen so much as thrust upon her. Her cousin had been lynched in 1943. Her father was shot and killed by a white relative in a dispute over some cows. There were three witnesses, but the grand jury in her native Baker County did not indict the suspect. Sherrod became an activist with the Student Non-violent Coordinating Committee, registering voters near her hometown. Her husband, Charles Sherrod, was instrumental in leading the Albany Movement, which attracted Martin Luther King Jr. to town. But when Stokely Carmichael rose to lead SNCC and took it in a black-nationalist direction, the Sherrods, committed to nonviolence and integration, faced a weighty choice. Carmichael himself had been committed to nonviolence, until the killings and beatings he encountered as a civil-rights activist took their toll. Sherrod, with a past haunted by racist violence, would have seemed ripe for recruitment to the nationalist line. But she, along with her husband, declined, leaving SNCC in order to continue in the tradition of King and nonviolence.

Her achievements from then on are significant. She helped pioneer the farm-collective movement in America, and co-founded New Communities—a sprawling 6,000-acre collective that did everything from growing crops to canning sugar cane and sorghum. New Communities folded in 1985, largely because Ronald Reagan's USDA refused to sign off on a loan, even as it was signing off on money for smaller-scale white farmers. Sherrod went on to work with Farm Aid. She befriended Willie Nelson, held a fellowship with the Kellogg Foundation, and was shortlisted for a job in President Clinton's Agriculture Department. Still, she remained relatively unknown except to students of the civil-rights movement and activists who promoted the rights of small farmers. And unknown she would have remained, had she not been very publicly forced out of her position by the administration of the country's first black president.

Through most of her career as an agriculture activist, Sherrod had found the USDA to be a barrier to the success of black farmers. What hurt black farms the most were the discriminatory practices of local officials in granting loans. Sherrod spent years protesting these practices. But then, after the election of Barack Obama, she was hired by the USDA, where she would be supervising the very people she'd once fought. Now she would have a chance to ensure fair and nondiscriminatory lending practices. Her appointment represented the kind of unnoticed but significant changes Obama's election brought.

But then the administration, intimidated by a resurgent right wing specializing in whipping up racial resentment, compelled Sherrod to resign on the basis of the misleading clips. When the full tape emerged, the administration was left looking ridiculous.

And cowardly. An e-mail chain later surfaced in which the White House congratulated Agriculture Secretary Tom Vilsack's staff for getting ahead of the news cycle. None of them had yet seen the full tape. That the Obama administration would fold so easily gives some sense of how frightened it was of a protracted fight with any kind of racial subtext, particularly one that had a subtext of black rage. Its enemies understood this, and when no black rage could be found, they concocted some. And the administration, in a panic, knuckled under.

Violence at the hands of whites robbed Shirley Sherrod of a cousin and a father. White rage outlined the substantive rules of her life: Don't quarrel with white people. Don't look them in the eye. Avoid Route 91 after dark. White racism destroyed New Communities, a fact validated by the nearly $13 million the organization received in the class-action suit it joined alleging racial discrimination by the local USDA officials granting loan applications. (Which means that her being forced out by Vilsack was the second time the USDA had wronged her directly.) And yet through it all, Sherrod has hewed to the rule of "twice as good." She has preached nonviolence and integration. The very video that led to her dismissal was of a speech aimed at black people, warning them against the dangers of succumbing to rage.

Acceptance depends not just on being twice as good but on being half as black. The community in which Obama is rooted sees this fraudulent equality and seethes.

Driving down a sparse country road, Sherrod and I pulled over to a grassy footpath and stepped out at the spot where her father had been shot and killed in 1965. We then drove a few miles into Newton, and stopped at a large brick building that used to be the courthouse where Sherrod had tried to register to vote a few months after her father's death but had been violently turned back by the sheriff; where a year later Sherrod's mother pursued a civil case against her husband's killer. (She lost.) For this, Sherrod's mother enjoyed routine visits from white terrorists, which abated only after she, pregnant with her dead husband's son, appeared in the doorway with a gun and began calling out names of men in the mob.

When we got back into the car, I asked Sherrod why she hadn't given in to rage against her father's killers and sided with Stokely Carmichael. "It was simple for me," she said. "I really wanted to work. I wanted to win."

I asked Sherrod if she thought the president had a grasp of the specific history of the region and of the fights waged and the sacrifices made in order to make his political journey possible. "I don't think he does," Sherrod said. "When he called me [shortly after the incident], he kept saying he understood our struggle and all we'd fought for. He said, 'Read my book and you'll see.' But I *had* read his book."

In 2009, Sergeant James Crowley arrested Henry Louis Gates Jr., the eminent professor of African American studies at Harvard, at his front door in Cambridge, for, essentially, sassing him. When President Obama publicly asserted the stupidity of Crowley's action, he was so besieged that the controversy threatened to derail what he hoped would be his signature achievement—health-care reform. Obama, an African American male who had risen through the ranks of the American elite, was no doubt sensitive to untoward treatment at the hands of the police. But his expounding upon it so provoked right-wing rage that he was forced away from doing the kind of truth-telling he'd once lauded. "I don't know if you've noticed," Obama said at the time, "but nobody's been paying much attention to health care."

Shirley Sherrod has worked all her life to make a world where the rise of a black president born of a biracial marriage is both conceivable and legal. She has endured the killing of relatives, the ruination of enterprises, and the defaming of her reputation. Crowley, for his actions, was feted in the halls of American power, honored by being invited to a "beer summit" with the man he had arrested and the leader of the free world. Shirley Sherrod, unjustly fired and defamed, was treated to a brief phone call from a man whose career, in some profound way, she had made possible. Sherrod herself is not immune to this point. She talked to me about crying with her husband while watching Obama's Election Night speech. In her new memoir, *The Courage to Hope*, she writes about a different kind of tears: when she discussed her firing with her family, her mother, who'd spent her life facing down racism at its most lethal, simply wept. "What will my babies say?," Sherrod cried to her husband, referring to their four small granddaughters. "How can I explain to my children that I got fired by the first black president?"

In 2000, an undercover police officer followed a young man named Prince Jones from suburban Maryland through Washington, D.C., into Northern Virginia and shot him dead, near the home of his girlfriend and 11-month-old daughter. Jones was a student at Howard University. His mother was a radiologist. He was also my friend. The officer tracking Prince thought he was on the trail of a drug dealer. But the dealer he was after was short and wore dreadlocks—Prince was tall and wore his hair cropped close. The officer was black. He wore dreadlocks and a T-shirt, in an attempt to look like a drug dealer. The ruse likely worked. He claimed

that after Prince got out of his car and confronted him, he drew his gun and said "Police"; Prince returned to his car and repeatedly rammed the officer's unmarked car with his own vehicle. The story sounded wildly at odds with the young man I knew. But even if it was accurate, I could easily see myself frightened by a strange car following me for miles, and then reacting wildly when a man in civilian clothes pulled out a gun and claimed to be a cop. (The officer never showed a badge.)

No criminal charges were ever brought against Carlton Jones, the officer who killed my friend and rendered a little girl fatherless. It was as if society barely blinked. A few months later, I moved to New York. When 9/11 happened, I wanted nothing to do with any kind of patriotism, with the broad national ceremony of mourning. I had no sympathy for the firefighters, and something bordering on hatred for the police officers who had died. I lived in a country where my friend—twice as good—could be shot down mere footsteps from his family by agents of the state. God damn America, indeed.

I grew. I became a New Yorker. I came to understand the limits of anger. Watching Barack Obama crisscross the country to roaring white crowds, and then get elected president, I became convinced that the country really had changed—that time and events had altered the nation, and that progress had come in places I'd never imagined it could. When Osama bin Laden was killed, I cheered like everyone else. God damn al-Qaeda.

When trans-partisan mourning erupted around Trayvon Martin, it reinforced my conviction that the world had changed since the death of Prince Jones. Like Prince, Trayvon was suspected of being a criminal chiefly because of the color of his skin. Like Prince's, Trayvon's killer claimed self-defense. Again, with little effort, I could see myself in the shoes of the dead man. But this time, society's response seemed so very different, so much more heartening.

Then the first black president spoke, and the Internet bloomed. Young people began "Trayvoning"—mocking the death of a black boy by photographing themselves in hoodies, with Skittles and iced tea, in a death pose.

In a democracy, so the saying goes, the people get the government they deserve. Part of Obama's genius is a remarkable ability to soothe race consciousness among whites. Any black person who's worked in the professional world is well acquainted with this trick. But never has it been practiced at such a high level, and never have its limits been so obviously exposed. This need to talk in dulcet tones, to never be angry regardless of the offense, bespeaks a strange and compromised integration indeed, revealing a country so infantile that it can countenance white acceptance of blacks only when they meet an Al Roker standard.

And yet this is the uncertain foundation of Obama's historic victory—a victory that I, and my

community, hold in the highest esteem. Who would truly deny the possibility of a black presidency in all its power and symbolism? Who would rob that little black boy of the right to feel himself affirmed by touching the kinky black hair of his president?

I think back to the first time I wrote Shirley Sherrod, requesting an interview. Here was a black woman with every reason in the world to bear considerable animosity toward Barack Obama. But she agreed to meet me only with great trepidation. She said she didn't "want to do anything to hurt" the president.

QUESTIONS TO CONSIDER

1. According to Coates, how has the need to appear "twice as good, half as Black" impacted President Obama's first term?
2. How does Coates portray anger as a political force in America? Who uses (or rejects) political anger and why?

30.2 BARACK OBAMA, STATEMENT ON THE PARIS CLIMATE AGREEMENT (2015)*

The first significant step to address climate change was the UN Conference on Environment and Development, or Earth Summit, held in Rio de Janeiro in 1992. Its Declaration called environmental protection an "integral part of the development process," one that "cannot be considered in isolation from it." Further steps to balance economic development and environmental preservation were outlined in 1997 in the Kyoto Protocol. In 2015, after years of intense negotiation, the Paris Climate Agreement—the most important international treaty aimed at mitigating climate change to date—went into effect. The United States was among the 195 countries that signed the accord, only to have President Donald Trump announce in 2017 that the United States would pull out of the agreement. However, President Joe Biden signed paperwork that recommitted the United States on his first day in office. In this statement following the original adoption of the Paris Agreement in December 2015, President Barack Obama (b. 1961), who worked vigorously to get the agreement drafted and signed, reflects on this "turning point for the world."

* The White House, "Statement by the President on the Paris Climate Agreement," December 12, 2015. https://obamawhitehouse.archives.gov/the-press-office/2015/12/12/statement-president-paris-climate-agreement.

In my first inaugural address, I committed this country to the tireless task of combating climate change and protecting this planet for future generations.

Two weeks ago, in Paris, I said before the world that we needed a strong global agreement to accomplish this goal—an enduring agreement that reduces global carbon pollution and sets the world on a course to a low-carbon future.

A few hours ago, we succeeded. We came together around the strong agreement the world needed. We met the moment.

I want to commend President Hollande and Secretary General Ban for their leadership and for hosting such a successful summit, and French Foreign Minister Laurent Fabius for presiding with patience and resolve. And I want to give a special thanks to Secretary John Kerry, my Senior Advisor Brian Deese, our chief negotiator Todd Stern, and everyone on their teams for their outstanding work and for making America proud.

I also want to thank the people of nearly 200 nations—large and small, developed and developing—for working together to confront a threat to the people of all nations. Together, we've shown what's possible when the world stands as one.

Today, the American people can be proud—because this historic agreement is a tribute to American leadership. Over the past seven years, we've transformed the United States into the global leader in fighting climate change. In 2009, we helped salvage a chaotic Copenhagen Summit and established the principle that all countries had a role to play in combating climate change. We then led by example, with historic investments in growing industries like wind and solar, creating a new and steady stream of middle-class jobs. We've set the first-ever nationwide standards to limit the amount of carbon pollution power plants can dump into the air our children breathe. From Alaska to the Gulf Coast to the Great Plains, we've partnered with local leaders who are working to help their communities protect themselves from some of the most immediate impacts of a changing climate.

Now, skeptics said these actions would kill jobs. Instead, we've seen the longest streak of private-sector job creation in our history. We've driven our economic output to all-time highs while driving our carbon pollution down to its lowest level in nearly two decades.

And then, with our historic joint announcement with China last year, we showed it was possible to bridge the old divides between developed and developing nations that had stymied global progress for so long. That accomplishment encouraged dozens and dozens of other nations to set their own ambitious climate targets. And that was the foundation for success in Paris. Because no nation, not even one as powerful as ours, can solve this challenge alone. And no country, no matter how small, can sit on the sidelines. All of us had to solve it together.

Now, no agreement is perfect, including this one. Negotiations that involve nearly 200 nations are always challenging. Even if all the initial targets set in Paris are met, we'll only be part of the way there when it comes to reducing carbon from the atmosphere. So we cannot be complacent because of today's agreement. The problem is not solved because of this accord. But make no mistake, the Paris agreement establishes the enduring framework the world needs to solve the climate crisis. It creates the mechanism, the architecture, for us to continually tackle this problem in an effective way.

This agreement is ambitious, with every nation setting and committing to their own specific targets, even as we take into account differences among nations. We'll have a strong system of transparency, including periodic reviews and independent assessments, to help hold every country accountable for meeting its commitments. As technology advances, this agreement allows progress to pave the way for even more ambitious targets over time. And we have secured a broader commitment to support the most vulnerable countries as they pursue cleaner economic growth.

In short, this agreement will mean less of the carbon pollution that threatens our planet, and more of the jobs and economic growth driven by low-carbon investment. Full implementation of this agreement will help delay or avoid some of the worst consequences of climate change, and will pave the way for even more progress, in successive stages, over the coming years.

Moreover, this agreement sends a powerful signal that the world is firmly committed to a low-carbon future. And that has the potential to unleash investment and innovation in clean energy at a scale we have never seen before. The targets we've set are bold. And by empowering businesses, scientists, engineers, workers, and the private sector—investors—to work together, this agreement represents the best chance we've had to save the one planet that we've got.

So I believe this moment can be a turning point for the world. We've shown that the world has both the will and the ability to take on this challenge. It won't be easy. Progress won't always come quick. We cannot be complacent. While our generation will see some of the benefits of building a clean energy economy—jobs created and money saved—we may not live to see the full realization of our achievement. But that's okay. What matters is that today we can be more confident that this planet is going to be in better shape for the next generation. And that's what I care about. I imagine taking my grandkids, if I'm lucky enough to have some, to the park someday, and holding their hands, and hearing their laughter, and watching a quiet sunset, all the while knowing that our work today prevented an alternate future that could have been grim; that our work, here and now, gave future generations cleaner air, and cleaner water, and a more sustainable planet. And what could be more important than that?

Today, thanks to strong, principled, American leadership, that's the world that we'll leave to our children—a world that is safer and more secure, more prosperous, and more free. And that is our most important mission in our short time here on this Earth.

Thanks.

QUESTIONS TO CONSIDER

1. In his statement, President Obama declares that "this agreement sends a powerful signal that the world is firmly committed to a low-carbon future. And that has the potential to unleash investment and innovation in clean energy at a scale we have never seen before." He made this assertion in 2015. Thinking of your own life, is the "low-carbon future" a reality, or is it still in the future?

2. Obama praises the cooperation between the United States and China in addressing climate change. Taking into account international affairs today, do you think the United States and China are cooperating to solve the world's problems as they were in 2015?

30.3 NICHOLAS FANDOS AND EMILY COCHRANE, "AFTER PRO-TRUMP MOB STORMS CAPITOL, CONGRESS CONFIRMS BIDEN'S WIN" (2021)*

Throughout his presidency, Donald Trump (b. 1946) repeatedly cast doubt on normal electoral processes and expressed sympathy for violent behavior. Most famously he excused the white nationalists who incited a struggle that left one person dead in Charlottesville, Virginia, in 2019 by calling them "very fine people." He also repeatedly called the 2020 presidential election into question in the months before voting took place in November. Because there was not yet a vaccine for the ongoing

COVID-19 pandemic, some states encouraged voters to submit ballots by mail to avoid large gatherings at polling locations, while President Trump repeatedly cast doubt on the legitimacy of voting by mail. When the election took place and it appeared that Trump had lost, the president then engaged in dozens of lawsuits in an attempt to prevent votes from being properly counted in states where he had been defeated. On January 6, the day that the US Congress met to certify the results of the 2020 election, Trump held a rally in Washington in which he repeatedly disparaged Congress, the election, and his own vice president, Mike Pence. Rally attendees then attacked the US Capitol to prevent the ballot certification. The assault eventually led to nine deaths.

WASHINGTON—Congress confirmed President-elect Joseph R. Biden Jr.'s victory early Thursday morning, overwhelmingly repudiating a drive by President Trump to overturn his defeat after it culminated in a mob of loyalists storming and occupying the Capitol in a shocking display of violence that shook the core of American democracy.

There was no parallel in modern American history, as insurgents acting with the president's encouragement vandalized Speaker Nancy Pelosi's office, smashing windows, looting art and briefly taking control of the Senate chamber, where they took turns posing for photographs with fists up on the dais where Vice President Mike Pence had just been presiding. Outside the building, they erected a gallows, punctured the tires of a police SUV, and left a note on its windshield saying, "PELOSI IS SATAN."

The attack by rebels carrying pro-Trump paraphernalia stopped the electoral counting for several hours and sent lawmakers and Mr. Pence fleeing. But by the time the Senate reconvened in a reclaimed Capitol, one of the nation's most polarizing moments had yielded an unexpected moment of solidarity that briefly eclipsed partisan division.

Republicans and Democrats locked arms to denounce the violence and express their determination to carry out what they called a constitutionally sacrosanct function. They refused, by resounding bipartisan majorities, to deliver Mr. Trump the election reversal he demanded.

Mr. Pence, breaking with the president he has loyally served, made Mr. Biden's victory official just after 3:40 a.m. in Washington, declaring that Mr. Biden had received 306 electoral votes to Mr. Trump's 232 and would be inaugurated the 46th president on Jan. 20.

"To those who wreaked havoc in our Capitol today, you did not win," Mr. Pence had said earlier. "Violence never wins. Freedom wins. And this is still the people's house."

Senator Mitch McConnell, Republican of Kentucky and the majority leader, said the "failed insurrection" had only clarified Congress's purpose.

"They tried to disrupt our democracy," he said. "They failed."

In a statement just before 4 a.m. Thursday, the president finally conceded, saying, "Even though I totally disagree with the outcome of the election, and the facts bear me out, nevertheless there will be an orderly transition on January 20th."

Still, the process opened bitter wounds within the Republican Party that are unlikely to quickly heal. While some Republicans who had planned to join the effort to overturn Mr. Biden's victory agreed to drop their challenges after the Capitol siege, Senator Josh Hawley of Missouri pressed forward, keeping both chambers in session well past midnight.

An objection to Arizona's results lodged by Senators Ted Cruz of Texas and Tommy Tuberville of Alabama just before the violence broke out in the Capitol failed overwhelmingly in the Senate, 6 to 93. The House turned it back on a vote of 121 to 303, but more than half of that chamber's Republicans supported the effort to overturn the election results.

A challenge to Pennsylvania's results backed by Mr. Hawley ended in lopsided defeats, as well. Skipping debate altogether, senators voted to reject it 7 to 92. The House moved more slowly, but eventually voted 138 to 282 to do the same.

The upheaval unfolded on a day when Democrats secured a stunning pair of victories in runoff elections in Georgia, winning effective control of the Senate and the complete levers of power in Washington. And it arrived as Congress met for what would normally have been a perfunctory and ceremonial session to declare Mr. Biden's election.

From the start, Mr. Trump's allies, acting at his behest, had been determined to use the session to formally contest the outcome. Driving a painful wedge among Republicans, they trumpeted his false claims of voting fraud and initially gave voice inside the Capitol to those who ultimately forced their way in, stopping the process in its tracks.

Lawmakers and Mr. Pence mostly took shelter together near the Capitol, amid violent clashes between protesters and law enforcement, but small groups reported being stranded for a time in offices and hideaways throughout the building.

Capitol Police, reinforced by the F.B.I. and National Guard in tactical gear, successfully retook the Capitol complex just before 6 p.m., after more than three hours of mayhem. Mayor Muriel Bowser of Washington had declared a citywide curfew from 6 p.m. Wednesday to 6 a.m. Thursday, and a public emergency lasting until after Mr. Biden's inauguration.

The siege was the climax of a weekslong campaign by Mr. Trump, filled with baseless claims of fraud and outright lies, to try to overturn a democratically decided election that he lost. He fought the result in court with dozens of spurious lawsuits that he lost. He outright pressured Republican leaders in key battleground states to reverse the will of the voters. And he fought, at last, to turn the congressional counting into the site of his final stand.

"We gather due to a selfish man's injured pride, and the outrage of supporters who he has deliberately misinformed for the past two months and stirred to action this very morning," Senator Mitt Romney, Republican of Utah and the 2012 presidential nominee, said after the chamber reconvened. "What happened here today was an insurrection incited by the president of the United States."

Far from discouraging confrontation, Mr. Trump had encouraged his supporters earlier Wednesday to confront Republican lawmakers going against him to side with the Constitution.

"We will never concede," he told a group of thousands gathered near the White House, inveighing against members of his own party preparing to finalize his loss as "weak Republicans, pathetic Republicans" whose leadership had gone "down the tubes." He then repeatedly told them to march to the Capitol where the vote tallying was about to get underway. The violence began a little more than two hours later.

In a speech just before the violence broke out, Mr. McConnell, the most powerful Republican on Capitol Hill, forcefully rebuked Mr. Trump and members of his own party, warning that the drive to overturn a legitimate election risked sending democracy into "a death spiral."

"The voters, the courts and the states have all spoken," said Mr. McConnell, the majority leader. "If we overrule them all, it would damage our republic forever."

Yet even as he spoke, it was becoming clear that the vicious cycle had already been unleashed. Within an hour, Mr. McConnell was in the grip of his Capitol Police detail and being rushed out of his chamber with other senators as members of his own party chanted curses to his name.

Mr. Biden, in his own remarks, demanded that Mr. Trump intervene to tamp down an "unprecedented assault" on democracy. He called for a televised address by Mr. Trump to "fulfill his oath and defend the Constitution and demand an end to this siege."

"This is not dissent. It's disorder. It's chaos. It borders on sedition, and it must end now," Mr. Biden said. "I call on this mob to pull back and allow the work of democracy to go forward."

Mr. Trump initially stayed quiet as the mob rampaged through the Capitol. When he did make himself heard, it was to call for support for law enforcement in a tweet that concluded, "Stay peaceful!" But not long after, he released a brief video repeating his disproved claim that "the election was stolen" and speaking in sympathetic and affectionate terms to members of the mob. Later, he absolved the mobsters of their gross assault, effectively arguing that their actions had been warranted.

"These are the things and events that happen when a sacred landslide election victory is so unceremoniously & viciously stripped away from great patriots who have been badly & unfairly treated for so long," Mr. Trump wrote Wednesday evening in a tweet, which Twitter later removed. "Go home with love & in peace. Remember this day forever!

The mob of Trump supporters was already massing by the thousands on Capitol Hill when Congress convened in joint session at 1 p.m. Under normal circumstances, the counting of electoral votes is little more than a glorified paperwork exercise.

But with Mr. Trump's refusal to concede, his allies had planned a series of as many as six objections to the electoral votes of battleground states Mr. Biden won, turning the session into a messy final parliamentary stand.

The president had also intensely pressured Mr. Pence, who as vice president oversees the counting, to go rogue and unilaterally throw out the votes of key battleground states Mr. Trump lost. Shortly before the session began, Mr. Pence denied him in a bold statement after four years of loyal alliance.

"I do not believe that the founders of our country intended to invest the vice president with unilateral authority to decide which electoral votes should be counted during the joint session of Congress, and no vice president in American history has ever asserted such authority," he wrote.

Once the counting got underway, Senator Ted Cruz of Texas and Representative Paul Gosar of Arizona quickly lodged the first such objection to Mr. Gosar's home state, sending senators and House members to their respective chambers for up to two hours of debate on Mr. Trump's baseless fraud claims.

About 2:15 p.m., as the House and Senate separately debated the objection, security rushed Mr. Pence out of the Senate chamber and the Capitol building was placed on lockdown after the demonstrators surged past barricades and law enforcement toward the legislative chambers.

"We now have individuals that have breached the Capitol building," an officer told the House.

In a scene of unrest common in other countries but seldom witnessed in the history of the United States capital, hundreds of people in the mob barreled past fence barricades outside the Capitol and clashed with officers. Shouting demonstrators mobbed the second floor lobby just outside the Senate chamber, as law enforcement officials placed themselves in front of the chamber doors.

For a time, senators and members of the House were locked inside their respective chambers. Just outside the locked doors, Mr. Trump's supporters violently tussled with the police. A woman inside the building was shot and later died, the District of Columbia police said. Three others died of "medical emergencies," authorities said. Multiple officers were injured.

As the mob closed in, senators were rushed into the well of the Senate and down into the basement where they left the building via an underground tunnel.

"This is what you've gotten, guys," Mr. Romney yelled as the Senate was first thrust into a lockdown, apparently addressing his Republican colleagues who were leading the charge to press Mr. Trump's false claims of a stolen election.

On the other side of the Capitol, Representative Steve Cohen, Democrat of Tennessee, yelled out to Republicans on the House floor: "Call Trump, tell him to call off his revolutionary guards."

Multiple lawmakers reported that the Capitol Police had instructed them to take cover on the House floor and prepare to use protective hoods after tear gas was dispersed in the Capitol Rotunda of the Capitol. Shortly after, the police escorted senators and members of House from the building to others nearby, as the mob swarmed the hallways just steps from where lawmakers were meeting, carrying pro-Trump paraphernalia.

Representative Nancy Mace, a freshman Republican from South Carolina, described seeing people "assaulting Capitol Police." In a Twitter post, Ms. Mace shared a video of the chaos and wrote: "This is wrong. This is not who we are. I'm heartbroken for our nation today."

In the early afternoon, the police fired what appeared to be flash-bang grenades. Rather than disperse, the demonstrators cheered and shouted, "Push forward, push forward." One person shouted, "That's our house," meaning the Capitol. Other people repeatedly shouted, "You swore an oath."

When the violence broke out it was Mr. Pence, sheltering in the Capitol, not Mr. Trump who approved the deployment of the D.C. National Guard, according to Defense Department officials. Mr. Trump initially rebuffed and resisted requests to mobilize forces, according to a person with knowledge of the events. It required intervention from Pat A. Cipollone, the White House counsel, among other officials, the person said.

At the White House, officials—including two from the East Wing and a top press aide—began submitting their resignations, with more expected to follow in the coming days.

"I don't recognize our country today, and the members of Congress who have supported this anarchy do not deserve to represent their fellow Americans," said Representative Elaine Luria, Democrat of Virginia.

Other Republicans laid responsibility squarely at the feet of the president.

"What he has done and what he has caused here is something we've never seen before in our history," Representative Liz Cheney of Wyoming, the No. 3 House Republican, said on NBC. Ms. Cheney said that the chaos unleashed on Capitol Hill would "be part of his legacy."

"What we are seeing today is a result of that—a result of convincing people that Congress was going to overturn the results of the election, a result of suggestions that he wouldn't leave office," she said.

QUESTIONS TO CONSIDER

1. What threats does this sort of mob violence, especially when encouraged by an elected leader, pose to democracy?
2. How does this article convey the gravity of the January 6 attack?

30.4 VISUAL SOURCE: MICHAEL WILLIAMSON, RAINBOW WHITE HOUSE AFTER GAY MARRIAGE SUPREME COURT DECISION (2015)*

The 2015 Supreme Court decision in *Obergefell v. Hodges* requiring states to issue marriage licenses to same-sex couples was a major victory in a decades-long struggle for the acceptance of same-sex relationships in the United States. In the first half of the twentieth century, sexual activity between same-sex couples was outlawed in numerous states, making it very difficult to live as a gay American. Activism by and on behalf of gay Americans increased beginning in the 1960s, encouraged by a counterculture that rejected norms of heterosexuality and gender. Recognizing the marriage of same-sex couples came to be seen as a core issue of the larger gay rights movement, as legal recognition of same-sex relationships would protect gay Americans from discrimination. Thirty-one states, predominantly in the South, Midwest, and Great Plains regions, have state constitutions that ban same-sex marriage, although these clauses have been inoperable since the *Obergefell* decision. In recognition of the *Obergefell* decision, the White House was illuminated in rainbow colors, as the rainbow is a common symbol of support and affirmation for the LGBTQ community.

* The Washington Post/Contributor

QUESTIONS TO CONSIDER

1. Why was it significant to illuminate the White House in this manner? What message was the Obama administration expressing?
2. Why is legal recognition of same-sex marriages of such importance to LGBTQ Americans?

30.5 VISUAL SOURCE: DAVE GRANLUND, *MARCH MADNESS* (2016)*

The Republican Party sometimes refers to itself as the "Party of Lincoln," in reference to Abraham Lincoln, the first president to run as a Republican and commonly regarded as one of the best American presidents in history. In this cartoon by Dave Granlund, Lincoln is portrayed as one of a variety of Republican opponents of Donald Trump who did not want Trump to represent the party in the 2016 election.

---

* Dave Granlund, Courtesy of Cagle Cartoons

By mid-March 2016, only three candidates remained in the Republican primary race for the presidential nomination: Texas senator Ted Cruz, Ohio governor John Kasich, and Donald Trump. Trump had won major states such as Florida, making him a front-runner for the candidacy, despite lacking experience in elected politics in general and in the Republican Party specifically. His coarse language and the sometimes violent nature of his campaign events drew repeated criticism, including from Republicans. For these reasons many in the party regarded Trump as an unacceptable candidate, regardless of his popularity with voters.

QUESTIONS TO CONSIDER

1. What is the significance of juxtaposing Trump with Lincoln in this cartoon? What does Lincoln represent and how does that contrast with Trump's campaign?
2. Why would being the "Party of Lincoln" be important to Republicans? Why would Donald Trump pose a threat to that image?